What Read

The Blind Eye – A Sephardic Journey

From 15th century Portugal to 20th century America, this moving and well-crafted novel explores one woman's search for her roots, and the revelations that will change her life forever.–Victoria Zackheim, Author, *The Bone Weaver*, editor of *He Said What?* and *Exit Laughing*

"*The Blind Eye* is brilliant with visuals and characters so real you feel their heartache resonate off the page. Terrifying, and at times maddening, this amazing read put me right there in the adventure. Ms. Fine's research and artful prose allow us to step into a piece of history that cannot be forgotten." – Deborah J Ledford, award-winning author, *SNARE*

". . . an engaging story that unravels history."–Lois Rudnick, author of "*Mabel Dodge Luhan: New Woman, New Worlds*," Professor Emerita

"As an expert on Judaic history I was very impressed with the accuracy of the story. Loved the settings and even the humor! The whole family is reading it!" – Shai Shalom, *Jerusalem guide*

"*The Blind Eye* is an absorbing dramatization of the horrors Jewish people endured during the expulsions from Spain and Portugal at the end of the fifteenth century. Marcia Fine has created a cast of characters readers can identify with, both in the past and in the present. She shows the family and cultural links that bind us all to the history of our people, no matter what our ethnic origins. This is a fast and moving read. I highly recommend it." – Toby Fesler Heathcotte, EPIC Metaphysical Fiction Winner

"Why do Book Clubs love Historical Fiction? Because you learn so much about the history of the world–while reading a compelling story. And why do book clubs love Marcia Fine? She is not only a great writer and wonderful story teller, but a meticulous researcher. Her historical fiction is so gripping, members of my book clubs cannot stop talking about her! Three cheers for Marcia Fine!" -- Marsha Toy Engstrom, Book Club Cheerleader

"…powerfully written story with a depth of emotion based on real times. It brought me to tears . . . and rage. It offers the lessons we need to learn today." – Susan Brooks, Thought Leader, Author, International Speaker

Marcia Fine steps into the world of the fifteenth century. Her vivid portrayals of affected families bring into sharp relief the pain and betrayals of dislocation. -- Virginia Nosky, Author, *Blue Turquoise, White Shell*

"Marcia Fine's detailed research pays off in her narrative about the expulsion of the Jews from Spain and Portugal in the late 15th century - the same time that Columbus was commissioned by the 'evil' Queen Isabella to explore new lands. The loyal devotion of families to their religious customs and traditions, despite threats on their lives, makes this an informative, literary novel. It authenticates a forgotten history of a people who suffered at the hands of the Inquisition." – Jan Smith, Intuitive Counselor

"From one who never reads historical novels – I loved this book! It was riveting and very easy to read; the story flowed, educating, while never getting bogged down in excessive historical details. Totally enjoyable!" – Roxanne Henderson

"A mesmerizing account of the Jews in Spain and Portugal during the Inquisition, the "*Blind Eye*" is important reading for everyone, Jews and non-Jews alike. I couldn't put it down, and finished it in two days. I've recommended it to several people, and it will make wonderful gifts for family and friends." – Ellen De Domenico, Public Relations

"The historical information was fascinating and powerfully woven through the plot. I loved the flawed yet likeable characters." – Kate Timmerman, Artist

"I finished reading *The Blind Eye* and was crying at the end. It is a very moving story. Very insightful time of history. I want to learn more." – Susan Bulfinch, Mediator

"This was a fascinating, fast-paced story of a remarkable and horrific time in world history. The characters and their connections were well conceived, and the author did a brilliant job of research. I will recommend it to all my friends." – Gloria Robinson

"I LOVED the book...it was so riveting. It's amazing how this story was told. Wow. Very impressive!" – Tracey Cuervals, Author

"I would finish a chapter with tears in my eyes for the suffering of Grazia and Bellina and the next chapter would have me laughing with Alegra." – Janet Welk-Forsch

The Blind Eye

A Sephardic Journey

Marcia Fine

L'IMAGE PRESS

Scottsdale, Arizona

L'IMAGE **|P** PRESS

Scottsdale, Arizona
www.Limagepress.com

The Blind Eye
Copyright © 2012 by Marcia Fine
First Published by Author House 7/18/07

Cataloging Publication Data Doctors
ISBN   –   978-0-9826952-3-4
Library of Congress catalog card number: 2007902405
Scottsdale, Arizona
www.Limagepress.com

Cataloging Publication Data
1. Historical fiction 2. The Inquisition 3. Cuban women 4. Spanish exodus
5. Lisbon 15th century 6. Recife, Brazil

Publisher's Note:
This is a work of fiction. Names and characters are fictional. Events and places are based on actual history.

Cover and interior design: Kim Appis
Photography: SMF Photography

www.marciafine.com
www.theblindeye.com

This book is dedicated to those who came before us and those who will carry on the tradition.

~ Abraham and Liberty

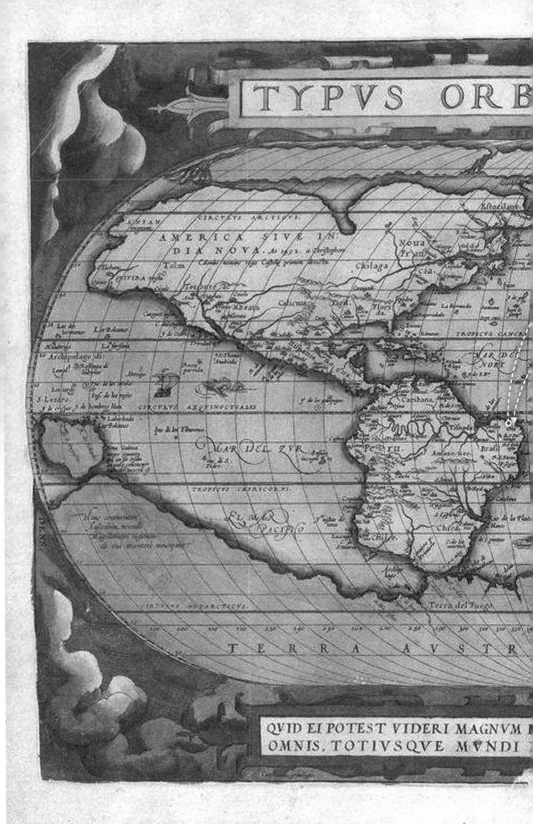

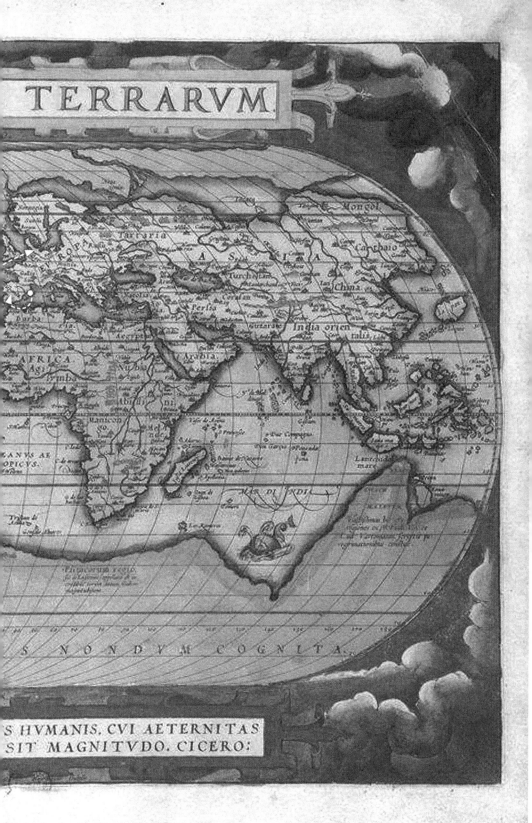

TERRARVM

S NONDVM COGNITA.

S HVMANIS, CVI AETERNITAS
SIT MAGNITVDO. CICERO:

Chapter One

Grazia

Edict of Expulsion: 31st of March, 1492

Accused of ritual murder in Granada and not under jurisdiction of the Inquisition, the Church orders expulsion of all Jews and Marranos from Spain within four months.

Granada, Spain

2 Ab 5252 (4 August 1492)

"Hermando, no. Please. Hanna's still a girl. She made a mistake." My mother appealed to my father even as she, too, made preparations for our long journey. The air in the front room of our home that served as our place of trade reeked with anger and frustration. Despair replaced hope. Three months had passed since the Edict of Expulsion on the thirty-first of Adar. Originally we were to leave on the first day of Ab but the monarchs in their cruel contempt gave us one more day.

"No!" my father shouted, gathering stacks of Byzantine silks and flax linen. Furious, he stuffed them into large hemp bags. A swath of crimson tapestry fell to the floor.

"But Hanna's only fourteen."

"Old enough not to be a fool. Pregnant by a common *marrano* who believes in their Holy Ghost? What kind of a Jew is that?" My father made a disgusted noise as he reached toward his top shelves. "Her chances of marriage are finished. She can rot like old cheese in the convent. I will never see her again." My father grimaced, a sure sign of his fury. He dismantled the showcase of his wares, until now, the finest in Granada. The shelves normally filled with a variety of textures of wool, rough for the working class and creamy soft for the wealthy, stood bare.

"Hermando, lower your voice. Grazia has big ears." I faded back behind the door. I didn't want them to know I'd been privy to their conversation. They had been arguing about Hanna for weeks, my beautiful sister, the one with sea-green eyes, fair skin and a face so uncommon people stared as she passed in the street.

My mother renewed her plea. "Melt your heart for your daughter, *le sangre llama*. Our blood is calling."

I pressed myself flat against the wall and peeked around the corner into the room loaded with our possessions. Lanterns cast monsterous moving shadows. My father shoved a carved wooden bench with his foot. The pillows my sister and I had embroidered with strawberry designs fell to the floor.

"We've survived threats and excessive taxes before, leaving with only what we can carry. We cannot abandon our daughter." My mother lowered her voice, "Jews do not cast out their children. Or their grandchildren."

"Yes, they do! Even New Christians. Coming with child before a proper wedding? I will not accept her. What kind of a daughter brings such shame to her parents? Let the nuns take care of her and the baby. Ach. A bastard." He spit toward the floor, part of the spittle spraying his worn leather vest.

My father's hands moved in a jerking rhythm of folding, smoothing, matching hems, and stacking the luxurious cloths into piles. A colorful palette of blue, purple and green silk thread that embroiderers bought by the ounce sat jumbled in a corner, their vividness dimmed in the soft light.

Once, he took me with him to see how fabrics dyed into rich colors, crimsons and azures of varying shades that picked up the light. Men, ancient and sharp-featured, almost beetle-like themselves, stood on stools stirring vats of boiling insects, their long poles occasionally splashing a rainbow across their clothes.

My father mumbled to himself, "What's the difference if their church takes one more after all they have stolen?"

My mother, expressing her frustration and despair, delayed the packing of herbs and spices—mint, cumin, paprika, ginger, cloves, salt and pepper. As a cook she was extraordinary, preparing everyday fowl and vegetables into something delicious for our weekly feast.

She enhanced her recipes with pine nuts, garbanzos and my favorite, pistachios. I nibbled a few of the small green delicacies that had fallen on the mosaic tile floor in the back room, one my father had labored over with a few friends when we first moved to Granada from Baeza. Now she sat nearby transferring her tasty treasures from stoneware jars into small cloth bags, her lips pursed. I was supposed to be doing the same with dried apricots and dates but instead I hid behind the door.

Without provocation my mother sobbed into a handkerchief. She got up and stumbled by me, her soft velvet slippers a slight moan on the stairs to her room.

I could not comfort her. Nothing would replace Hanna. I went to my room, the one I no longer shared with my sister. Although I missed the warmth of Hanna's body in our bed and the sweetness of her nature, a part of me reveled in the solitary comforts she left behind—my own room with nothing to share and the sole attention of my mother. I undressed to my body linens and slipped beneath the sheets, wiggling my toes.

Foggy memories glided by me as I drifted toward sleep—the last time Hanna, my mother and I went to the *mikvah*, the ritual bath of rain water collected in a cistern for our *nidda*, the monthly cleansing.

We waited for three stars to be visible before we left. Hanna searched for them through the window, her face angelic in the moonlight. Of course my sister's lie that her menses had passed when none had come for a few months did not occur to me until later. I sank into dreams, not unlike lowering myself down the tile steps of a full immersion into the natural water, over my head, holding my breath, erasing my soul of jealousies.

Sounds of packing, barrels rolling and the noisy street awakened me. It was to be the last time in my feather bed, head propped into a pillow, cocooned under the canopy. I had mixed feelings about the journey to Portugal. It frightened and thrilled me. There, my parents said in hushed voices, merchants were welcomed, even Jewish ones.

Although ostensibly converted, we still practiced our ancestral faith and identified ourselves as *conversos*. We despised the ugly word *marranos* meaning swine. We were New Christians with the thought that maybe someday we could practice the Laws of Moses without fear.

The plan to gather with other families in Seville had been made weeks ago. Many were associates of my father's textile trade. Others forced to flee planned to exit from el Puerto de Santa Maria, not far away. My father had decided on a sea route to Portugal.

My mother came to me at dawn, the first crevice of light splitting through the shuttered window. She touched my shoulder, setting a small candle in a clay dish next to my bed. The flickering light danced shadows on the walls. I hesitated. My father told tales of his travels through villages and cities in Spain, Italy, Portugal and France to purchase exquisite cloth from cottage industries, fending off sleep for days. "Lurking wolves or robbers will get you if you close an eye," he told us.

"Get up. We have to go." My mother hurried out of the room, her skirts swishing. She left me a piece of bread and goat's milk. Normally, we ate only once a day, but I knew she was worried about our journey. I felt my way around the room, touching the furniture, a small carpet under my feet, dressing by rote, the fog of sleep still in my head. I couldn't eat anything.

I met my mother in the back room as she removed the large fire bell and stirred the smoldering embers. The square brick fireplace and oven above it was our family hearth. A piece of green velvet draped across the top to contain the smoke. We stood next to each other, lifting our skirts for warmth. She glanced at me, her eyes filled with tears and then turned to hold me. This time her sadness was not about my unfortunate looks or my narrow prospects.

"What about my sister?" I asked, searching her face.

"Hanna's gone. Your father will not have her under his roof or any other. Maybe he will soften with time." She cast her sea-green eyes downward, heartsick, a hand stroking her ivory throat.

"How will she find us?" A parent never lets go of a child, but I felt a small satisfaction that I was here and Hanna was not. I tried not to think about the baby born a few months ago, a girl without a future. My mother, who had made secret visits to see her, had told me it had been an easy delivery.

"I will find a way." Her voice cracked on the last word. She shifted away, her shawl wrapped tight around her shoulders. Soon my mother and father's voices faded into the clamor outside, hordes of people in sorrowful departure, their possessions rattling, pots clanking, mules braying, children crying, wailing from those being cast out of a place that had been their home for centuries.

A fishmonger screamed, "Cod and pickled herring. Buy it now." A parrot must have been rocked in a cage because its shrieks and squawks drowned out the fish woman. The steady squeak of wagon wheels churning through rocks and mud made me pause. Someone's household goods crashed to the street followed by wild cursing, their possessions trampled, abandoned.

We were being sent away even though we were part of the Church. At least we pretended to be. My father taught us to murmur in Hebrew as we entered any Catholic Church, "I enter this religious house, but I do not adore sticks or stones, only the God of Israel."

"I have to go to her," I heard my mother say.

"No time. She has shamed our family. Forget her. We have one daughter now." My father's words cut with a hard edge.

"She needs me."

"Where were you when she and this boy were together?"

The door slammed. My father groaned as he lifted something heavy. It fell and broke against terra cotta tiles and he cursed.

My mother called, "Grazia, hurry. The wagon's almost loaded."

In my hasty exit I glanced back at our lovely home with its second floor terrace and tiled roof. The home of most of my childhood. I felt a lump in my throat and ran to the wagon. Dressed in my finest tunic, I wore a belt with its leather pouch slapping against my side–a few coins, a carnelian brooch from my grandmother, salve for my lips. I had polished my shoes with fat from the joints of a calf we slaughtered for the spring festival of *Shavouth*.

Animal blood and fat were forbidden in our home, but my father saved it in a barrel outside. The cooler air slapped my face as I pulled my skirts up and tumbled into the back of the wagon with our belongings.

Huddled behind barrels and stools with three layers of skirts bunched beneath me, I settled into a spot. The sewage of the street: rotten food, people's waste and a decaying animal, assaulted my nose. I sneezed. Bags of textiles were piled on, more pieces of furniture on top of that. I shivered in the cool morning air. My father grabbed the round iron ring, slamming our front door with the finality of no return. The bell that had been installed to warn us of strangers, tinkled. He stomped his feet as he came to the back of the wagon, lifting more bolts of material tied with thin pieces of rawhide on top of the load, moaning with each heavy roll. Finally, he pushed in our washstand with the cabinets, trapping me in a column of possessions.

Suddenly, a soft bird whistle sounded next to me. It stopped. Wagons filled with pots and pans rattled by; livestock, loud and complaining were tied to the back. I leaned my head to the side, closing my eyes, the thought that I would never see Hanna or meet my niece sliding by me. Did the baby have green eyes or plain brown ones like mine?

In a few minutes the bird sound repeated its tune. How could one of God's creatures feel joy at a time like this?

I wiggled around in my small space and peered out the wagon's rough slats. At first I saw nothing. The small song cut through the din. I moved again pushing a three-legged chair to the back, my fingers brushing a plush velvet cushion. The scraping sound alerted my father.

"What are you doing? You can break something," He hit his hand on the side to scare me.

"I am sorry, Father."

Through the bottom of the wagon I heard movement. Maybe a deserted dog. With all the confusion I would not be surprised. A rat? I was terrified of them and the diseases they carried. They gnawed everything and sometimes stole food, even though my father set traps.

"Grazia. Quiet. Your father cannot hear me." My mother crouched next to the wagon on the side away from our house.

"What are you doing?"

"Tell your father I went ahead. I will meet you at the dock."

"How will you find us in this chaos?" Wagon wheels creaked along the narrow street splashing mud. A horse neighed then stopped next to her to relieve itself. The plopping excrement would soon draw flies. She looked filthy.

"Speak up," I told my mother. "Are you there?"

"Grazia, when you get to the ship your father will be busy unloading. Distract him if you do not see me."

"I want to go with you." I made an attempt to stand and could not steady myself in the tight space.

"No. Keep him occupied with taking care of our goods and loading the ship. He will be busy returning the donkey and wagon."

"But where are you going?"

Then I understood.

"Your father can not know where I am." She said the next words, with resentment brimming, "How does he expect me to abandon a daughter?"

"I want to see Hanna, too." I made another effort to lift myself and could not move.

I admit that when my sister was first banished a certain delight swept over me in my excitement to have her space and extra clothes. But in recent weeks I missed her, the melody of her voice, lips puffed as though stung by a bee, dark lashes settling on high cheekbones. She had been my companion, my confidante, my solace against an angry father.

I watched through the slats as my mother pulled at her heavy cape, one that inspired envy among the neighborhood women, rivaling those worn by the royal court. A magnificent garment trimmed with gold brocade and ermine, a fist-sized mother-of-pearl button closed it at the neck. The hood covered her hair, her light eyes shifting to watch for my father. It sailed out behind her as she blended into the crowds, fading as she rushed off into the rising sun.

"Estrella, where are you? It is time to leave." My father sounded agitated, his voice hoarse from layers of ballooning dust.

I hesitated.

He repeated his request. "For God's sake, woman, I have enough to do without playing cat-and-mouse games."

I called out from my cell in a small voice, secretly delighted at my mother's boldness. "Padre, she said she will meet you at the dock."

"What?" His voice roared like a stricken animal.

Thank Goodness he could not see my sly smile. "Father, let's go. She says she will find us."

No response. I jumped when his fists hit the side of the wagon shaking it back and forth for a few moments. A stool balanced on top fell into the street and was broken apart by a wagon's wheels.

"She went to see that bastard child. I know it."

"No, Padre" I lied, "I think she went to place a stone on her parents' graves."

"God damn her," he said, climbing into the front of the wagon with a heave.

And so we left in the dank early morning air on the same day as the destruction of the Temple in Jerusalem and the beginning of our *diaspora*, an auspicious sign rumored to be an evil omen. Our gray shroud of misery made a hazy exodus down narrow winding streets, past the Church of San Juan de los Reyes with its minaret of two hundred years, up the hill to the El

Albaicin, the Moorish quarter of the city, en route to the Plaza Nueva and its Arab baths known for their tiny glazed tiles inlaid with precision. Torches held high by our Christian neighbors in front of their homes accompanied by an occasional jeer cast an eerie red glow.

I stopped peeking out when we reached the Alhambra, a former palace and fortress, and closed my eyes. Now, a source of pain, it was used by the Catholic monarchs for a Christian court and the signing of the Edict of Expulsion.

I saw only one processional of condemned *Judaizers*, New Christians like us who could not leave the old ways behind and were caught, perhaps by a vigilant priest who scanned the chimneys for the lack of a fire on the Sabbath or a suspicious servant asked to prepare a bath on a Friday night. My parents would not let me watch any others.

These poor souls, their pale, fearful faces, "the damned" as they were called, were marched to their deaths by fire. Paper tunics and pointed hats, bright white in the glaring sun, predicted an excruciating end. The citizens gathered and cheered for the spectacle, priests following the doomed, offering repentance and death by hanging if they would recant. My body shuddered. A mournful violin played a familiar song in a minor key, the tune fading into the distance.

We had limited choices for our exit: north to Navarre where we were not wanted unless we converted again, east to the sea or west to Portugal where Don Vidal ben Benveniste of Sargossa, our elected spokesman, a scion of Jewish nobility and a man of culture, pleaded with Pope Benedict in Latin and negotiated with King John II. The man who minted gold coins for Aragon and currency for Castile, a favorite of the court, had us admitted for one ducat each and one-quarter of our goods if we only stayed six months.

I rocked back and forth, bouncing along, the clip-clop mirrored by the sounds and smells of a lively city casting out its loyal inhabitants. Dust created by horses' hooves and wagon wheels sprayed my face and hair. The sounds of cows, drums, and tambourines filled the air. Surrounded by wails from the elderly, sighs from my father, and cries of displacement from the young, we made our way with thousands of other disconsolate souls, their packages and bundles of meager possessions balanced on weary shoulders. On the way some gave up and entered churches to convert.

I steadied myself by putting my fingers through a large crack, peeking through the slats. A rabbi herded miniature brides and grooms dressed in traditional white veils and black coats down the street. Orphans could not be left behind so children as young as ten were married to each other. Even little girls found husbands.

Chapter Two

Alegra

Miami, Florida
July 10, 1998

"**I**rma, I covered your condo and Mercedes last month. You haven't paid me back for that."

The dial tone buzzes in my ear. I squint at my mobile phone in the bright sunshine. Traffic has stalled on Le Jeune Road heading toward the airport. Did I accidentally hit a wrong button? No, my baby sister hung up on me. Oh well. I've just saved myself five minutes of manipulation.

Irma's full-time job is corralling her next rich victim/husband. As a veteran of two marriages and a broken engagement which left her with a four-carat pear-shaped diamond, her sole means of support has been her settlements. Men make fools of themselves to be with her. Then they do anything to get away, which usually involves plunging themselves into financial ruin. Now that she's blown through her last sucker's money, she's on the prowl again.

I've never married and probably won't. Saul's my boyfriend of eight years who teaches history at Coral Gables High. He spends most nights grading papers, watching CNN or doing errands. We only see each other on the weekends. My sisters say he's a momma's boy. I say he's saving money living at home with his mother. I'm bit of a nerd myself. I'd rather curl up with a good book than go dancing or shopping.

Following airport signs toward *Arrivals*, I slow down behind a yellow Cadillac without a driver. Miami has lots of headless people operating vehicles. This one stops every few feet, red taillights blinking like a fire alarm. Cars behind me start to honk and one driver speeds past us yelling,

"*Loco!*" and giving me the finger. I make my way around the recalcitrant car and glance into the driver's side. An ancient guy with a shiny lobster-head lifts his arms high and grips the steering wheel. He peeks between the spaces, a child in charge of a tank. I move past him.

In the steamy heat I search for Marta, my eldest sister returning from a trip to California. Florida's humid weather is unbearable. No one wants to get out of an air-conditioned car.

The airport, a confusing tunnel of construction and multi-layered garages, has sawhorses with blinking yellow lights blocking lanes. Sweaty cops, pens ready to write tickets, patrol the area. Stifling exhaust fumes from vans with their rental car company logos emblazoned on the sides, circle endlessly. It's hard enough to maneuver all the obstacles without trying to park.

My sister, Marta, a doughy silver-blonde, motions to me, her wrist laden with gold bangle bracelets. She's wearing a shiny black track suit trimmed in turquoise that billows in the waves of hot air. Usually she wears a white nylon uniform for her job as a phlebotomist at Felicity Labs. Maybe that explains why when it comes to dressing, she goes overboard.

Marta endures endless jokes about being a blood-sucker, but she loves her work. She was promoted to head of the vampires a few months ago. She said it was because she's shown up for the last five years. "These jung people, they don't wanna work," she told me at the time of her promotion. Why can't she pronounce "young" after all these years?

"Alegra, *aqui, aqui,*" she yells, waving her arms at roaring engines and honking horns. Carbon monoxide from the bus in front of me stings the back of my throat. As I slip my Pontiac close to the curb, Marta takes small steps forward in her wooden platform shoes and leans in the passenger side, her bosom heaving. "Help me with *mi maleta*. Ay, I'm so hot," she says, fanning herself with her ticket folder.

I pop the trunk and get out. Marta opens the door and plops herself into the passenger side. Shit. I thought she would help me. I struggle with the large Louis Vuitton knock-off, balancing it on the edge of the bumper and finally dumping it into my trunk. It's not a very good copy. I'm sure the real ones don't have purple handles. Knowing my sister, she probably wore one-tenth of what she took with her. I've never seen the point in packing all that stuff or her marathon shopping trips for that matter. She comes home with the same outfit every time – more tracksuits. As though she exercises. As if.

The car engine jumps into action. "Why didn't you help me with that thing?" I speak in English and Marta responds in Spanish, a living statistic of someone who has resided here most of her life and has little command of the language.

Marta leans her head back against the seat, exposing her fleshy neck, its creases cluttered with gold chains. She's five-foot-three and one-hundred-and-fifty pounds. Her hand creates quick flutters with another makeshift fan, a tabloid screaming the headline, "Julio's baby has two heads" or something like that.

"It's too heavy. I have problems with my back. The pain pills don't help. The chiropractor said …" Her rapid recitation of complaints tumbles out in Spanglish, a unique combination of half-words and phrases in English and Spanish. A serious hypochondriac, she thinks the result of every patient's blood test belongs to her. Certain weeks she has lymphoma, which she miraculously cures with herbs; the next month she's got a rare blood disease that disappears by drinking smelly tea prescribed by an acupuncturist. The thought of needles gives me the willies, but she's not afraid of them.

"You know, Alegra, I may only have six weeks to live. Pray for me," she says, breathless with worry.

No point in arguing with her. After our parents died she appointed herself family matriarch, which included adopting my mother's "A" ailments – arrhythmia, anemia and asthma.

I want to ask her about her trip and Stefan, my nephew who recently married, but she continues with her litany of complaints. Recently she's been convinced she's got a brain tumor from dyeing her hair black for thirty years. When I suggested she stop and go *au naturel* she screamed at me, "You think I want to live with ugly grey hair?" No, die with shoe polish on your head. Her solution was a recent change to a strange shade of blonde.

"Los Angeles may have more traffic, but it's cooler than here, I can tell you that." She adjusts the air-conditioning vent toward her face.

"How was Stefan's wife?"

My sister's mouth sets itself into a prim line, which means the two small points painted above her top lip disappear. "I don't know why he couldn't marry a *Cubana*. What could he possibly see in that insipid Anglo with stringy hair?" She pauses. "Besides, she hates me."

Maybe because Cuban women are bossy and controlling?

I sigh and re-grip the wheel. Here we go, another saga of slights, hurts and damaged pride. Ever since my nephew, Stefan, a tall Ricky Martin look-alike, brought home an alien-sized model from South Beach with large collagen lips, my sister has been fighting with him. Ludmilla's German accent and vacant blue-eyed stare drives her wild. And I haven't gotten to the plastic chi-chis she exposes to the world as she parades up and down the beach in a thong hoping a photographer will notice her.

Ignoring the protests of his mother and father that maybe he should consider someone with a bit more substance, Stefan staged a quickie wedding, danced all night in the clubs and flew off with Ludmilla the Lips to LA.

"She's so fake," claims my sister. In our family all the women are well-endowed: me, my sisters, my aunts, even sweet Mama, may-she-rest-in-peace, so anyone who has to pay for bosoms is suspect. "How can he want to touch those plastic balls?"

"Maybe he likes them."

Marta can't accept that. She makes a tsk-tsk sound and settles her *chi-chis* into a comfortable position with a few hand jiggles, adjusting them to look like a soft pillow, her line of cleavage sprinkled with freckles.

"The least you could do, Alegra, is get a little sex appeal. Buy a good bra. Look how Irma fixes herself up." Right. Irma, my role model with two ready-to-launch rockets in a low-cut number and cloying perfume wafting from her valley of flesh. When I'm with her I pretend not to be.

I feel Marta's disapproval. "Alegra, you need a hairstyle, contact lenses, some make-up. Why don't you fix yourself up? Let Irma take you chopping and you'll attract a decent guy." First of all, it's shopping and secondly, if Irma dressed me I'd look like a hooker and the pimps would be circling the block. I don't want a different guy. In fact, I'm considering no guy since Saul canceled our quickie Bahama cruise to stay home with Mama.

I stop at the light on Calle Ocho, part of the Latin culture of horny men and hot women. Better known as Little Havana, Latin rhythms pulse into the street accompanying women who jiggle and sway down the sidewalk. Men with pencil-thin mustaches sip dark, sweet coffee at the cafes, smoke cigars and play chess. Some stroke their pleated cubaveras in lust for the women.

When the first wave of Cubans came to South Florida in 1959, many people duplicated the businesses they had in Cuba. Our parents settled a bit farther up the road in Coral Gables. Their ten Havana dry cleaning stores had been distilled into one enterprise off Miracle Mile where my sisters and I gathered after school and weekends to work. The laments about Batista's corruption and Castro's confiscation stayed with them.

Eighth Street, an authentic transfer of culture, ignores the fact that it's located in America. The signs are in Spanish, the help speak no English, and the goods appeal to the Latin lifestyle.

My mother used to love to shop here, bustling from store to store with her netted shopping bag, dark hair poufed high, gray streak in the front and a floral dress covering her knee-hi stockings. She'd share gossip, bargain for goods, all without any knowledge of English. I'd trail behind, embarrassed at her flirtations and old world ways, but thrilled with the treat that waited for me at Cafe Madrid.

I'd start to salivate from the aroma before the garlicky steak covered with a mound of *papas fritas* ever hit my mouth. The elegant, elderly waiter, shirt starched eggshell white, would set down the plate with a flourish. After drowning it all in catsup, I'd eat in silence.

Mama, bags at her feet, would pat her perspiring upper lip with the napkin, her fork playing with the fried bananas that were my dessert and sipping Cuban coffee, a thick syrup loaded with sugar.

"Alegra, of all my daughters, you have the most sense," she'd tell me. I never knew if she meant it because I was the quiet, plain one or she was pleased to have me with her.

A horn honking behind me breaks my reverie. As we cross Eighth Street and travel farther south on Le Jeune past Dixie Highway, the scenery shifts from commercial businesses to lush Saint Augustine lawns, thirty-year-old pastel houses perched on concrete blocks set back from the street and enormous banyan trees with shaded canopies of green. Picturesque red tile porches are surrounded by yellow oleanders, pink and coral bougainvillea and white hibiscus.

With the seat belt stretched across her ample body, my sister adjusts her bra with a snap. "Can't you turn up the air? I'm so hot. I haven't eaten all day. I might faint. They're re-paving Hardee so don't turn here." With the last command she reaches out to tap the steering wheel with a purple talon embellished with a gold Aries charm.

I interrupt her litany. "Irma called me for money," I say, ungluing my sticky legs from the vinyl. I turn onto Madeira, a tree-lined street of candy-colored homes, their windows covered by elaborate wrought iron bars, caged protection from Miami's underbelly of crime.

"What? I can't hear you. Alegra, why don't you speak up? What kind of a *Cubana* doesn't speak clearly? You mumble." I hunch over the steering wheel at my sister's criticism.

The car jerks to a halt in the concrete-ribbon driveway next to the side of Marta's house. The chut-chut-chut sound of rotating sprinklers greets us. The iron in the water has turned the turquoise paint a discolored orange where it hits the house.

My shirtless brother-in-law, Sammy, opens the metal screen door holding their Rottweiler's collar. Rambo's drooling growl is directed at my car.

Marta waves and pushes open the passenger door, propping it with her foot. Gripping the doorjambs, her fingers splayed so as not to break a nail, she leans back and hoists herself forward, the acetate of her pants folded into the crack of her behind. She rolls like a football player ready to take his prize down the field, landing face down on the damp lawn. With a moan she turns over on her back.

"Marta," Sammy yells, hustling down the steps, the waistband of his shorts way below his jelly-belly. Rambo senses his chance, lurches and breaks free. He leaps onto Marta humping her leg wildly, his drool making a stain on her clothes.

"Get him off me," Marta yells.

"Hey," I shout, slapping my hand against the outside of my door. Rambo bares his teeth and emits a low growl when he sees me leaning out of the car. This is one mean canine.

"Can you get her suitcase?" I call to my brother-in-law. I spring the trunk with the lever inside the car.

Rambo leaps at me, a monster in action. Barking and drooling, his paws hit the side of my door with the noise of a jet breaking the sound barrier. I jump.

"For God's sake, Alegra, he won't hurt you. He's just friendly," Sammy says, picking up the choke-chain and jerking it.

Marta flails her arms. "He's ruined my outfit."

A neighbor opens her casement window with a screech. I catch part of what she yells, "Lock up that dog. *Peligroso … policia.*"

"Alegra, help Sammy with the suitcase. We both have bad backs. God help me, I might need surgery. Goddamn that dog," Marta says, propping herself on an elbow, frosted hair disheveled like a day-glow mop.

I've got to get out of here. With caution I open my door, hunch low, and, with the car hiding me, head toward the back of the Pontiac. I pull the twenty-ton fake Vuitton out, flopping it in the dank grass. Rambo smells meat, growls, and leaps out of Sammy's grip again. My sister, still in recovery on all fours with her rear in the air, curses.

The enraged dog closes his jaws around my ankle.   Crunching sends chills through my body. Pain shoots through my leg and the world swirls around me in green and black, a wetness filling my moccasin. I fall against the car and slide into the trunk.

"Sammy, get her in the car. Help her," yells Marta.

"She IS in the car."

"No, you *gordo*, so she can drive."

"You hold Rambo while I see if she's okay," says my brother-in-law. The dog yelps hoarsely, then coughs.

"I can't get up," says Marta, falling into the grass.

I curl into the fetal position to touch my ankle, bringing my fingers up to my face. Warm, sticky blood and throbbing pain. Marta's used to blood, but it panics me. I wish Sammy would close the trunk and dump me in the Miami River with the rest of the bodies wearing cement shoes.

"Alegra, get out. I'll take you to the *clinica*," says my brother-in-law, his image wavering in front of me. He looks very short. Barefooted and without his Cuban heels I think he's Danny Devito.

I close my eyes with the pulsating pain.

My sister screams, "The damn dog's choking. He's vomiting on my pants."

I can get to the ER myself. Anything is better than these two bozos taking care of me. I grit my teeth. I can do this.

"Give me a hand outta here," I say, reaching out. Sammy half-lifts, half-pulls me out.

I limp to my side of the car as fast as I can move, grab an old towel from the back seat and wrap it around my ankle to stanch the bleeding. Agony swirls around my leg as I fumble to start the car.

Marta calls out, "Thanks for picking me up. Sorry about the dog. I'll call you later, *hermana*." Then she turns and screams at Sammy, "You idiot, I told you to get rid of this God-damned dog. Pick up my designer luggage. It's getting ruined from the sprinkler."

Chapter Three

Alegra

July 13, 1998

Stretched out in my Barcalounger with my throbbing ankle elevated on a pillow, I click from channel to channel. On seven the broadcaster with extreme make-up reads our daily dose of murder with a slight lisp and on four, a twenty-year veteran with a bad toupee and sun-damaged frown lines squints at the camera. I settle on a Bill Moyers Special on PBS about environmental toxins in the home and mute the sound. The only toxins I have are my sisters. Never mind. I drown in a dark tide of misery, petting Butter, my calico nestled into my lap,

When the phone rings I don't want to pick it up. Without caller ID I never know who it is. I try to guess. Irma wanting to borrow money with another sob story? Marta with an ailment? Or maybe it's Saul, my boyfriend of broken dreams.

I hope I don't end up as a little old lady with no one to take care of me. I might be sorry I became a recluse. Sigh. At least my medical bills are covered by Burger King corporate headquarters. I work as an admin-assistant at the Home of the Whopper. And, let me tell you, I've seen a few.

"Alegra? Remardo here. You still sick?" Doesn't he remember I'm not ill. I just can't walk. "You've missed a week. Your temp's here, but I need you back to prepare the agenda for the franchise conference. She can find *nada*."

An acid bubble circles my stomach and burps its way up. The thought of a thousand franchise owners gathered in the gaudy ballroom of the Fountainbleu, jabbering in foreign languages, all of whom are committed to challenging management, gives me instant heartburn.

"Mister Remardo, I can't put any pressure on my ankle yet." The tetanus shot they gave me hurts every time I move and I wince. Thank God I didn't have to get a rabies series in my belly from that maniacal animal. Miraculously, he'd had his shots.

"I don't want to pressure you, but I can't set up this conference without you. Either come back *rapido* or I might have to look for a permanent replacement. You'll be back this week, right?"

"But Mister Remardo. . ." Click.

I struggle to sit upright brushing Butter off my lap. I've saved most of what I make and have a cushion I inherited from the sale of my parents' store, which my sisters blew through in a few months, but I don't want to lose my job. My Spartan life suits me. Change means turmoil.

When the phone rings again, I figure it has to be Saul. He's the only one who hasn't aggravated me in the last few hours.

"Hey, it's me, kid. Feeling better?" There's noise in the background so I know he's calling from the teacher's lounge.

"Not really. My boss called and threatened to fire me."

"Maybe you should limp back to work."

"Hey, that's not very sympathetic." I visualize him, bushy eyebrows half-hidden behind his over-sized square Cuban glasses, pencil in his shirt pocket, a bit rumpled, thinking he's giving me a helpful suggestion. Instead he's annoying me. Is this love? I'm not sure. I've never gotten mushy, fluttery, sinking-to-my-knees feelings. The truth is I can't be with my own company all the time.

He clears his throat. "Listen, I hate to do this. I know you were counting on getting out this afternoon to the doc office and a few errands, but. . . Mama has a migraine."

"Saul, I have no way to get there." My voice rises with a screech.

"Honey, I know. I can't leave her alone. She's nauseous. The light bothers her eyes. I can't leave her sitting in the dark."

What about me? I'm in a black hole of misery. I drop my head back and roll my eyes. I'm fed up. This is going nowhere. I must be crazy to put up with this for an occasional movie. That Mama gets to pick.

"That's fine. I'll take a cab." I don't click him off. When the nagging beep stops I doze off.

Chapter Four

Grazia

3 Ab 5252 (5 August 1492)

My father and I entered a cramped room after most of our belongings were stored in the ship's belly. In limited space, stepping around each other, we piled bundles of food and clothing into the corners. I handled them with care, placing my mother's sardines, wrapped in a thin layer of lambskin tied with string, on top of our bed. Ginger, saffron, parsley and peppermint permeated the room, familiar aromas that she created. Did she remember the almonds and pine nuts as a topping? Please, dear God, let her come soon.

My mother's valuables, sewn into fancy pillows from my father's finest fabrics, littered the bed. Her jewelry, stuffed into padded linings behind embroidered pastoral scenes, pressed against each other. A violet cushion of waxed linen, a method my father used for water-proofing, held gold and silver *kiddush* cups. Family heirlooms, table-covers embroidered with delicate flowers and grapevines, silver candlesticks and more were sewn into bedding, secret wrappings for our treasures. "Thieves and pirates will not know what lies beneath us as we lounge," my mother told me as we sewed them. Even my father's prayer books remained disguised behind Christian covers.

"I paid extra not to share with another family. No privacy, eh?" My father's face, lined with exhaustion, appeared swarthy in the dim light. His sweaty beard curled into the cowl of his hood, his tunic soiled from our day's journey.

I sat down on the bed. How could we sleep here? Perhaps I could walk the decks and find a place to doze later.

"Where is your mother?" My father was agitated, pulling at his bottom lip. My heart stopped. I shrugged my shoulders and fingered the soft leather purse that hung from my belt. He glared at me, his jet-black eyes accusatory.

"Do you know where she is?" I could not speak. I knew it would come to this. Where was she? She promised to be at the dock. He pulled me up by my shoulders, his face close, breath foul. "Where is she? Did she go to see that tramp sister of yours?" My eyes widened and I shook my head from side-to-side. "Liar."

He shook me until my teeth rattled. One hand drew back to slap me. The door slammed open with a clamor. Before his flesh met my face I heard my mother's voice, shrill with anxiousness.

"Hermando!" Her cheeks were high with color, eyes flashing around the room.

"*Madre*," I pleaded, breaking from his grip and running to her side.

The velvet cape, its hood hiding her mahogany hair, fell to her ankles and a green-fringed shawl tied in a knot over her bosom, covered her shoulders. White fur framed her pale face. The commotion of the last months destroyed all of us, yet she seemed serene. Instead of putting her arm around me she pulled the cape closer to her body.

"Where were you? I thought the ship would leave without you." My father was accusatory in his voice and stance, not relieved enough to move forward and touch my rescuer. His sulky eyes flashed.

My mother's soothing voice, cooing like a love bird at the nest, said, "Hermando, compose yourself. We are all well."

Shouts of others getting settled, trunks banging walls, distracting noises and the cries of resistance for what people could not change rang in my ears. So many tears for those left behind, some tragically burned at the stake. A horror I witnessed once in the past, ungodly screams and cheering crowds sanctioned by the Church, damaged my soul forever with nightmares. I shivered and it brought back the sympathy I felt for our compatriots and neighbors, don Marco Mendoza, two sons and their wives, abandoned, agreeing, as many did, to be pious Catholics with their children who would never learn sweet prayers. Another son was sacrificed to the church. What could ensure safety better than a priest in the family? Others, like us, insisted on one God and made a different choice.

My father's shoulders relaxed.

My mother placated him. "Come, let's find our friends, have a meal, watch the stars. The constellations will move across the sky wherever we are. A new life begins even if we object." As he stepped toward her, she pulled into the doorway. A wealthy patron in a brocade coat herded a group of musicians playing a familiar melody on string instruments. Others followed clapping and singing.

Her usually clear eyes were dusky as they shifted around the room. "Let us meet on the deck where Señor don Toledo plays cards." She motioned toward the water basin. "You go, Hermando. Give me a few minutes to freshen up. Grazia and I will meet you." She urged him out of our confined space, hands aflutter, shutting the door with resolve and leaning against it, her face fierce with excitement.

"Grazia, look what I brought." Her voice, husky with conspiracy, did not hide trembling hands as she unknotted her shawl, shifting the cape away from her body. Inside a sling swaddled in soft felt, slept a baby. Its translucent skin glowed with promise, the soft down of its sculpted head like the innocent feathers of a new bird. A benevolent smile transformed my mother's face and she lowered her eyes toward the newborn with pride.

"*Madre*, what have you done?"

"My granddaughter, your niece." She said this with pride, pulling away the layers from the child's tiny chin. "She's sleeping like an angel. I gave her wine to keep her quiet, something I learned from the secret circumcisions."

"*Madre*, have you lost your senses? Father will be furious." I leaned in to whisper, "The baby is a bastard."

Her face hardened. "Shush. Does it matter to God?"

"Father will never let you keep her. He will throw her overboard. Another mouth to feed. How do you plan to keep her alive?"

She clutched the infant closer to her chest. "Help me keep her hidden. A wet nurse waits below. Later we can slip away to see her." My mother's mouth twitched in fear and determination.

"*Madre*, this is crazy. I am afraid of *mi padre*, of what he will do to you and me if he catches us."

"He will not catch us." She lifted her chin in defiance.

"Yes, he will. I know him. He'll strike us with fury." A wistful sadness crossed her face and I relented. "*Madre*, why did you do this?"

Her eyes locked into mine with resolve. "I have lost sons in childbirth. I left my beloved daughter behind. I refuse to leave a grandchild."

I stepped forward to kiss the baby cuddled between us, sinking into compliance. The baby smelled sweet and clean and I was drawn into her spell. "Oh, *Madre*, I will help you."

Chapter Five

Alegra

August 7, 1998

I escape for three reasons: Irma, Marta, and the termites. But I digress. Late on a Monday afternoon, with my leg propped up, still unable to put weight on my ankle and bored enough to tune into a *novella* on the Spanish-language station, I descend into mediocrity. Graciela's pregnant and leaving Antonio for an Anglo who looks like Brad Pitt and stealing money from his father's *zapata* store.

The phone rings.

"Alegra, I have an idea for you," says Saul. Saul has a post-nasal sinus drip and sounds particularly stuffy.

I emit an internal groan. "What?" I know he can hear the irritation in my voice and I feel bad about it, but on the other hand, sometimes he has a high PIA factor. That's for pain-in-the-ass.

"A former professor of mine from the University of Miami is looking for a research assistant." He clears his throat and coughs. "Sorry. My allergies." I hear him gulp. I can't stand phlegm.

"What does that have to do with me?" I reach into a bag of chocolate-chip cookies from Andalucia bakery. Any hope of staying fit during this disaster collapsed when the doctor told me, "Six weeks until you can put weight on it and another six before you can exercise." Not that I exert myself much, but sometimes I take a stroll around the block of my Coconut Grove neighborhood.

"Here's the number. Just call Professor Guzman. Maybe he has something you can do from home." I don't feel motivated to do anything, but Saul knows I like to make and save money. Can I do without it? Get it used? Do they sell it on e-Bay? I search for the pen and paper I've squirreled in the side pocket of my green vinyl monster, one of my few indulgences. I'm proud to say I'm the only person I know under sixty who has a Barcalounger.

I write down the number to appease him without much interest in calling Professor Guzzie or whatever his name is. In this depression I think about combing my hair for an hour. A dark fog wraps itself around my head. I can't get past how wretched everything's turned out. The piece of paper drops on the floor.

Days later when the debris around my chair looks like an urban garbage dump, I pick up the note with the number and stuff it in my bathrobe pocket. My sisters are coming over today. I wish they wouldn't but I can't stop them. Marta's convinced she can cheer me up and I'm sure Irma has an agenda.

In the bathroom mirror my face looks sallow and blotchy. I haven't plucked my eyebrows in a year and there's soft fuzz on my top lip. If I don't make some minor improvements my sisters will sit on me and do damage. I get out the razor that I shave my legs with when necessary. By the time they arrive I'm decorated with little bits of toilet paper.

Marta bustles in wearing her favorite tracksuit and carrying a large casserole wrapped in tin foil. A piece of white dimpled flesh separates the top and bottom of her outfit. She says with delight, "Potatoes au gratin."

"A whole potato dish?" An entire meal of starch? My sister takes my surprise as an opportunity to explain her potatoes.

"It's from a box. All I had to do is add the potatoes. The cheese was included in powdered form. Mmmm. Smell it." She offers me a corner where she's peeled back the foil. It's the aroma of chemicals in processed food.

"Cheese and potatoes? I'm on the sugar diet–cake and cookies."

"It's good for you. Cheese has fat in it so it makes your skin look nice. God knows you could use some help in that department." She gets up close to me and squints. "What happened to your face?"

I turn away from her examination. "Thanks, it looks delicious."

Irma waits behind her in skin-tight jeans and a halter-top, a studded belt wrapped around her hips twice. She prances by me. "I'm the diet-conscious one so I brought you a tofu salad. It's from Epicure." That's the expensive gourmet market on Alton Road. Unfortunately, tofu gives me gas. No way I'm sharing it with Saul.

Marta sets her casserole dish down in the kitchen and turns to me, hands on hips. "What the hell happened to you? Another dog fight?"

"No, I was getting rid of a few hairs and. . ."

"Haven't you heard of electrolysis?" Irma asks me as she fluffs her salad.

I hear her mutter under her breath, "How can a sister of mine be so dumb?"

I could give her one of my smart retorts, but what's the point? I really don't care what Irma thinks about my sub-standard grooming habits. A ragged red bit of toilet paper from my face drifts to the floor.

I lead them to the family room. Irma says, "Why do we have to sit in here? It's stuffy. Let's sit in the living room." She turns and heads, hips swinging, toward my unused room and stops in the doorway. "Oh. I forgot you've never taken the plastic off Mama's furniture."

Irma stares into my living room, a 1950's Cuban museum sans the red velvet rope. A burgundy brocade sofa takes up most of the wall between antique tables with green leatherette tops. Plump pillows with black tassels fill the corners of the couch. An oil painting of a ship in a storm fighting white-capped waves hangs over the sofa. Two gold filigree lamps with ivory shades and fringe, complete the room except for Mama's purple glass grapes in a bowl. The pile on the carpeting leans in one direction because I backed out of the room when I vacuumed a month ago.

Marta elbows her way into the doorway. "*Mi Dio*, Alegra, why don't you use this room? It's a mausoleum." She tramps across the carpeting leaving gross footprints. The couch makes a crackling noise when she sits down. She smiles, satisfied, that she's done something to annoy me.

I hobble over and lift up her arm. "No, I want to sit in the family room."

Marta doesn't resist me but she mumbles in Spanish that I'm crazy. Irma follows us, a smirk on her face. Listen, their places aren't so great either. Irma moves all the time and sticks with white (how much decorating talent does that take?)and Marta thinks red velvet wallpaper is sexy.

My house isn't that great but at least I own it. Mama and Poppa told me over and over not to pay rent. I know if I live frugally I'll always have enough.

They settle themselves into my family room furniture and I climb into my cocoon of a chair with its steel reinforcements. I hear a breaking noise from a few lost potato chips as I pull back the squeaky handle to recline.

Marta leans over to pat my knee. "So, *hermana*, how are you feeling?"

Before I can respond that my throbbing ankle keeps me awake at night and I'm depressed as hell, Marta cuts in, "I don't know how much longer I can work with my bad back. I need to go for an MRI. Consuela drew my blood yesterday and I think I'm anemic." Her hands run up and down her arms as though she's cold.

Irma dismisses her with a wave, "You always have something wrong with you. I have real problems." She leans forward, arms on knees, "I'm one payment away from my Mercedes being repossessed."

"Why do you need such a fancy car when you haven't got a pot to piss in?" asks Marta, playing with her rings.

"Are you counting my money?" Irma raises her voice and twists her body toward Marta, eyes dancing with displeasure. She jabs a fake French-manicured nail at her. "You've got a helluva nerve."

"Please stop it," I say. "I don't need to listen to an argument. I thought you came to keep me company."

Marta turns away from Irma, "Yes, *hermana dulce*, we're here to cheer you up."

The only thing that would cheer me up is if they left.

Irma, cooing in a baby voice, says, "Can I fix you a plate?" I agree just to get them separated. Irma prances into the kitchen, her walk suggestive enough to inspire the comatose. How does she get those jeans down to pee?

"I don't know why she can't get a job and work like the rest of us. Don't loan her any more money," Marta says to me in confidence.

"I hear what you're saying in there," says Irma, coming out of the kitchen, a plate piled high with tofu salad and potatoes. "You're always putting me down. Since we were kids you had it out for me. Even Papa said so."

Marta stands up to look Irma in the face. "*Mierdo*. I am so tired of your accusations. You've never worked a day in your life. Sammy and I hustle our backsides to make a living. What did you do with mama's money? Pissed it away on your expensive car and punta clothes."

Irma shoves the plate into my chest. She positions herself, hands on hips, in Marta's face. The fight continues above me. "Like it's not work finding a husband?"

"Yea, you worked on your back." Marta turns, crossing her arms on her chest.

I hunch over the plate shoveling food into my mouth even though I'm not hungry. Potatoes and tofu are better than watching the two of them. My sisters' spat, a continuation from childhood, hasn't changed much over the years. In the past I tried to be the mediator to avoid upsetting Mama. The difference is now I don't care.

I pull the handle on the Barcalounger and jerk upright, my head bouncing like a pogo-stick. After setting the plate on the floor, I squiggle out of the chair and, with an exaggerated limp, head into my bedroom dragging my left foot behind me. I lock the door, crawl onto my bed and put pillows over my ears. Soon I hear Irma knocking. In a wooing voice she calls, "Alegra, Alegra, do you have any pain pills?" I ignore her. "I have a terrible headache."

I don't know when they left, but it's dark outside when my bursting bladder tells me it's time to get up. I hobble to the bathroom.

When I finish I grab the crutches leaning against the wall and tuck them into my armpits. How am I ever going to learn to use these? I stumble through the house and turn off the glaring yellow light outside and maneuver myself through the door, flopping on a lawn chair. I drop the crutches into the dewy grass and take a breath of fresh air scented with night-blooming jasmine.

The phone rings. Oh, well. Probably one of my nasty sisters anyway. I'm beginning to feel more like Cinderella every day. I close my eyes and try to think positive thoughts. Not a one floats to the top. Everything seems bleak. Only the thought of constellations, a favorite of Poppa's, soothe me.

He'd reach for my hand when I was a kid, his clothes still smelling from the dry cleaning store and say, "Alegra, in Cuba the stars shine even more brightly. Castro can't steal freedom in our heart or beauty in the sky." Then he'd put his arm around me and chew on his cigar. We'd sit in our backyard for hours staring up.

In the early evening an oblivious Orion, easy to identify by the three stars in his belt, leans back on his right elbow with Taurus, the bull, glaring down at him with his eye sparkling. Later, as Orion rises, club overhead, he threatens Taurus. Most of the night they stare at each other, and then toward morning, Orion's club reaches overhead with Taurus backing away into the horizon.

Lost in the heavenly drama, I feel calm. With my crutches tucked into my armpits, I venture back inside. A blinking red light reminds me I missed a phone call. I press the button and my answering machine makes a whirring sound. Irma pesters me to get voice mail, but I don't want to learn all the new technology: voice messaging, call waiting, three-way calling. Too overwhelming. It whirls to a stop.

"Alegra, this is Mister Remardo. Uh, I'm sorry to have to do this on the phone ..." I hear a scuffling noise and a cough. "...but I have to let you go. With the convention coming and the amount of work I'm responsible for, I. . .

Listen, you've got severance pay and sick leave coming plus unemployment. I can write you a recommendation. I wish you the best."

The dial tone bawls at me, a taunting kid with his tongue out. I push the rewind button and listen again. It's the same. "That coward," I stammer. Firing me over the phone. What an outrage! I hammer my fist on the aqua Formica counter. No job. No real boyfriend. One ankle. I'm a mess. I'd like to march in there and tell him what I think of him. I'd like to remind him of all the times I saved his ass. I'd like to.

It's then that I notice a few clay-colored cocoons nestled in the crease of my kitchen ceiling and wall. I clump and hop around the kitchen like a madwoman, slamming the closet door open, grabbing a broom to dislodge the suckers, whatever they are. How dare they take up residence in my home?

The straw of the broom doesn't dislodge them so I turn it around, a violent baton twirler, and stab at them with the other end. At first I tap the hard wood tip on them. Nothing. Then I try to push at the edges, lose my balance and fall on the linoleum floor. My throbbing elbow broke the fall. I lay flat, tears rolling into my hair and let out a noisy, sloppy sob. Sometimes a huge cry is the only alternative. When my runny nose drips onto my chin, I decide I can't stay on the floor any longer. I try to get up and collapse in a heap on my rear, terrycloth slippers pushed to the baseboards. It takes me ten minutes to crawl into the family room and drag myself into my favorite chair.

The next morning it's all still bleak but I decide to take action. I'm going to file for unemployment, tell off my sisters, buy myself a half-gallon of Rocky Road and ignore Saul. But first, I call No Cucarachas Extermination Company.

"Lady, it's a good thing you didn't dislodge the nests yourself. Could be wasps. Who knows? Our technician, Luis, can get out there this afternoon."

Next, I reach in my pocket for the crumpled piece of paper and call Professor Guzman. Maybe it's time for a change.

He's not in, but the secretary for the history department gives me an appointment for an interview tomorrow. I have no idea how I'll get there and negotiate a campus with distant parking spaces, grass and stairs, but I'm determined.

A few hours later Luis, a well-built young man, arrives in a brown uniform with a pencil behind his ear and a flashlight hanging from his belt. I show him the problem in the kitchen. He nods.

"I'll have to inspect the rest of the house and outside."

I feel so insulted. Like I'm not a good housekeeper. "I don't have any bugs. Just those few pods up there. Think they've got body snatchers in them?"

He looks at me with an arched eyebrow and speaks to me in Spanish. "Señora, what you've got is no joke." He begins to inspect the rooms, opening closets, poking into everything, even my dirty clothes hamper. How embarrassing. I hope I turned my underwear right-side out. Worse, I wear the nylon old lady kind that comes to the waist. Silent and serious he pushes up the square to the attic crawlspace in the hall with my broom.

"There's nothing up there," I say, "except global dust balls."

He gives me a knowing look as if to say, "That's what you think." He asks, "Do you have a step-ladder?"

I limp into the kitchen and drag a step-stool out of the broom closet. Paper bags from the grocery store leap out and I do my best to stuff them back in. I pull it behind me, the way Marta dragged me around as a kid.

He places and adjusts it a few times, climbing up and sticking his head through the crawl space. He shines the flashlight into the corners. From where I stand it's all pipes and insulation and cobwebs.

After he gets down he gives me a dark, hard stare, as if to say, "Your mother would be disappointed in you."

"What?" I've given away my power.

He shakes his head. "Señora, lo siento. You have termites." He takes the pencil from behind his ear and scribbles on a pad. "The boss'll do an estimate later. It'll cost you. . . ." He stops to chew on the eraser and add numbers. "Now, mind you, this isn't the final number. You can't hold me to this because the boss has to come and measure."

Sweat beads up on my head and between my breasts. "For crying out loud, tell me. How much?"

"Five thousand dollars."

"You're kidding." No job and a five thousand dollar expense? Deflated, I cave, my knees buckling. I reach for a piece of furniture.

"Don't worry. That includes all the subterranean digging outside and the tenting."

I look up. "Whoa, tenting?"

He gives me an exasperated smirk. "Señora, you have to move out for a few weeks. We tell people its okay to move back in after a week, but if you have respiratory problems it's a bad idea. I wouldn't advise it." He shrugs his shoulders with indifference. "Any pets?"

I nod yes.

"You'll have to board them. Fumes can make them sick, too. And be sure to remove all those hanging spider plants."

"But my cat doesn't adjust well to new situations."

"Yea, Lady, I hear that all the time. The boss'll call you to schedule it. I'd say do it as soon as possible. You've got a real problem. You know all those antiques you got in the living room?" My eyes widen. Mama's furniture? He tucks his pencil behind his ear. "That's where the nests are." With that my screen door with the wrought iron palm tree slams and locks automatically.

I touch the walls and furniture to guide myself into the family room and settle into my chair. Could it get more devastating? My house under a yellow plastic tent filled with noxious fumes? Moving out for a few weeks means spending money for a hotel. I can't go to a dive. Between the drug dealers and the burning goats from the island people practicing *santeria*, Miami can be dangerous. Besides, without a job extra expenditures seem like punishment.

My other choices are: Saul, Marta or Irma. Saul's out. Living with his migrained mother dressed in widow-black would be torture. She'll think I've moved in to trap Saul into marrying me. I'd be cooking and cleaning and waiting on her in a day. Five-foot tyrants do not rule my world.

Next on the list is Marta. I could handle Sammy, my Neanderthal brother-in-law, but do I really want to move into a house with a killer dog? I haven't recovered from the last injury. That leaves Irma. The fancy condo and the strong smell of perfume are manageable, but smoking and whining? Gheez, I don't know.

Of course, that's my only alternative. Living with Irma. Temporarily. Will it sever a life-long relationship?

I can hear her after a week when she starts introducing me as "her housekeeper" to her dates and offers to buy me a uniform. "Think of how impressed these guys will be. Money begets money," she'll tell me. Right. A gimpy maid.

I'm using a cane to get around, pressing my weight onto my right leg. I can drive, too. And, just so you know, the interview with Professor Guzman at the university went badly.

His office, tucked away at the end of a long hallway in the Old Main Building, smelled like musty clothes. I stored my crutches in the hall and limped to the door. With a timid knock I entered when I heard a "come in."

A professor around fifty with a halo of grey hair wore half-glasses and a bow tie. He sat behind a cluttered desk. Bookshelves climbed to the ceiling and a cherry wood pipe sat in an ashtray. I smiled.

"Come in, come in. Sit down. Which one are you?"

"Alegra Cardoza," I answered with hope. He gave me a puzzled look. "I should be on your schedule." I got up to lean over his desk and pointed to my name on the piece of paper he held. I realized my bosom was showing so I slapped my hand against my chest and sat down. "Saul Carasco sent me." He looked confused. It made me nervous that he had no idea who I was. "Your former student?"

"Oh yes. Now I remember. So what are your qualifications to be a research assistant?"

I cleared my throat to sound professional. "I don't actually have any. But," I added, sitting straighter, "I'm very efficient and reliable. I've been the assistant to the VP of Burger King."

"I'm not selling hamburgers." His swivel chair squeaked as he turned around and searched a file drawer.

"Yes, I realize that, but I'm used to handling many tasks and Saul says I'm pretty bright. May I ask what you're researching?"

"*Marranos.*"

I had no idea what that was and I'm sure I appeared confused.

"*Conversos.* Crypto-Jews who lived hidden in Spain. Fifteenth century."

"Oh. Interesting." Hey, I needed a job.

"Listen, do you mind if I'm direct?" I shook my head. He leaned toward me, flipping through a pile of index cards. "I have someone else in mind. She's getting a graduate degree in history. Knows who *Marranos* are." He stood up, offering his hand. "Thank you very much. My best to Saul. He could have been a great scholar."

So I didn't even get the minimum wage job with the professor. Dejected,

I made mental plans to transport Butter and pack my bag to move to Irma's, hoping the antiques wouldn't disintegrate in the toxic fumes.

It takes me a few days to get it together and after I settle in to her eclectic condo, I start going through the help-wanted ads, calling temp agencies and drinking a lot of Cuban coffee.

Irma sleeps 'til noon every day. Three weeks to the day after I arrive, she emerges from her bedroom with Butter wearing a rhinestone collar, a sleek black sleep mask on top of her head, barking orders.

"Coffee. No cream. Two sugars." She groans, pulling her fingers through her hair from the bottom up so it stands out. "I have no money for my hair appointment with Rosario. Can you buy some color and help me with my roots?" She sinks into a chair with her legs apart, satin mules dropping off her feet. "Drive the Mercedes around the block so the repo guy can't find it in the lot." She lights a cigarette, takes a drag and I start to cough. "I told him you borrowed it the last time." Butter curls into her lap, that rotten slut.

"Me? Why me?" I fan my face with my hand and back away from the smoke. I can't believe my life. Another stupid scheme. How did we come out of the same womb? Mama and Papa would be appalled. If I wasn't related to this woman, I'd, I'd. . .

"When you move the car, bring back another pack of cigarettes. You know the kind I like. The French brand." She gets up and parades out to her balcony with its great ocean view, robe flapping open in the breeze. I follow her outside to view the sky spread with fluffy clouds.

"Since when am I your errand girl?"

"Since you're staying here." She turns to me touching my cheek. "Come on, *mi hermana*. I'm just in a rough spot. My check will be here this week from the lawyer. Just do it."

"Do you have change for the parking meter?"

Her hand with the cigarette brushes me aside. "You take care of it for me. I'll pay you back." Right. If she ever paid me back all the money she's borrowed, I'd be able to bankroll a rescue mission to Africa.

Inside I grab my purse, take her keys from the imitation Louis the Fifteenth hallway table with its gigantic arrangement of red silk poppies and head toward the glass elevator. Outside, I move her car to a public lot a few blocks away, pile coins into the meter, and begin my walk back to

Ocean Towers. I trudge down the sidewalk, my ankle not fully healed, but grateful to be mobile.

Collins Avenue, lined with swaying palm trees, has an inlet of water on one side with houseboats and yachts floating side-by-side and tall condominiums hiding the beach view on the other. Since the fifties it's been a prime real estate address.

I remember Irma's hair color and cigarettes and the fact that no stores are within walking distance.

I make a momentous decision. Butter loves Irma. I am not going back. Ever.

I hail a cab and climb in. The taxi driver asks, "Where to?"

I have no idea. He turns around to give me a dirty look. "Lady, where ya goin'?" A recent New York transplant no doubt.

"University of Miami in Coral Gables." How dare that professor not hire me? I'm going to go back and ask him why. Losing a bit of bravado, I mumble, "Maybe someone else needs a highly efficient bi-lingual secretary."

"Lady, ya got a hundred bucks for this trip?" I open my purse and check my wallet. The good thing about being tight is you always have mad money squirreled away.

Chapter Six '

Alegra

August 10, 1998

"**D**id we have an appointment? Where's my blasted calendar?" Professor Guzman begins to rummage through the mess on his desk, lifting papers, dropping books on the floor, turning over piles of exams and computer print-outs. He looks up at me, eyes blinking, forehead crunched into a confused furrow. "Is your laptop set up to take my files? The Symposium requires hand-outs for all the participants. I hope you have those ready. Also, call my housekeeper and tell her to take the fish home with her."

He turns his back to me and dives into a beat-up leather briefcase, oblivious that I'm standing there with my mouth open. "The special food for the lion fish is in the cabinet."

The smell of stale French fries from a forgotten lunch wafts toward me. Crumpled packages of catsup are strewn across the desk and a large drink drips puddles on the papers bleeding ink into a Rorschach design. A small fan whirrs on top of a tall filing cabinet and lifts corners of papers in a pop-up rhythm.

It's obvious he thinks I'm someone else. "Professor Guzman, I'm not. . ."

The door opens. A middle-aged woman in a cardigan sweater and red frizzy hair hangs through the entrance with an envelope in her hand. On the frosted glass of the door, near Harold Guzman, Ph.D, painted in black lacquer letters, dust and fingerprints zig-zag across, crab tracks dancing across a beach.

"Professor Guzman, a young woman dropped this off for you. Said it was urgent," says the messenger. She holds out the envelope but his back is still to us. "I have to get back to the phones," she says to me with a disgusted look, shoving the missive in my direction.

When the door closes, he turns, his eyes darting around the cramped space. "What? Who was here?"

"A woman left this for you." I pass him the manila envelope.

Distracted, he tears it open and unfolds a white piece of paper, his eyes skimming across the page. I notice a small stain on the front of his shirt.

"Shit," he says, slamming it down on a pile of books. "That flimsy-assed girl studying Churchill. Well, she doesn't know it but I just became her Gallipoli. She'll never get a recommendation from this department. I can black-ball her from every historical review in the country. In Europe. In the world." His neck muscles bulge into thick purple cords. He looks ready to explode, banging his fist on the desk, files spilling onto the floor.

"Sir?" He doesn't hear me. I feel claustrophobic in the tiny office with a madman. His rant becomes louder, spittle spraying from his lips. "That academic idiot. Fuck her. I'll destroy her. I'll. . ." He sputters and little wet spots hit some papers. He rotates to the bookshelves and starts to bang his head. Maybe he ran out of horrible things to do to her.

"Sir?" I ask with trepidation, trying to get his attention. I ease back toward the door, poised to flee if I have to.

He whirls around, "Who the hell are you?" His forehead beams tomato-red.

"Alegra Cardoza. Saul's friend? Remember I interviewed with you a week ago? The position was filled, but I stopped by to see if maybe you know of another professor who needs some help." I stop and then stammer, "Maybe you," nodding toward his mess.

"Do you work on the computer?" he asks, smoothing back a few stray hairs from his fading-to-pink forehead.

I step forward. "Oh, yes sir, I know Excel and Word and I'm a whiz on a search engine. And I type one hundred forty words a minute."

He looks mollified. "I'm not interested in speed. Can you organize my notes?" He's annoyed with me.

Suddenly, I realize he's interviewing me and I stand taller. "Yes, I'm very efficient."

He stares at me and I smooth my skirt, swallowing hard. "Are you a quitter?" he asks, reaching for a pencil and bouncing it between two fingers until it flies out of his hand.

"No, I finish everything I start. Ask Saul." Okay, I've just dumped my sister so mentally I escape into dusky crevices of guilt.

He purses his lips, tapping them with his finger. "If you can leave in three days for Spain and get everything ready for my symposium, you've got a job. If not, you're out of here."

"I can be ready," jumps out of my mouth as my eyes bulge and my heart leap-frogs inside of me. All my anxiety about sisters and termites sails away. "How long will I be gone?"

"Three months."

Chapter Seven

Alegra

August 12, 1998

I don't even care what the professor is paying me. With neither of my sisters speaking to me and Saul angry at my quick departure, I make arrangements for a cab to take me to the airport. I leave my disloyal cat at Irma's, abandon the Pontiac in Marta's driveway and place my keys in an envelope that I slip behind her screen door.

Rambo growls and begins a barrage of barking when he hears me. I bare my teeth and growl back, slamming my hand against the turquoise entryway. His paws hit the inside with such force that he could knock it down. I flee in terror. I clutch my hand to my chest and run down the porch steps to the waiting taxi, the maniacal animal howling after me.

I feel like a prisoner escaping from a Georgia chain gang. Sweaty with anticipation, fearful of failing and apprehensive about being locked up with the nutty professor for three months, I take a deep breath to calm myself. I've never done anything with such impulsive abandon.

When the Iberia Airlines plane lifts off, I press my forehead to the window, watching the hazy pink Miami skyline fade away, its ragged coastline of beaches and hotels blurry in the twilight.

The professor ignores me, busy with his briefcase and papers. Periodically he moves his glasses from his nose to his head, his pocket to the front of his shirt. Eventually they drop to the floor.

So far he hasn't asked me to do much. He gives me a quizzical look as though he doesn't remember why I'm here and falls asleep with his mouth gaping, snores thundering and bowtie askew at his neck.

I snuggle under a navy blanket and can't sleep worrying about what I left behind. Will Butter miss me? Probably more than my sisters and Saul. Did I do the right thing dismissing my life? Saul started a fight the night before I left when I stopped over to say good-bye.

We stood in the vestibule of his home. "I'm going to miss you," he said, hugging me close to him, his big, hairy arms around my back. He removed his square glasses and hung them on the front of his shirt. Without them he looked bewildered, confused. His belly, a soft cushion hanging over his khaki pants, bounced against me, a teddy bear of protection. Blue specks dotted his bushy brown hair and his T-shirt smelled from paint. Mama had him painting kitchen cabinets.

"You'll be fine," I said, giving him a playful push.

"No, I won't. I didn't know when I referred you to the professor you'd be taking off like this." He sounded sulky.

"Saul, it's the opportunity of a lifetime for me." Or my own personal disaster. I looked up at him hoping I was in focus. His eyes seemed watery and I turned away. "You don't take me anywhere. What's the difference if I'm here or not? It's a cyber-relationship anyway."

"E-mail is the best way for me to keep in touch with you. You knew when we started dating I wasn't going to be a typical boyfriend. We share intellectual pursuits. What about that?"

I stuck my neck forward and squinted at him. "When's the last time we talked about a book or we didn't have to see a movie your mother wanted to see—one without sex, violence or bad language and in Spanish?" My voice reverberated with sarcastic mock-horror.

"Don't bring my mother into this."

"Saul, how can we have a relationship when there's a vampire sucking us?"

"Are you saying my mother's a vampire? If you were open to Mama's suggestions–"

"Saul, that's it. Your mother is not going to control what I think and believe. I should be good enough just the way I am." I touched my perspiring neck.

"I think you should go. Have a nice trip," he said, turning me toward the door. He kissed the back of my head and gave me a gentle push. I heard the click of the extra security lock and thought, 'Maybe I should go back in to make things better.' But what was the point?

Instead of confronting the real demons in my head, I curse the hibiscus bushes on Saul's front lawn, his mother, Irma's feathered mules and the idiot dog who bit me, "Damn it. I'm tired of nothing going my way. I'm not a doormat. I'm outta here."

I doze to the monotony of the engines. Then it hits me. I'm going 3000 mile with a sloppy professor who probably doesn't know my name and wants me to do a job I may not be qualified for, in a place where I know no one. Now there's a plan. I recite a convincing monologue where, afterward, everyone comes to me and apologizes for all their wrong doings. It doesn't make me feel any better. I'll show them, I say over and over again.

A cheery flight attendant, an apron covering her uniform, breaks my reverie by holding tongs, a steaming towel dangling from the end of them. Plastic food is on its way. Tears stack up in the back of my throat. I press the button to lean my seat back and close my eyes. I miss my chair. The cabin lights are dimmed and I drift away. A few hours later I'm awakened by the pilot's voice announcing our altitude and more tongs with a hot towel in my face.

As the plane descends I'm in awe of the mountains and the shadow of the plane reflected in front of them as we approach in the early morning hours. After the long flight to Madrid, I disembark behind Professor Guzman who is still stewing about his previous research assistant. "Damn history major."

He hasn't bothered to use the packet of toiletries so graciously given to us by the airline. Salt-and-pepper stubble covers his face, his clothes are rumpled and his electric-socket hair looks like a halo from hell. I brush away lint from my clothes, real and imagined.

We notice a man with a two-day growth of beard in a shiny dark suit holding up a cardboard sign with "Guzman" on it. After introductions and luggage retrieval, including a giant box with the Professor's hand-outs, he herds us into a boat-sized black car and whisks us to our hotel, the Madrid Continental, the site of a three-day symposium.

"Excuse me, Professor, what are our plans?" Without air-conditioning I lower the window. The air is heavy with humidity like Miami and I feel apprehensive sitting in the back seat with this stranger. What have I gotten myself into? He's mentioned we're scheduled to stay in a colleague's home in the hills overlooking Granada for a few months, but I don't have any details.

"What?" He's disorganized, searching through papers in a battered briefcase, checking for his wallet, dropping his passport and clip-on sunglasses near our feet. I see why he needs an assistant.

I repeat my question.

He blinks at me with surprise, an unexpected alien who's landed in his vehicle. "I gave you our itinerary months ago." He's a bit snippy.

"Sir, you only hired me this week."

The vehicle stops short among horns honking and screeching tires. I brace against the front seat. His briefcase flies off his lap, contents and all his papers fluttering around the back seat.

In the hotel's marble lobby, The Professor, as I call him, comes alive. He barks orders about checking the ballroom, posting the schedule, viewing signage, testing microphones and setting up his brilliant hand-outs entitled, "Eating Habits of Crypto-Jews and the *Diaspora* from the Iberian Coast during the Fifteenth Century Inquisition."

I write down everything I'm supposed to do and count baggage. Uh-oh. I'm one short.

Professor Guzman is greeted warmly by some fellow academicians and launches into a tirade about his no-show history major.

I re-count the pieces. Frantic, I search for our driver in the slick suit and he's gone. Of course it's the box of hand-outs that are missing, hi-jacked by intellectual terrorists from a rival faction of nerds. Seriously, I can't find them.

Chapter Eight

Grazia

4 Ab 5252 (6 August 1492)
En route to Portugal from Spain

I preferred the ocean to our land journey, the dusty tragedy of our expulsion resonating with the cries and turn of every wheel. The sea changed color like the tail feathers of wild geese in the wind. Blues blended into the night sky and inky blacks, shiny as a crow's head, folded into the horizon. I stared for hours into the deep waters, the ship tossed by waves, rocking my spirit.

I hurried with coins Mama gave me for my niece's wet nurse. Fragments of languages float by me from the others on board. Greek, Italian, Portuguese, German, and Spanish flowed from people's mouths as they strolled the decks. Castles up high fore and aft are filled with arrows. Will we be attacked?

I nibbled a meal of bread, yellow *barenja*, and chicken livers. Two gentlemen leaned on the handrail next to me speaking *Ladino*, a jargon of Spanish and Hebrew that my father used in business. In fact, all the congregants in our secret temple spoke it plus other languages: Arabic, Portuguese, Dutch or French, a necessity for survival with shifting circumstances and business travel. Their voices sounded familiar as they whispered in the darkness. I hid my identity in the hood of my cloak.

". . . tired of cold, dark Sabbaths, afraid to have the servants stir a fire. I want to live in the open," one man said, voice grouchy with frustration.

After a silence I heard, "Yussef, why will the Catholics do business with us in the new country if we reject Christ and deny Mary's virginity?"

"We are New Christians." He turned and faced his friend.

"I am not a believer no matter how many times they sprinkle water on my head. Better to live as a Jew. Whatever we do we are not accepted. We live together in the same *barrios nuevos*, never changing our habits. Does moving us to a new country make anything different?" I heard him cluck his tongue then sigh. "I yearn for the past."

He waved his friend away. "Do what we have always done. Pretend. Forget their saints and holy pictures. Do business with the Moslems." I lost snippets of conversation in the wind, my father's scraps of fabrics floating away. "Ach, stick with what you know. Maybe it is time to switch from textiles to coffee and tobacco when we settle in the new place. Let Guzman have the textile trade."

The other responded with enthusiasm. "It is almost Sukkoth. The observant need myrtle, palm, willow and citrons for the festival. Maybe this year we will not have to hide our booth."

The festival that celebrated the forty years our people wandered the desert made me nostalgic. We used to re-construct the symbolic temporary shelters with friends in the forest decorating them with palm fronds and citrons. Has our wandering changed? The two men shifted away from me.

I glanced at the sky to spot the sprawling Ursa Major. It looked brighter here than on land. The stars created a loose bear that cradled The Big Plough. I pretended my humble wagon or perhaps a golden chariot towed me away from my troubles. The pattern of the blue-white stars consoled me. Maybe God lived there, observing us all. It gave me something to clutch while my life had no roots.

My parents resented being ordered out of our home. Could we continue to live two lives? One for the outside world as pious Catholics following the church's rules, and one inside as Jews, complicated and defiant. Forever labeled *conversos*, not fitting one place or the other, we were doomed.

Though I knew the pageantry and grandeur of the church, my mother taught me our blessings, festivals and recipes to remember for our children's children. She was passionate about our link to the past and women's duty to preserve it. But my father's scholarly father, a man whose funeral was attended by hundreds, shared stories I remembered most from my younger days.

One Sabbath we consumed a meal prepared in the woods. I asked him, "Why do they despise us?"

He responded in his baronial voice, lips rosy against his snowy beard. "In our Torah, the holiest of books, it tells the story of a prophet of the Gentiles. As exalted as Moses in his time, Bilaam was known for two characteristics, one blind eye and his hatred of the Jews. With his good eye he prophesized the fate of the Christians, but with the unseeing one he saw only the Jews. It is the same clouded eye of injustice that accuses us, tossing us from place to place far from the land of Abraham."

I dwelt on the blind eye at times, wondering what made a man despise another for his beliefs, but I never reached a conclusion. In frustration I sighed and left to look for my mother.

We were at sea a few days and my mother and I had managed to fool Papa. He had no idea she had smuggled a baby on board. It exhilarated me to have a secret and scared me, too. What would happen when we disembarked? She would have to tell him. I feared his reaction.

The first time we visited the child she named Bellina, I choked on the stench in the hold. I was appalled at so many people crowded together without fresh air. I cupped my hand over my face to keep the stagnant odors from burning my nostrils.

Later I crept by myself to the bottom of the ship avoiding people. Many were sick from the motion, bending over the side. I placed a handkerchief over my nose as I approached the hold. My mother, in an appliquéd dress of black, met me at the bottom. She gave the guard a coin to let us through. I followed as she strode to the corner of the room where a plump young woman hunched against a wall nursing a child. Two more young ones clung to her skirt, their faces camouflaged in the filmy light.

"The baby, please," my mother told the woman whose dark hair was covered by a scarf. When the wet nurse pulled away her cotton gown, a pink child appeared.

"Almost finished." The baby's cheeks were round as ripe apples.

My mother lifted her and placed her over her shoulder with a small cloth, patting her back and cooing. The baby burped. We laughed, sitting on a low bench.

"Look." My mother unwrapped Bellina and turned her over on her lap, resting her full belly in her hand. "The mark."

I stared at a pear-shaped blue stain at the base of the infant's spine. "What?" I traced it with my finger.

"It proves she is of our people."

I was confused.

"You and your sister had one, too, at birth." She clutched a little at the thought of my abandoned sister, yet she continued. "Sometimes they fade, but all Sephardim have them. Sometimes a dark gray, sometimes blue, but always near the base of the spine or on the back or leg. It shows we belong together."

"Mama, the baby is beautiful, but what if Papa finds out?"

"Give the woman coins from your pouch." She turned away with a smile. "I have paid her with a necklace of garnets." She handed the baby back, kissing her head. "It will work out." I followed her through the smelly hold with my fingers cupped over my nose and mouth.

Chapter Nine

Alegra

August 19, 1998
Granada, Spain

The lost box of symposium hand-outs never appeared. Somewhere, some place another professor is impersonating the wild-haired Dr. Guzman and using his research.

We've settled into a contemporary home on loan from one of his colleagues. The elaborate structure turned out to be an architectural feat carved into a hillside. I have my own quarters at one end and he has the master suite at the other.

A large living room, white leather love seats and marble tables, overlooks a terrace with a spectacular view of the Sierra Nevada Mountains. A wall of glass runs the length of the room. A kitchen with modern appliances and tile counters separates us. Our office is in the corner of the main room with a desk and bookshelves. We share his laptop. Sometimes I work on my notes and organizing paper files at the tiled counter in the kitchen.

This morning the professor's tennis game at a neighbor's court takes priority over academic pursuits. An unlikely sort to play a sport, I've watched him a few times and he's surprisingly coordinated. A fluid serve and competitive spirit drive him to win.

I usually walk in the morning, work a bit, have lunch, a brief siesta and then tackle the computer in the evening. He spends his time writing, reading or trying to keep his pipe lit. All in all, it's relaxed, especially since the home comes with a cook who prepares *tapas* for us in the evening.

I'm learning to love the assortment of appetizers–garlic lamb chops, eggplant wrapped in peppers, *cerviche*. I enjoy a glass of wine with Professor Guzman at sunset on the deck although we don't banter back and forth much. The silence makes us both more likeable. My sisters would be proud that I'm wearing cotton skirts and tops trimmed with lace purchased from the *mercado* in town. Nothing fancy, but the bright colors match the bougainvillea that cover the wall surrounding the property. It forces me to think in cerise, plum and tangerine instead of black and white. Is this what Marta meant when she said live a little?

Yesterday the post-it note on my desk said:

Research Mongolian spots

alfajor (macaroons)

Andres Bernaldez

barenja (do eggplants come in white and yellow?)

15th c. *mikvahs* and *minhag*, Sephardic rituals

kosher slaughtering

hammocks

He's left me lists like this before. I spend hours looking up this stuff – God knows what for–and he's so uncommunicative I don't dare ask him why. After all, I like it better here than running errands for Irma or worrying about whether Saul's mother is going to have a migraine and kill our weekend plans. I don't miss any of them except Butter and he only loved me as a favor for feeding him. Well, Irma's doing that now.

The other day when I gave the Professor the information on hammocks, he was upset. I thought it was something I said so I hurried to explain. "Columbus brought hammocks back from the Bahamas. He got the idea when he saw the natives sleeping in swaths of cloth strung between two trees." I busied myself in the file cabinet. "Probably kept the bugs from crawling on them," I added over my shoulder. When he was silent I turned around.

He looked annoyed, his bushy eyebrows meeting in a frown. "*After* Columbus? Are you sure?"

I stood taller. "Yes, I'm sure. The first ones were from the bark of the Hamak tree, hence..."

His fist hits the desk with a thump. "Damn. That means they weren't used on the caravels in the 1490s."

I had no idea why this mattered. "What's the problem?"

"Never mind."

I wandered into the kitchen area and picked through a bowl of fruit. I'm not used to anyone snapping at me. At first I was upset but as I peeled a banana I found it curious.

I shake off most of what he says because it doesn't make sense to me, but hammocks? Most of what he requests is available through Google, Judaica and Catholic encyclopedias installed in his computer. I figure he's starting on the next symposium, although I can't figure out the focus. Anyway, he's already researched Sephardim and their food. Doesn't matter. Just so I can relax and not think about Miami. By now the termites must be dead.

I return to his desk searching for today's list. The disorganized Professor. While I'm straightening his mess of papers, folders, and professional journals into piles, I move post-it notes, abandoned coffee cups, a Spanish phone book, pipe paraphernalia that includes a large ashtray overflowing with pipes and cellophane bags of tobaccos, I stop to sniff the cherry one with its woodsy fragrance. That's my favorite.

A manila envelope peeks out from another stack of papers addressed to him in his own handwriting. I don't hesitate. It only takes a moment to undo the metal grip on the back and slide out a sheaf of papers titled "The Blind Eye". Thumbing through it, I'm intrigued. Maybe it's not my business, but I haven't spoken to another soul since I've arrived, except the cook. His desk is considered part of my domain.

Curiosity makes us do strange things—like open someone else's mail. I begin to read the professor's loopy handwriting. He has abbreviations for many words, leaving out vowels in others and switching between English and Spanish. It takes me a few minutes to realize I'm not reading a personal letter or historical notes. It's not a research paper or an academic treatise for the next conference.

I sit down in his desk chair without a trace of guilt. It takes a little while until I realize it's a story. I've been duped.

I'm not quite sure why I'm simmering, but somehow I feel cheated. I thought I was doing something important, contributing to historical significance or aiding important research. I might as well be a secretary back at Burger King. It shouldn't matter, but it doesn't sit right with me.

I've had this happen before, where something bothers me, never crystallizing so I can verbalize it. I just know it's gnawing at me like those damn termites in my walls.

I sit in the Professor's chair, waiting, my feet propped on the desk, which, by the way, is now in perfect order, including sharpened pencils and his four types of breath mints. I've set up a color-coded file system for him with no hope he'll use it, but I'll be able to find everything. Hours pass and

I doze. It's funny how even when you're sleeping you can tell someone is staring at you. My eyes flutter open and he is standing in front of me.

I remove my feet from the desk. He looks chagrined, picking through old messages on a spindle perched at the edge.

"Professor, with all due respect, you hired me as a research assistant." I cross my arms over my chest.

"Yes, and you're sitting in my chair." He pulls off his clip-on sunglasses and a sweat-stained visor and drops them in front of me.

"I found *The Blind Eye.*"

"So?" He gives me a look that says it's none of my business.

"So you're making up stories and not writing a historical paper. Why am I researching all this?" My voice gets high-pitched when I'm nervous so I lower it.

He turns away. "Do I pay you on time?"

"Yes, but, this isn't serious work. I was led to believe. . . ."

Without warning, hands thrown in the air, he explodes. "Who are you to say what's important? An impudent without a sense of history or your traditions. You don't even know how your family got to Cuba. It was most likely via Turkey before the First World War because they didn't want to fight or be persecuted."

"What are you talking about?" I'm sure I look unhappy and confused. He takes my expression as an opportunity to get louder, pulling his shirt out of his waistband and flapping it to air himself.

"Where do you think the fine name Cardoza comes from?"

"I have no idea. What does that have to do with anything?" And, a bit more haughty, I add, "I'd appreciate you lowering your voice. My hearing is excellent."

"You think you can judge my work without knowing your past? You're like the rest of the ignoramuses I teach who have no sense of historical continuity."

I stand up. "Where I've come from or what I know is of no consequence to you as long as I do my job." I'm snippy and I know it. I haven't lost *every* argument with my sisters.

"There's a rich tapestry of ancestry you've buried in your oblivion." His fuzzy eyebrows leap and his voice bellows. "What's the use? You're fired."

That shocks me. Embarrassing tears flood my eyes. I come out from behind the desk and run to my bedroom on the other side of the house. Fuck. Why did I antagonize him like that? Maybe I'm supposed to go home anyway, but it doesn't feel great to have messed up a free vacation. I pull my bag from under the bed, scrape open the drawer of an ancient carved dresser and toss in my colorful wardrobe.

I hear footsteps and the professor stands in the doorway.

"Alegra, stop. Don't leave. I-I apologize. Stay for dinner. Let me explain what I'm doing, why I'm passionate about getting my research out in a different format. Maybe you can help."

I snuffle. It would be a sign of weakness to stop and get a wad of toilet paper to blow my nose right now. "I don't think I can stay. It's time for me to get back to Miami. My family misses me." I lie.

Professor Guzman, his hair in its usual disarray, steps forward. The dim light yellows his tennis whites and the worry lines on his forehead seem more pronounced. He doesn't have his glasses perched on the end of his nose or on top of his head.

He smiles a little. "Have dinner with me in town. At Le Bistro. I remember you mentioned you'd like to try it."

I put my hands on my hips. What makes him think I can be bought with dinner and a flamenco guitar?

"I don't think so." I turn back to pack my suitcase, pressing a pair of brown leather sandals into the sides.

"I'll tell you what. Bring your suitcase with you to dinner. If you don't want to stay, I'll pay for a night at the pension so you're closer to the train in the morning."

I think for a minute, my head tilted to the side. The offer appeals to me. I try not to grin. "That sounds fair, but I'm not making any promises."

"Would you mind making the reservations for eight-thirty? I'm going to take a siesta." When I turn around he's trying to smooth his Einstein-like hair with his hands. "I'll see you later."

I end up driving to town because Guzman can't locate his glasses. It's not far and on the bumpy ride he steadies himself against the dashboard with his hands and squints. I know he can't see anything so he'll have to take a cab home. I'm leaving. He'll have to get his friend to get the car.

Le Bistro drips in ambience. We're seated outside on a large terrace near a waterfall that flows into a small pool. Guitar music floats on the breeze.

After narrowing his eyes at the menu for a few minutes, the Professor waves over the waiter. A handsome young man with the deportment of a bullfighter appears in a starched white shirt and tight black pants. His slicked black hair reminds me of patent leather.

"Sangria, *por favor*."

The waiter brings the pitcher, orange slices floating on top, the handle decorated with a gardenia. I don't wait for a toast and take a sip. The red liquid slides down my throat. I remove my glasses, fold them and place them near my bread plate.

The waiter rattles the memorized specials. "Tonight's meal includes gazpacho, fresh catch of the day, seasonal vegetables and the house specialty, caramelized flan with fresh kiwi and berries."

I nod, the professor nods and my blurry Antonio Banderas leaves to place our order with the chef.

"Alegra, take off your glasses. If I can't see, why should you?" The professor's crinkly eyes, a light hazel, dance in the candlelight.

For a moment mariachis belting out "Que Linda" overwhelm the room from another part of the restaurant and drown out the guitar. I remove my glasses, placing them on the table, blinking for clarity.

He's wooing me! Since Antonio has disappeared, I'm open. I had no idea sangria, ambient lighting and soft music would make me so easy. Mind you, I'm not talking about any funny business. It's just that leaving no longer seems attractive. In Saul's last letter he wrote his mother had the shingles and Marta emailed there's a garbage strike encompassing all of Dade County.

The Professor breaks the silence. "Through my research I found my family came to Cuba from the West Indies and before that Brazil, just like the first Jews who settled America in September, 1654."

"But, excuse me, Professor, what..."

"Call me Hal."

"Hal, what does this have to do with..."

"Those twenty-three Sephardim who arrived in Manhattan on the Dutch ship Sint Catrina were from a Dutch colony in Recife, Brazil and had spent years looking for safety. How can people know what they lost unless they learn the story? History evaporates in two generations. Do you know your great-great-grandparents names, where they came from, why?"

I shrug my shoulders. I'm not as interested in my past as I am the present.

"What does that have to do with hiring me under false pretenses?"

He sighs in exasperation, his impatience evident. "First of all, I never made specific what you'd be doing and secondly, what difference does it make? Research is research. Besides, I need a female opinion." He softens and gives me a slow grin.

"Sir, with all due respect, I wouldn't know a good novel from a bad one. I'm part of the Latina culture. I watch novellas and read magazines, which are mostly fashion and ads." I don't know why I'm making myself sound so dumb. I do read books. Maybe I want an escape hatch.

"Alegra." He says my name, a growl from the back of his throat, and reaches across for my hand. I don't move it out of the way. "I am impressed with your intellect."

I puff myself up a bit at the compliment.

"You're the best assistant I've had." He lets go of my hand as the waiter, who smiles at me, clears dishes and re-fills our glasses. Self-consciously, I pull my hair behind my ear.

"I'm interested in your opinion of my first attempt at fiction. I've investigated *conversos* for years and how they survived under repressive conditions. Why not turn it into an appealing story?"

I asked a question I'd wanted to know for a while. "Are you religious?"

"I rejected all organized religion in college. Certain family customs struck me though. My mother closed the drapes and lit candles on Friday night. My grandparents wrote specific instructions on how to dispose of their bodies, including cleansing, wrapping them in white linen and using a pine box. Jews have great respect for life."

"But who's going to be interested in reading about things that happened ages ago?" A slip of hurt passes across his face. "I mean, what's the point?"

"The history of the Jews during the Inquisition is similar to that of the 1930s in Hitler's Europe." He counted off on his fingers. "Badges, hiding, scrambling to survive. Our idea of one God hasn't been let go of in 5000 years." He shook his head.

I bristle. "Are you assuming I'm Jewish? Aren't there employee privacy laws that you can't ask how old someone is, if they have kids or their religion?"

"Probably but we're not on American soil. Besides, what difference would it make? Many Catholics trace their roots back to the Expulsion."

I take a sip of sangria. "Aren't you assuming a lot?"

"Maybe."

I sit quietly, my body sinking into a resolve. "Does there have to be an orphan in your story? It seems like such a cliché." Maybe it's the sangria or maybe it's because I'm challenged, but I'm finding the evening stimulating.

"Ah, so you are caught up in my manuscript."

"Would you like some fresh ground pepper?" asks the waiter. I nod yes, stealing another look at him.

Chapter Ten

Grazia

4 Ab 5252 (6 August 1492)
At sea en route to Portugal

My mother's touch felt cool in the darkness. She slept between me and my father, his snores grinding against the rhythm of the caravel. The ship, favored by explorers, was one he admired. Sometimes he treated me as his son, taking me to the docks to watch the loaded vessels leaving for their discovery of new worlds. Before, it was Hanna. A grain of guilt rubbed against me.

My mother stroked me again. I moved closer to the edge of the bed, my fingers dragging on the floor.

"Grazia."

I shifted my body, my head turning toward her, the softness of my Egyptian cotton undergarments grazing my skin.

Her lips touched my ear, a butterfly flutter. "Take Bellina to the deck for fresh air. Wrap her against the night chill."

I groaned in annoyance.

She shook my shoulder. "Ssh, he will wake."

Rolling myself into a ball, I hugged the quilts to my body. I did not want to get out of bed to walk a baby. Bellina knew me now, tiny fists reaching toward my face, a smile on her moist lips. But she was not precious enough for me to leave the warmth of a bed.

I shook my head back and forth. "*Madre*, no. Not now."

Her fingers gripped the upper part of my arm, nails pinching my skin. "Yes, before he stirs and the decks fill with people. Take the woman a bolt of cloth hidden beneath my cape. Your father will not miss it."

I had serious doubts she could hide a baby from him much longer. What would happen when we arrived in Lisbon?

She pressed her icy fingers on my back. I stumbled out of bed. My father grumbled a few words, flinging his arm across her. I froze. Minutes passed. When his breathing became steady again, my mother urged, "Take my wrap for the night air."

Weary, annoyed, I crawled on the floor toward the door, pulling myself upright when I felt the velvet of my mother's garment. Her luxurious cape felt heavy on my shoulders, silky satin lining glimmering in the darkness, felt slippers warming my feet. With fabric for the wet nurse tucked under my arm, the hood covering my hair, I opened the door with stealth and slid into the corridor, my heart thumping.

Small lanterns illuminated the low ceiling. In the dim light, I crept through hallways, my annoyance abated. Alone at night, a rare experience. Fear pushed bile up my throat.

One other time I found myself alone with only the moon to guide me. We had gathered at our Cousin Catalina's home on Friday afternoon for our Sabbath bath, a chance for community with friends. With the servants sent away and the stew prepared, Catalina poured heated water into a large ceramic tub in the middle of the kitchen.

After blessings she sprinkled rosemary and orange peels into the steam, the fragrance swirling into the air. We took turns cleansing ourselves before changing into fresh clothes, sharing stories and combing each other's hair, all in preparation for the Sabbath bride. My mother showed me how to clean under my nails with a small sliver of wood, throwing the parings in the fire. A knocking at the back door interrupted us and we jumped.

"Señora, my shawl."

Catalina, her eyes darting around the room, whispered, "Estela, my cook." She coughed. "A moment. I am not well."

Even as she motioned us to hide everything from our Judaizing, we glanced at each other in panic. A group of women together on a Friday aroused suspicion. Discovery could mean death. My mother tucked her prayer book in the folds of her skirt; my cousin Reina grabbed spices and placed them behind her; two older women took a bowl of garbanzo beans with them into another room.

She knocked again, louder. "Señora, the night air is chilling me. I need my shawl." Was it a ploy to expose us? Did the priest send her?

Catalina, frantic, knew there was no time to empty the bath. "Ah, Estela, I have come down with a fever. Perhaps contagious." With deer-speed she peeled off her white linens and picked up her dirty clothes from the floor. "I will have to bathe again," she whispered to us.

My mother sat, her expression calm, knowing this could be our last Sabbath. She turned to me and with a soft voice and said, "Grazia, go home and tell your father I will be late. Set our table."

I reacted with surprise that she could think we were going to survive this.

"Grazia, go. The Lord waits for us."

I tip-toed to the front door and slipped outside, standing in the darkness, afraid, even though I knew the way. Beggars, thieves, rabid dogs. Anything could stop a female alone at night. I searched for the moon. Once found, I ran, its light guiding me, my heart racing, feet careless of mud or garbage. Papa had to know of our danger.

Hours later, when *mi madre* returned, I learned Catalina passed Estela her shawl through a crack in the door, a cloth over her face for the feigned illness. Estela tried to peek inside, offering her services to prepare a soup, but Catalina declined. Her opportunity to buoy a suspicion with an accusation could mean a reward of Catalina's goods. When the others felt secure in her dismissal, they assisted Catalina in re-heating water, saying the blessings and bathing again.

The ship rocked with a heave and jolted me back to my mission. Wide awake, alone, I relished my freedom, taking long strides. The ship is mine, I told myself, as I swung my elbows out from my sides. Until I heard voices. Men's voices. Would they want to know what a young woman was doing wandering a ship alone at this late hour? Frightened, I crawled under a stairwell to wait, crouching in a corner. As they approached I recognized Enrique Torres, a merchant with a limp who traded with my father.

From my vantage point I stared at his special shoe, one that fascinated me because of its lift in the heel and a space cut for a deformed toe. My heart, thrashing like trapped bird's wings, almost crashed outside my chest. I held my breath and put my head between my knees to erase any sound, hiding the white of my face.

The men stopped to chat, their words muffled.

Saying a silent prayer to God Almighty that the black cloak blended into the murky space, a movement startled me. The tickle of short legs scurried across the top of my foot. I jerked, pulling my legs under me. A small gasp escaped my lips. Rats, or even a small mouse, petrified me. My meticulous mother who associated rats with pigs said a person could die if a rodent touched the body. My hand leaped to my chest to steady its drumming.

Breaths came short and fast and I blinked in nervousness.

"What? Who is there?" The two stood in front of me.

I sunk into the sheltered shadow, pressing against the stairwell, the cloth clutched under my arm. I did not want to be discovered. What if I had to explain why I was moving around the ship?

"Ah, Enrique, forget it. A lover on a mission."

"Who is that hiding? Show yourself," said Señor Torres in a loud voice.

With my finger I wiped sweat from my top lip. Pulling the hood close around my face, I put my head down and aimed between them, a bull charging a fence. I jostled them and the unbalanced Señor Torres fell.

His friend knelt over him offering an arm. "Are you hurt? Who was that?" he asked.

"I recognize that cloak," said Señor Torres. "Only one man's wife dresses with such elegance. . ."

I made my dash, disappearing around a corner, throbbing with anxiety. I prayed they did not follow me. Or start rumors about my mother. "*Shema Isroel*," I whispered under my breath as I ran. I looked behind me. No one. I leaned into a doorway, heaving. I hurried down the staircase that led to the hold.

In the obscure light people covered the wooden floor. They leaned into one another, mouths drifting open in slumber, their bundles uncomfortable pillows. I picked up the hem of the cape to step over dozing mounds of flesh, so many bodies, contorted limbs, broken marionettes. A large man sleeping on his back exploded thundering snores. A few children giggled nearby. In one corner a woman whimpered, a trapped kitten caught in a burlap bag readied for drowning. A few men rocked back and forth, swaying in prayer, lips reciting forbidden words. The smell of spoiled food overwhelmed me as I made my way to a fussy Bellina. The wet nurse rocked her, looking up at me, her tired eyes waiting for relief. I set down the fabric. She handed me the cranky baby.

"I am taking her upstairs for air." She nodded and stroked the indigo damask with her fingers, raw hands worn with work.

I saw no one as I carried Bellina upstairs, down corridors, past four masts, their triangular lateen sails bloated by wind, to the rounded stern. I peered out over the vast ocean, stopping for a moment to play with the precious baby, touching her precious nose half-hidden in her wrappings.

She took a deep breath and with a tiny sigh, settled in and closed her eyes.

I paced back and forth close to the rail, wandering and singing a low song. I repeated the Prayer of Dreams: *yo soy tuyo y mis suenos tuyos seran.* "I am thine and my dreams are thine." Maybe someday a sweet child would belong to me if I married.

Alfonso, the young man my father betrothed me to, one of soft eyes and thick brows, stole my heart. His hands appealed to me—long, graceful fingers with spotless nails that slipped in and out of his coat for a hidden candy or a childish trick. The way he held himself, proud yet shy, revealed someone not handsome but kind.

I was no beauty, my plain features a disappointment to his mother. A discussion of a dowry for me began—rare fabric, jewelry, money. Alfonso was from a fine family, educated, required by our laws to learn Hebrew for prayer. My father lamented that Christians could only listen to Mass, not read it, another cause for prejudice.

Alfonso and I hoped for a wedding. After a secret seder in 1495, held on a different day so as not to arouse suspicion, we celebrated Passover in their attic. Shortly thereafter, his mother and father were accused by neighbors of not being true New Christians.

Stories were whispered to the authorities that incited an investigation. Details began to pile up—animals slaughtered with forethought, their blood caught in a pan outside, a banked fire and cold partridge on the Sabbath, a grandmother who kept watch as she sat in their front window with a spindle pretending to weave while they made preparations for the day of rest. They fled in the night, leaving their home behind, knowing the outcome of an *auto de fe*, the grand tribunal where many were sentenced to prison or death by fire.

Without warning a pinch on my shoulder spun me around.

"What are you doing here without a chaperone? Whose baby is this?" My father stood before me, furious, waiting for an explanation.

I had none. I could not explain my mother's complicated plot, one that had lured me into a spider's web of deceit.

"Answer me," his voice bellowed. I shrunk back to the rail, opening my mouth. Nothing came out. Petrified, I felt trapped in a nightmare. He wrenched Bellina from my arms, holding her over the railing. She began to wail, instinctive of her danger.

"Oh my God. *Padre*, no, do not hurt her." I grabbed at my father's arms without touching Bellina. He pushed me away with his elbow. I faltered, tripping on my feet, falling to the deck.

A white figure ran toward us, arms and legs flailing with urgency, screaming, a black hole for a mouth, hair streaming like uncombed skeins of yarn.

"Hermando, stop. No." My mother reached us, stumbling, heaving, pleading with him, her litany of no's desperate.

My father lifted the baby high, dangling her above the water, her cries louder. Bellina's blanket slipped away and floated into the abyss, a breeze lifting the corners.

"You defied me. This is *her* baby."

Tears spilled down my mother's pale cheeks. My place was not to interfere in family matters. I cried for the helpless child, slipping away from the rail. When my father realized my complicity, he would reach for me.

His voice roared. "*Her* baby?" He raised his eyebrows and his eyes flashed in anger. Bellina shrieked, her cries piercing me.

The ship rolled with a shifting of the sails and we lost our footing for a moment. A few drops of rain fell on my shoulders.

"You cannot kill. It is a sin. Remember the commandments," my mother begged.

"Do the commandments say anything about daughters and wives who defy the head of the household?"

My mother dropped to her knees, shivering without a cloak. Her pained face glistened with sweat in the small bit of moonlight. "Hermando, for the love of God, I pray you realize your power. Let the child live." My father's expression, still angry, softened a bit around the mouth. She made her case. "Another child for us in old age. In a new place. No one will know or care. Our lives are uprooted, turnips pulled from the ground."

Bellina's cries filled the silence. Her small feet with perfect toes hung over the bottomless sea. A lifting of the fingers, the lurch of the ship, a loss of balance and she would be gone. I began to sob, my hands covering my face. A clap of thunder startled me and I looked up. Bold lightning ripped across the sky. My mother closed her eyes, my father's mouth turned down in frustration and he moved away from the edge. The heavy scent of rain filled the air.

"Get up."

My mother, with my help, rose from her knees staggering with grief.

"Cover yourself," he said, handing the baby to her. "You have betrayed me. We will all be punished for your defiance." As he turned away, Señor Torres and his friend approached.

"Señor Guzman, good to see you. You are wakeful also. Meet Enrique Cervantes. Perhaps we can do business together at our new destination." He leaned in with a confidence. "A friend of the Columbus family. Wool weavers, too."

"Perhaps," my father growled, glancing at us over his shoulder and striding away.

My mother hugged Bellina and threw her head back, eyes toward Heaven. "Thank you, *el Dio*." She clutched the infant to her breast. I placed part of the cape around her shoulders for warmth. Bellina's breath smelled sweet.

"*Madre*, careful. It's *Dios*. Remember the plural is for the Father, the Son and the Holy Ghost."

Raindrops began to fall in earnest and we hurried for shelter.

Chapter Eleven

Bellina

My story, one of truth and lies, hardship and unexpected events, remains a mystery. I am a motherless child.

I do not recall the packing before our exit from Granada, the wailings of my grandmother and the shouts of my grandfather as he hammered barrels together for piles of fabric. Grazia has told me of velvet for draperies, felt for hats, silk and linen for garments and material woven through with metallic-wrapped threads that looked like spun gold in colors of ruby, sapphire, amethyst, ebony and iridescent pearl–the colors of *mi abuela's* jewels, ones hidden under her skirts.

At five I was fluent in Spanish and *Ladino* as well as Portuguese, the language of our adopted land. Usually accompanied to the market by my grandmother or Aunt Grazia, on a particular day I was entrusted to go by myself to negotiate rope, fruit and sweets. In my childish head a magnificent adventure awaited me filled with hidden treasures and secret dangers.

"Do not give them the lace unless it is not enough," my grandmother said as I prepared to leave. I fingered the rough texture of it in the pocket of my dress.

As my grandfather banged nails into raw wood with a vengeance, he cursed the queen who started it all. He prepared boxes of white linens to be shipped to other *conversos* for burial purposes. He lifted his head and pushed himself up from the corner of a wooden box, rough hands torn and bruised.

"What? Give away my goods? I walked through Lyon for days to find silk lace until the sun faded. Novices worked into the night. I was almost killed by a robber. This is what you toss aside?"

My grandmother stepped between me and my grandfather.

"Quick," she told me, her hand on my back, "Go."

I hesitated.

"Hermando, our coins are few." *Mi abulela*, a handsome woman of thirty-eight years looked worried, her green eyes darting from him to the door. Long fingers slicked back her jet-black hair, poking the bun low at the nape of her neck. Her voice softened, "Everyone wants your lace."

She shooed me out the door.

He came to stand in the doorway, hair disheveled, his velvet waistcoat covered with saw dust. He wiped his arm across his brow. I heard him say, "When will our fate be tied to our talents and virtues, not the flaw of our birth?"

I skipped through the stalls with ease, paying for the goods with a few small coins and the lengths of lace from my grandfather's stock. Many vendors knew me, greeting me with respect, the granddaughter of Señor Hermando Guzman, an educated man with business acumen, a man with proper lineage.

But, as sure as I was about whom my grandparents were and where they came from, I had many questions about my own parentage.

The story of my origins changed at each telling. Sometimes my mother with the green eyes ran away with her husband, sometimes her husband abandoned her, sometimes she was lost and nuns took her in, but she always, and my grandmother's voice would sink to hushed tones when she told me this, my mother always died in childbirth.

Often my grandmother made herself the heroine, running down the colonnade, through the market in Seville toward the dock, a tiny baby clutched to her bosom. Sometimes my Aunt Grazia saved me from unknown terrors and swarthy strangers. When I asked about discrepancies in their stories, they clucked their tongues at me. What were their selfish reasons for keeping me, a female? To pass on our leaky heritage, a belief system punishable by death?

Later, when I asked about my mother's special robes and garments I needed to wear for celebrations, my aunt and grandmother made excuses. The absence of a trousseau, the lovely lace and linens that brides savored and kept in families for generations, were gone.

"No," my grandmother would say, shaking her head in sorrow, "we buried it with her. A very sad day. God did not mean for children to perish before their parents."

My aunt said they had to be left behind when we fled Spain.

I romanticized my parents' passion, the sacred parting kisses, her pale alabaster skin and his muscled shoulders. In my fantasy a lock of dark hair fell onto his forehead, banded in worry. Sometimes it was darker. The kisses faded into her body writhing in pleasure and then into the pain of thrusting me into the world.

Later, I had fleeting dreams that others held me, one whose milk kept me alive with the rocking of a ship or that a swirling sea invited me to rest. I sensed my arrival, both wanted and unwanted, made me loathed and adored. Had I created a social conflict for my family? I held my version of a loving mother and father close to me. As I matured my questions became more urgent, until finally my grandmother and aunt said, "Enough." I repeated their stories, adding my own details.

"– and my father was handsome, the son of prominent people?"

They would glance at one another, intent on their embroidery or hand-stitching around a collar and nod. My grandfather, silent and serious, sipped his sherry.

Chapter Twelve

Bellina

The high-born home I grew up in coveted secrets. On Fridays my grandmother shopped early in the day, stopping into the Cathedral of Santa Maria, the ancient church off the square in the main part of Lisbon, three towers marking the sky. With a distracted wave at neighbors, she rarely stopped to chat. We kept to ourselves. Once, when I tagged along, I overheard her say to Aunt Grazia, "Someone must see you going into the church. If no one is around mention it to the shopkeepers. Good Catholics keep the faith."

Preparations consumed us as we washed, cleaned and cooked for the Sabbath eve and the next day. We refreshed the wicks in our lanterns, took baths, dressed in white linen, all under threat our holy rituals could expose us. So many of our kind had been tortured or burned by Fray Tomas de Torquemada's zealots because a jealous neighbor cast a whispered suspicion, that we trusted no one. The promise of our success invited envy. The Church confiscated our goods and shared them with others, enriching the Queen's coffers.

With a surreptitious eye I spied on my grandmother. In the morning she took a special knife kept apart from the other utensils. With a swing of her arm she sharpened it against a stone. Then she went into the backyard and caught a chicken from the few penned up. She amused me chasing the fowl, alternating between kind and coaxing words and curses about poxes, hunching and reaching for a fast bird. In the end *mi abulela* always won, the squawking fowl wedged next to her body, her lips pressed in determination.

With a deft move the knife appeared from her pocket and she tilted the bird's neck back. The sharp instrument went across its throat faster than a blink and the cackling struggle ended. After a few headless runs around the yard she hung the carcass on a hook, blood draining into a dish until it sometimes spilled over. She disposed of the earthenware bowl later. My job was to cover the stained earth with ashes from the fire. When she brought the bird inside, she removed any trace of blood, placing it in a wicker basket to be roasted later in a pan of salt water.

I watched from a small stool in the corner of the kitchen. A few stray feathers skittered around the floor with the movement of skirts. Grazia was learning how to braid *challah*, a soft yellow bread we tore into pieces and passed at the table. "*Madre*, tell me again. What do the humps on the bread mean?"

My aunt, with olive skin a touch too dark and midnight eyes a bit too small, was not a beauty. Her pie face with its beaked nose and thin lips showed little expression and her short body appeared lumpy in places, as though she was hiding balls of cotton thread on her hips.

My grandmother's gaze was sincere. "The braids symbolize peace, truth and justice. The twelve camel-like humps remind us of the tribes of Israel. Some day we will gather in Jerusalem and be free."

Grazia dropped her head. I could barely hear her as my grandmother moved pots to boil water and finished plucking the chicken, the pink pimpled skin slapping a board.

"*Mi madre*, when will I marry? Is no one interested from our community?"

"Your father pursues this, but with another edict imminent, our priorities are elsewhere." She looked up as the chicken's feet fell to the floor, a few more white feathers drifting in the air. "It will be when the time is right. God takes care of these things. Hurry, we must finish and go for our Sabbath bath before three stars appear in the sky."

My grandmother moved a small rug with her foot, bent down and lifted a loose floorboard in the kitchen. With great care she reached in, removed a package and unwrapped two burgundy velvet bags. *Mi* abuela placed ornate silver candlesticks on the table.

"Bellina, wash your face and hands, change your dress to the white one and wait for us. If someone knocks on the door, make sure it is your grandfather. We expect him soon." I resented that I could not go with them because I was too young, but I looked forward to *mi abuelo*'s arrival, his pockets often filled with sweets.

Many times I touched the intricate scrolls on the candlesticks, my finger tracing the grooves on the length of them. "From Granada," my grandmother told me, "and passed to us with great danger. After the forced baptism. After they took away our books and burned our Torah."

When she spoke to me in Spanish her words tumbled like traveling clowns and vagabonds, more fluent than her stiff Portuguese. "Bellina, these candlesticks graced my family's table, passed from one generation to another, back to King Solomon when we first arrived in Spain, descended from the tribes of Judah and Benjamin." Her eyes watered.

In a shaky voice she continued, "After the riots in 1391 and the destruction of our quarters, we were forbidden to ride in carriages or wear jewelry, allow silk or brocade to touch our bodies. At great risk, we saved these." She touched the candlesticks, her head dropping in despair. I reached out and touched her dressed hair, urging her to continue.

"I met your grandfather because he was from a family of renowned merchants who traded with the Indies. Mine were physicians who intermarried with the Spanish court." Her voice, bitter, sounded hoarse. "Some good that did us. We did not offer a child to the church as other families to bribe for influence. Our dignity could not be compromised."

She opened her collar to show me a ruby necklace of miniature butterflies hidden against the safety of her alabaster skin. With a flick of her wrist she folded it into a six-pointed star. My eyes opened with wide amazement. Again, she turned it back to crimson butterflies.

"No one can tell Dona Estrella what to wear. Despite their cruel rules we observed the Sabbath, God's special day of rest, read our books behind Christian covers, attended church on Sunday and still it was not enough. Our true faith is our secret."

"*Mamacita*, we have to go." Grazia pulled her from her intense reverie. "Fortuna is waiting for us in her cellar. The door will be closed after dusk and the water cold. Hurry." My grandmother leaned down and brushed her lips on the top of my head.

When they returned we gathered around our table covered in a cloth of embroidered silk, vines of grapes and bountiful fruit stitched with care, our countenances shiny from scrubbing.

Mi abuelo stood tall at the head dressed in a spotless shirt, snowy hair combed away from his forehead. He traveled often, making a special effort to be home for the Sabbath, bathing and clipping his hair with precision. The Lord respected cleanliness.

With the padlock bolted and the servants dismissed, we lit long tapers, whispering the blessings.

My grandmother dressed in white linen, a white silk scarf wrapped around her head. She covered her eyes with her hands while we recited the prayers over the wine and the *challa*. The lines on her face softened in the candlelight as she waved her hands toward her in a circular motion to bring in the clandestine Sabbath, our Holy Bride, the day of rest and private thoughts, a culmination of the week's work, a reminder of God's gifts.

Afterward, satiated from the chicken that had been cooked to sweetness with a Moor's raisins from the market, and drowsy from the fragrant wine, my grandparents spoke of our painful history, tales of injustice and escape, persecution and death, the bells tolling in a constant call to Mass. Scared and confused by their stories, I questioned the necessity of learning the *Credo* and the *Pater Noster* if this was our true faith?

"It is the way it is," I was told. Murmurs of agreement meant a completed meal. My grandmother and Grazia began the clean up while my grandfather carried me to bed, the dusk of sleep dragging me toward clouds.

As he settled me into the spongy bedding, my eyes heavy, he smoothed the top coverlet with his large hands. He had scrubbed them of dyes that stained his fingers.

"I bought this piece of silk velvet for you, a *cisele*, something new with a pattern of repeated flowers. The color of your eyes, meadows of *verde*."

My eyes, light green with small flecks of brown were like my grandmother's. "Leaves with small acorns in a tree," said Grazia in a soft moment. "Your mother, Hanna, had unique eyes as lovely as an illuminated sea. Mine are ordinary and dark, like untilled soil."

Sleepy, I asked, "Why is this our true faith?"

"It is the God of our fathers."

"Why?"

He exhaled a deep breath. "Do not divulge this to anyone. We follow the first religion in the Bible even though it is against the law."

"But why did we leave *Espana*?"

"The evil Queen."

"Did we do something bad?"

"For eight hundred years we lived in religious harmony with Christians and Muslims, a time of *convivencia*." His storyteller's voice faded. *Mi abuelo*, head in his hands, leaned forward, his light shirt taut across his rounded shoulders.

"What happened?"

When he continued his voice sounded flat. "We were cast out. She took everything we had." He raised his head and looked at me. The places around his eyes remained puffy and lined, the top lid with its hooded fold closed with deliberateness. Now he choked out the words, "They unified Spain and made a dynasty of Aragon and Castile. The King and Queen came to our grand city of Granada in 1492 with three thousand cavalry and two thousand musketeers. The Moorish King Muley Boabdil greeted them at the entrance of the Alhambra with fifty Moors and gave them the keys."

I could not grasp the impact. He kissed my forehead. As he left he said, "Was it more important than people's lives? We were not in the plan. I traded my home for a donkey and a cart."

Chapter Thirteen

Grazia

19 Nisan 5253 (15 April 1493)
Lisbon, Portugal

Edict: Friday, 19 of March, 1493, all parents of Jewish heritage living outside the walls of Lisbon in all villages and the countryside therein are required to bring children between the ages of four and fourteen to Lisbon.

"A bad omen," said my father, his voice, anguished, his lips, taut. His ledgers were spread out in front of him at our kitchen table. He reached for his calamus, a reed pen he dipped in ink, striking it across the page. "Maybe Bellina is in danger."

My mother sat next to him sorting scraps of fabric, smoothing them with her hand. "Hermando, you worry too much."

"I sense evil," he said, looking up, his melancholy eyes shaded with distrust. He had aged, his shoulders slumped with unspoken burdens and a lifetime of labor. "A garrison of soldiers moved into the city as the criers read the edict. They seek lodging with our compatriots."

"Bellina is too young. Your concern is unfounded," said my mother, answering too quickly.

By now Bellina was part of us, although I resented her at times. Babies required patience and I had none. When Hanna was sent away I thought I would be the focal point of my parents' attention, especially since it was past my time to marry. But they were consumed with survival and my priority passed.

I stood at a small sideboard salting a piece of meat that had been drained of blood. After seasoning it with saffron, I put it in a pan with onions and cabbage. I stoked the fire, the iron poker increasing the flames. My mother taught me how to enhance the flavor of our food, even when the offerings were meager. A salad of lettuce and celery from our small garden soaked in vinegar.

My mother brought up another topic, but my father ignored her. "Maybe on your travels up the Iberian coast you can seek a young man for —" My back was to her, but I knew her eyes were shifting to me.

"*Padre*," I said, moving closer to the table where my parents sat, bowing with my interruption, "I saw many priests and nuns gathering at the Augustinian monastery in the square when I was out earlier."

"What do they want with the children?" He shook his head back and forth, a few spots of ink splattering across his page. "It is not good," he said, grumbling. He put his quill down, resting his hand in his chin. "You see? Something is going on."

"Hermando, you are always suspicious. The church has many events, always concocting something." Her fingers danced through fabric, the needle and thread moving with haste.

"I fear it is worse than another *auto de fe.*" His voice sounded heavy and scared. He turned to me, waving a bag. "Grazia, I want you to take these to sell tomorrow morning. Be careful, listen, learn. We must know our fate."

My mother sighed at my father, rolling her eyes. She continued to sew, choosing the colored threads with care. Most often content to prepare food, observe the Sabbath and take care of Bellina, she tried to ignore the outside world. "What could be worse than their false accusations? I wish they would leave us in peace."

I thought like my father, fearful of another plot.

The meat simmered, juices sizzling as I stirred the pot, the aroma permeating the room. Later, after our meal, I fretted about my errand tomorrow, restless slumber elusive.

In the morning after the first cock's crow I rose and readied myself, walking through narrow streets to the city's main gates, my small bags for coins or amulets over my arm. My mother had fashioned them from scraps of silk and linen, embroidering a bird or a flower on them. Many *conversos* wore them under their clothes with a Hebrew letter written on a torn piece of parchment hidden inside, a reminder of our Torah, the true faith close to their heart.

With so many restrictions placed on us by the Church, any extra money would provide food for our meager table. A few of the brocade and leather bags hung on velvet ribbons around my neck. They bounced as I moved over cobblestones, around corners and under the shadows of buildings.

I wound through an alleyway on the Avenida Infante dom Henrique to a

Moorish stone fountain tiled in blue and white chips. It gleamed in the early morning light. Black-winged birds dove down to splash in the water for a quick bath before darting off to mischievous play.

I took a deep breath. The spring air felt cool. The scent of wild lavender wooed me, my head dizzy with thoughts of romance. Perhaps I would see someone of interest today.

Mothers, fathers and grandparents arrived in our cosmopolitan city, probably some with *matzo* hidden in their clothes, since it was the first day of Passover. Their precious offspring, dressed in fine clothes, little caps hiding their faces from the sun, looked around with innocent eyes. Families filed by me, feet plodding, tired from their trip through rugged goat trails that led to our port by the azure sea.

Fathers carried baskets of food, blankets and other belongings for a journey. Wagons negotiated the steep street, lifting dust that settled on the parade of people. Donkeys brayed. A peaceful calm, reminiscent of wind rustling sails, taunted the crowd. It was not the chaos of our hasty exit from Granada but an orderly processional of families dressed in their Sabbath best with purposeful faces.

A fly buzzed my head and I brushed it away. I stood with my wares at the main entrance, the only one left open for the travelers. I shouted, albeit awkwardly, "Bags. Small bags for your treasures. Bags for sale."

A few people stopped to make a purchase but most passed me by, herded by cavaliers and soldiers mounted on caparisoned horses and mules. The men wore silk doublets and fine cloaks, hoods closed around their faces. They did not seem friendly.

Surprised at how many brought babies, the edict specified children over four. I guessed they could not leave them at home. A mother, suckling her infant next to her breast, its tiny head hidden in a shawl, passed me. Suddenly, I recognized the young woman's moon face and high forehead. I used to play with her at our festivals in Granada.

"Gabriela?" I was hesitant it might not be her. I remembered her as a child, not a mother with a baby. So, she had married.

"Grazia! I lost you when we left Spain. Are you well? Your family? Your beautiful sister?"

"We are fine. Is this your baby?" I could not speak of Hanna. Had she heard?

Gabriela, beaming, pulled the covering away from the child's face so I could have a glimpse.

"This is Theresa. We've come from Belmonte." She nodded toward other family members, her husband, a thin, pale boy, his frame gobbled up by an oversized shirt and vest, smiled. Her parents stood behind him and an old grandfather on a wooden crutch with a crosspiece under his arm. His shaggy beard and broken teeth meant they were not doing well.

"Belmonte?"

"Yes, a village in the mountains. Not as beautiful as Granada, but adequate. We live together in a small granite house."

Two soldiers on horses appeared at my side. The silver gilt of their tabards and swords shimmered in the light. "Move along," one said to us in a deep voice, his chin doubled with fat.

I tried to protest, but they glared at me. My friend moved into the throng of people. I ran alongside the crowd, stumbling into a doorway, no longer able to draw attention to my wares.

Frightened, I pushed the iron grille of a courtyard gate in front of me. It gave way. I slipped inside as it latched behind me. Afraid to go home with my unsold goods, knowing my father would be disappointed, I counted my few coins. Worried, I examined the cracked façade of my hiding place. Wet clothes and coverlets draped out of windows and a dog slept under a bush.

I crawled behind a pile of firewood, my hands clutching my wares, my skirts spread out to cover my legs. A horse neighed. Movement had stopped.

After a time the quiet was eerie. My father's suspicions echoed. I lifted myself onto a planter of wisteria along the front, caught my toe in a brick and peered over the top of the wall. The soldiers had taken away all the donkeys and wagons.

A weary stillness hung in the air. Families gathered near the entrance of Santa Engracia's church surrounded by men on horseback. They waited, a hush lingering over the crowd. Soldiers blocked the entry and the only exit through which many had traveled. The heavy wooden door of the church creaked open and two priests and a bishop in ornamental robes and hats, large crosses hanging from their necks, stood facing the crowd. They appeared somber squinting into the light of the sun.

The one in the middle began, "Today is the beginning of a new era for you and your children. A better life. One closer to God and his Holy child."

Whispers flitted through the crowd, necks craning forward to hear. Men and women's eyes shifted to the soldiers nearby. They were used to pontifications from church members. Bodies shifted with restless movement, the shuffling of feet, the touch of an ear, a cough. Some hoisted their children higher.

He continued, "Your children are going to be removed so they may know the ways of the Father, the Son and the Holy Ghost."

Silence except for the swallows singing. Had they understood his words? A murmur traveled from the front to the throng in the back, a wave of shouts and cries breaking out. A woman fainted. The words of the edict rang the same as their never-ending church bells in my head.

A small boy with pink chapped cheeks standing in front of his father, the older man's hands resting on his shoulders, broke free from his father's grip to kick an apple. Another child's narrow foot returned it. The first boy pushed it with his toe again. It rolled in front of the bishop. The first child chased after it, scooping it up in his small hand. Looking up at the senior church official with wide eyes, he held his prize to his chest. The bishop reached down and picked him up, gripping him as he began to struggle. The apple dropped and rolled away.

"I proclaim the children ours," the bishop said with final authority. "You have done a poor job of teaching them the ways of the Church."

Mothers' screams and fathers' protesting shouts permeated the air. The sound of slick swords pulled from sheaths, firearms cocked and the inhaling of breath caused a giant gasp. The men were ready. The horses blew air from their nostrils and, clicking their hooves against the cobblestones, tightened the crowd.

Priests in black, and nuns, beatific faces surrounded by crisp white wimples, wooden crosses hanging from their waists, emerged through the church doors and grabbed for tiny limbs with silky fingers, their pale lips muttering words that promised treats.

Gabriela's round face stood out in the crowd. She held Theresa over her head as if to pass her to safety. The child, dressed like a miniature princess in a long gown of claret velvet, began to wail. A soldier's hands jerked the baby, pushing the infant toward the waiting clergy. They surrounded her diminutive body until she disappeared in the melee.

Soldiers held the wailing Gabriela by her arms as she cursed the church. "You evil bastards. May you all burn in Hell. May your Christ damn you."

I shivered with fear for her. They killed people for blasphemy. Many had their relatives disinterred and their bones burned for less. Gabriela screamed in anguish, twisting her body. Her eyes rolled back in her head and she lurched forward, vomiting in the street. The men held her as she raged, the spittle covering her face and then she went limp. They tossed her in the gutter, her body broken with grief. Her parents fell on her.

How can one describe the screams of children torn from their parents, babies wrenched from their mother's breasts, fathers fighting back with helplessness to protect their families? And the blood. Blood of parents in protest, grief and denial.

I squeezed my eyes shut. When I opened them, the scene seared its image into my mind forever, scarring and branding me, iron on a mule's flank.

And what of the neighbors, perhaps people to protest the cruel behavior of separating children from their parents and birthright? Priests repeated how important it was to believe in the Trinity or burn forever in Hell and how the children of non-believers must be saved. Saved from what? Believers who they thought were only pretending to believe?

Wooden shutters slammed open behind me. A woman drawn to the window looked over the courtyard to the street. Her impassive face spied dark clouds and she pulled in her washing, closing the iron latch with a finite noise.

Stunned, I slid down the wall and hid in my corner. Men's voices were quelled, but women still cried, their hollow wails echoing against the walls. The pandemonium subsided. A few drops of rain stained the ground near me before the sky opened up in a deluge.

The darkness of a heavy sky and evening pressed downward. Rain pelted me harder and harder. After a long spell it ended and I gathered what was left of my silken goods. Many had fallen apart in the water, dyes staining the ground. I tried the gate. Locked. I ran around the courtyard looking for another exit. Without one I climbed the wall, my foot finding a brick to get me over the top. I jumped. Some of my goods dropped. I landed in mud, the street littered with abandoned baskets, food and small shoes.

Some parents, their minds uncomprehending the events, refused to leave the churchyard, hands bloodied from pounding on the doors of the cathedral. No one responded. A few men's bodies lay crumpled against the walls. I ran toward the safety of home.

As I flew down Rua Dos de Ferro I heard mothers searching the streets, their voices hoarse with yelling for little Sellam or Donna or Palumbo. The rain began again, beating harder, soaking me, hair plastered to my face. My emotions were numb, a sleeping limb. I felt nothing. I pushed past compact houses with secure families eating dinner.

I arrived at home breathless, dirty, void of any feelings. I could not comprehend what I had witnessed. My parents were relieved to see me, asking questions, shaking me for answers. All I could do was lower my head. I could not repeat the horrors I had seen. My mother fussed over me removing my wet clothes and making me stand in front of the fire. My father left the room.

"Grazia, tell me what you saw. We have heard terrible stories." She covered me with a clean cloak and led me to my bed.

I trembled, the shaking uncontrollable. I curled up on myself, and for a short period of time, slept, awakening to the nightmares of children's screams. Twice I got up to check on Bellina, asleep in a small pallet near mine. Her face, lovely in repose, reminded me of the beatific angels painted on the church walls. As conflicted as I sometimes felt about my niece, I was glad she was safe.

My mother urged me again and again to share my anguish until finally, nursing me into the next afternoon, I spoke. "The soldiers, nuns and priests wrenched crying, bewildered babies and children away from their parents' arms." Then I broke down and was not able to continue.

"Tell me."

"Even my friend, Gabriela." I choked on another sob. "Some were baptized right then and there. In the street. With basins of holy water. Sprinkling drops on the heads of the innocent children while the soldiers held back their fathers and mothers wailing with grief." Tears fell so hard they spotted my lap.

My mother leaned back, shocked. She did her best to soothe me, holding me and stroking my hair.

"Mama, they took the babies. They killed those who protested too much."

She lifted her head, tears tracking down her face. She held me without offering explanation or solace. What could she say?

Weeks later we learned the children were sent to live on the recently discovered island of São Tomé off the west coast of Africa. They were to be raised as good Catholics, never again to see their parents or feel warm kisses or know the Laws of Moses. The despair I experienced watching children taken from their parents was horrific. I felt sick in my stomach. Even now it remains a dark cave in my soul that will hold me forever, never allowing me to crawl out and find relief. Seven hundred kidnapped children from Lisbon, our port city whose sea breezes cooled the air and absorbed screams of innocents.

Chapter Fourteen

Bellina

16 Tevet 5267 (10 January 1507)

I am no longer a child. My thoughts skip through the past as I huddle near the fire for warmth. An icy winter rain pounds the unglazed windows. Aunt Grazia says old ways are hard to break, that my grandparents' stubbornness, an unwillingness to let go of customs, caused their deaths as much as a rampant Church. Our duplicitous lives sift through danger every day, shifting sand covering tracks at the shore. I lie without remorse.

During our religious holidays the elaborate preparations were more secretive. My grandfather, often frustrated by the number of festivals the Church sponsored and the restriction of eating meat on Friday, complained bitterly. My grandmother would roast sardine heads and scraps of wool to mask the smell of beef cooking on a Sabbath eve. The smell haunts me still.

We, too, had dietary requirements. At Passover we required *Pascua do pao asmo*, Portuguese for unleavened bread. In Spain we bought it from Jewish bakers but Portugal had none. To get around this my grandfather contributed to a communal oven set up in a clandestine location to bake *matzo*.

A few days before the Christian celebration of Easter when I was almost six, my grandmother sent our two servants to watch the processionals, a majestic parade of priests, guild members, church participants and horses decorated with finery. As we stood in the warmth of our kitchen she gave me a bag of pistachios for the baker as payment for the *pan de la afflicion*, as she called it.

"Is it safe to send the child out during Holy Week?" my grandfather asked, sitting at the rough wood table, his hands twisting fabric scraps into small bundles. The small room in the back of the house with its square window was my favorite place with its smells and sounds. The fire, red and orange, sizzled when my grandmother pulled pots away from it. *Blancmange* sauce made with rice and almond milk and *hamin*, a combination of spinach and chickpeas, made my mouth water.

The night before, after everyone had gone to bed, my grandmother cooked *alfajor*. When she noticed me peeking in the kitchen, she invited me to sit at the table, breaking off a morsel. It was the most delicious sweet I had ever tasted.

"What is it?" I asked with my mouth full, savoring it.

"A recipe from my *manuel de mugeres*. Before our expulsion. Flour is forbidden at Passover so we use a paste from almonds and spices boiled in honey." A smudge of it hung near the corner of her mouth.

The next morning my grandmother cleaned lettuce leaves, soaking them in vinegar and folding them in half for a salad. My grandfather watched her in his blood-red silk *jubba*, a knee-length robe. I climbed on his lap to look for a treat which he sometimes hid inside his large sleeves. My small hands searched his body and found one. Laughing, I pinched his knees where the brown stockings gathered and wrinkled. He sighed and put me down.

My aunt Grazia sat embroidering a piece of fabric used as a cover for *matzo* near the window in the front room. Still unmarried, she was sometimes short with me, especially if someone thought she was my mother. Few guessed I was her niece. If a comment was made about the color of my eyes, she would glance in another direction.

My grandmother pushed a strand of hair away from her forehead. "What choice do we have? We need the unleavened bread. Our other purchases – new tablecloths, towels, dishes – are all hidden. I even bought a new knife." The blade glinted in the lantern light.

"Is Grazia not fit to go?" My grandfather sucked his bottom lip. A few pieces of purple and red velvet fell to the floor, wisps of fabric saved for pillows.

My heart rose in expectation. I was a pest, yes. Maybe I could be the one dashing through the crowds, past the street vendors to the baker's door. The password was "Hail Mary." My grandmother addressed my grandfather.

"Grazia will be noticed. Neighbors are already suspicious. The one with the wart on her face mentioned she did not see us at church." My grandmother continued her preparations.

"I will not waste my money on Masses for the dead." My grandfather folded his arms across his chest.

"Hermando, I must. The Salvedo family received a warning letter from the priest's bailiff last week because they have not been seen in church. Sadly, they have panicked and fled in the night."

He slammed his hand on the table. "All the more reason. The child cannot go." More scraps drifted to the floor, threads unraveling. I pushed back the urge to grab them.

"Hermando, we need *matzo*. The holiday cannot be celebrated without it. It is not far. Bellina knows the way. Who will notice a child?"

I looked down and prayed for him to say yes.

My grandmother stopped chopping nuts and moved toward a small crucifix hanging next to the door. *"Puy-puy."* The sound came from her lips, a spit without water.

My grandfather leaped up and grabbed for her arm. "For God's sakes, Estrella. What if someone saw you do that?" His face, close to hers and harsh as winter ice, looked unforgiving.

She responded with her soothing voice. "We are safe in our own home. Let the child go. She is smart beyond her years."

"How will the child hide the goods?"

My grandmother smiled with pride. She nodded toward me with her chin. "Show him the bag."

With discretion I lifted my skirts. A cloth bag attached to my waist held pistachios, payment for our unleavened bread.

"Please let me go. I will be careful." My foot tapped in anticipation, a chance to be away from adult eyes.

My grandfather lifted me close to his face, his gloomy countenance arousing fear in me. "Do not let anything happen to you. You are the one to carry the Law of Moses. Despite what they say at church there is no Original Sin. The soul is pure. Do not listen to their lies." He held me to him and then kissed my forehead. "Go, my child."

I hugged his neck with its scent of fresh lemons. He placed me gently on the floor. With a rushed hug to my grandmother's skirts, I hurried through the house, past an alcove with a large table and two smaller rooms where we slept. My grandfather followed me so he could lock the front door upon my exit. I slipped on my patines, new leather shoes with cork soles that would let me fly over the cobblestones without slipping.

Grazia looked up from her sewing, puzzled, "Where is she going?" I darted outside afraid I would lose the privilege.

Outside our courtyard wall I stopped to breathe. Incense and blooming hyacinths sprinkled the air teasing a sneeze out of me. Penitential hymns came from a processional that turned the corner. Girls my age carried pictures of the Virgin, their voices high in song. Boys followed with wooden crosses. Brotherhoods of men carried a large statue of Mary painted gold. Men and women dressed as biblical characters stumbled under heavier crosses. Orphans marched to raise money for charity. Penitents in tall white paper conical hats reaching the top of walls, marched behind them, eyes cast downward. I closed my eyes to the self-flagellators, bare backs bleeding and raw from hemp and branches.

I opened them to see the end. A priest's white cloak flashed by, fading with the smoke of his trailing torch. My throat felt dry. Children chased behind the procession, dragging sticks on the cobblestones and tossing a citron back and forth. A few big boys, high-spirited and rough, pushed each other. When they noticed me and pointed, I ran.

We lived on the outskirts of the *Alfama* district, an enclosed area with the *Castelo de São Jorge* on the eastern hill, a commercial section of the city. Many of the wealthier residents had moved to the western side because of earth tremors. My grandfather said we were lucky to have found such a good place, even though fishmongers and paupers were not our usual neighbors.

My rehearsed directions rang in my head: two alleyways down, Rua Rosa until *The Se*, left down the steps to Rua São João on the lower level with the lemon tree courtyard and then count four houses. My spirit felt strong. I could find my way. Lisbon was a city of narrow paths, steep streets and fountains. Landmarks guided me.

At first I strolled, turning my head to catch every movement and smell: a dog lifting his leg, hands shaking a cloth out the window, a falcon sailing overhead, the aroma of wild lavender, the ringing of church bells. Red and purple bougainvillea spilled over iron balconies brightening every façade. On the outskirts of the forbidden Thieves Market, *mi abuela's* warnings echoing in my head, I slowed my gait. At a stall in a shaded arcade a peasant woman wearing black with her front teeth missing, offered me a tiny piece of nougat candy from her basket. Made with nuts, honey and sugar in blue, green and yellow, my mouth began to water. I shook my head no.

"I cannot buy anything."

She offered it again. "For you."

I looked around. With no one watching I took the morsel from her palm. The candy melted in my mouth.

She leaned forward, a crucifix hanging away from her bony chest. "Jesus and Mary provide." With that she handed me a misshapen yellow candy. I slipped it into my pocket. "A child alone on a festival day? Where is your family?"

"My grandmother sent me out." What I said surprised me. I had been warned not to speak to anyone, take anything from a stranger, especially because it might not follow our dietary laws.

"Where are you going? I will go with you." She began to fold the corners of the cloth toward the center, the colored candies jumbling together. "Help me with my goods." With feeble hands she gathered baskets behind her. I felt sorry for her, the knuckles of her hands large as walnuts.

My heart beat faster. Suddenly her dark complexion, the wrinkled skin around her eyes, the claw-like hands scared me. A voice said, 'Run, run.' I took off with such haste my shoes carried me like magic wings.

When my feet became tired, I rested, unable to breathe. The earthen wall behind me felt cool even through the fabric of my clothes. My chest heaved as a panting mongrel. The white-washed clay of the buildings deflected the sun and beamed rays of light.

I reviewed the instructions. I had missed a turn. Panic raced through me, perspiration dribbling from my hair. I ran to the end of the street. *The Se, Sedes Episcoplis*, the grand church was not there. I darted up and down a few streets, turning corners looking for its two towers, a worried wetness covering my body. The sameness of the red-tiled roofs confused me. I could not even spot the Tagus River that wound behind *The Se*.

Tears filled my eyes and a sob swept over me. I sank to the ground in the shadow of a tiled doorway, pressing my face to my knees. Was I lost or confused? I dug into my pocket for the candy and put the whole piece in my mouth. Too big to chew, drool dripped onto my chin, the sweetness bursting in my mouth. I did not hear him until he was beside me.

"Look what I found."

Two older boys stood over me, ones from the processional. Fear crept up my chest to my throat and then my mouth leaving a bad taste. Hastily, I chewed the candy.

Hands grabbed at my hair and neck and I twisted away from their probing fingers, managing to get on my feet. The nougat fell from my mouth to the ground.

"Something to play with?" said the larger boy to his friend, his squinty eyes and dirty face staring at me. His head had been shaved. Lice. He bent down, sneering in my face. "Your name?"

I pulled back without a place to go. No sound came out. I was young, but I knew big boys could do harm. I shook my head back and forth, glancing around. No one to rescue me in the shadowy darkness of the buildings. Oh, how I wanted my grandfather at that moment. A black bird landed on the top of the wall behind my tormentors. It turned its glistening head to stare at me, an agate eye, yellow beak bright as corn. A complaining song lured its companion from the bough of a tree.

The other boy, light-haired and also filthy, hung back. "What will you do?" he asked the one who had me trapped against the wall between his arms. A piece of mud brick stuck in my back.

"Tickle her and see if she talks." When I moved my head to the side I saw bleeding sores on his hands that repulsed me. I gagged. Thoughts of my grandmother washing me in a tub in candlelight, kisses and blessings on my clean shoulders and neck, scattered like vapor.

More harsh words. "Fool. Let us get rid of her."

At that moment the bird flapped its wide wings and circled our heads, excrement flying through the air, showering the boys with wet pieces. A few spots caught my face. The boys looked up, cursing. Their distraction became my chance to escape. I ran toward the sound of tolling church bells with the boys yelling, rocks whizzing by me. I looked down every street for the Tagus River until I spotted *The Se* with its beautiful rose window nestled between two towers and white massive stone blocks. Relief flooded me while I rested for a moment and caught my breath. With that as my guidepost I knew where I was supposed to go.

The baker's door had a peephole. I said my Hail Mary to gain entrance. A petite woman with suspicious eyes checked the street to make sure I had not been followed. Disheveled, I straightened myself. Ushering me to the back of the house, she opened the door to a small orange orchard, the trees fragrant with blossoms. A hut stood in the middle of it. She knocked on the slatted door, wormy with holes, a few times. When it opened a sweaty man with a stained leather apron stretching over his protruding stomach, stared down at me. His fat jowls and fuzzy eyebrows moved as he spoke.

"Who do you belong to?" He wiped his mouth with the back of his hand.

I smoothed my skirt and spoke. "The granddaughter of Hermando and Estrella Guzman."

He eyed me a few minutes. "How can I refuse a beautiful child with eyes as green as the sea?" The question embarrassed me and I looked down. I turned my back to lift under my skirt for the pistachios. He turned the netted bag with the sweet meats over in his hand and shook his head. "This will not pay for eight days of *matzo*."

I shrugged. "It is what my grandmother gave me."

The baker shook his head back and forth, my heart sinking. My dangerous journey was for nothing.

"Ach." He turned inside the shed and came out with a square package wrapped in white cloth. "The best *matzo* on the Iberian coast."

I took it from him, walked behind the nearest tree, lifted my skirts, nestling the goods into the bag my grandmother made for me. I straightened, turned around and curtsied.

"My regards to Señor Guzman. Tell him I expect a piece of fine lace for my daughter's wedding after *Shavouth*."

I nodded.

"Be careful, child. Hooligans run the streets during pre-Lent processionals." I shivered with the thought of the bad boys and my escape.

I left, running, the *matzo* hitting against my legs. I slowed to concentrate on the correct path back to the safety of my family. It would be easy to get lost again. Shallow-pitched roofs and boxed houses looked the same. I re-traced my steps with ease, staying close to the alley walls and glancing behind me. I did not see the foot sticking out from a doorway that tripped me.

A voice said, "Look who we have. Again." A large hand with sores reached for me, catching my arm, pulling me toward him. I struggled and slapped at the air.

"A feisty one," he said trying to hold onto to me.

"Let me go." I flailed my arms in an effort to break free.

"Ah, leave her be." The light-haired one pulled on his friend's arm. I blinked, my heart drumming in my chest. Bird shit saved me one time, but what miracle would take me to safety now?

My struggle ended when he held me close. I smelled his unwashed odor. He pressed his body to me. A cracking noise froze us.

"What is it?"

Broken *matzo*.

Two sets of hands groped at my skirts, tearing at me. My secret bag dropped to the ground.

"A *Judiazer*! This cracker is for one of their festivals." The meaner of the two scratched his hairless head and a spot of blood appeared. "The priest will be happy to see her. Maybe even a reward." Fear gripped me and I began to blubber. I spilled tears, an overflowing bowl of grief. My nose ran wet to my chin. I could not wipe it because my arms were pinned. I shut my eyes.

"Ah, let her be. Who cares?" The other one shuffled his feet. "I need to join the processional or my mother will look for a switch."

The bad one turned toward his friend, sneering. "No you wretch. We can get in trouble if she is not reported." He pulled the front of my hair back and I squealed. "Look at the eyes on her." A filthy hand clutched my arm, grimy nails that had never been cleaned. I cried and coughed at his odor, my fate, the stupidity of it all.

They stood on either side of me and dragged me down the street toward the church, the crushed *matzo* hung around my neck for shame, the leather of my shoes scraping the cobblestones. A few people looked out their balconies at a helpless child. They said nothing. I refused to cry anymore, although my chest ached with tears.

"Once she talks the whole family will burn," said the one with bugs on his head, his voice boasting a prize. He re-positioned his grip on me. I became limp. One *patine* fell off, deserted in a muddy puddle.

Soon we were standing in front of *The Se*, its ruby glass gleaming. The façade, broken in places from earth tremors, stood regal and imposing.

Inside the dark church my eyes watered from the dust and musty smell. The boys, breathless from dragging me, loosened their grip. My shoeless foot felt cold on the mosaic tile floor.

Parts of the church were cordoned off for repairs. Aunt Grazia brought me here one time. As I took in the gloomy interior, carved cloisters surrounded by wrought iron gates blocked my view. Too dim for details.

Chicken bumps ran through my body. The boy without the head lice held me. "Find the priest. Look beyond the nave in the other chapels. It is a maze in here."

What would the priest do? Would I be arrested? My grandparents had nothing good to say about the authorities who ran the Church. I decided not to answer, gritting my teeth in determination.

The meaner boy stared at me. "You find the priest. I can watch the green-eyed devil." Even in the murky light I saw his sinister mouth.

My grandmother's kind visage warmed me, my bereft spirit flickering with hope. Perhaps God's angels cannot recognize different faiths and fly from place to place doing their deeds without prejudice.

The one who held me became firm. "Father Igreja stays in the back behind the altar." His fingers tightened around my thin arm and he pulled me toward him as if to prove to his friend he was in charge. I ached with the strength of these boys on a mission of fear.

"I am not leaving you here alone. Take her to the *Capela de Santo Idlefonso* where the dead people slumber. Scare her into behaving while we find a priest to terrorize her."

With the colors from the rose window fading through a small sweep of light, I whispered a prayer. Maybe their Virgin could help me. "Hail Mary, full of grace," I started. I murmured the *shema* in my mind. Candles flickered along the sides of the stone walls and the cold, dank air chilled me.

The two of them were not impressed with my recitation and, although I struggled, they pulled me through the somber interior. Two tombs appeared in front of me with carved stone figures, one, a bearded nobleman, sword in hand, and, the other a woman, clutching a prayer book. Their dogs stood guard faithfully at their feet.

"Wait here," the worst of the two said. "Watch she does not wiggle away or you will find me on your back." Then he said in a threatening tone, "If you move, the dead bodies of Fernando Lobo and his wife, Maria Vilalobos, will come to look for you. They hate children."

I gasped. Even walking dead people were being called forth to torment me.

"Go. I can take care of her."

I leaned into him, limp with exhaustion and fear. His grip loosened a bit and I wiggled into a more comfortable position.

"Stop," he said as I kicked my feet back and forth. Then he mumbled to himself, "The priest will be outside where the procession ended." He dragged me by the arm so he could get a better view of the entry. He wiped his wet nose with his sleeve.

He pushed me around, moving to the other side of me and grabbing the other arm.

"Why does he take so much time?" he asked under his breath.

Emboldened by my grandmother's words of how cunning I was, I searched for an escape. If I could distract him for a moment, I could run out the way he brought me in, dash down an alley toward the warmth of my home.

I practiced a small sneeze, bouncing my head toward my lap. His fingers tightened on my arm. If I could not escape soon, the other boy would return with the priest. It would be the end. I had to try. I gathered spit inside my mouth, faked a large sneeze and sprayed the liquid over his arm.

"Ugh. Disgusting Jew." He loosened his hold to wipe his arm on his clothing. I slipped off my other shoe. In an instant I fled. Instead of running toward the back and out the door where I knew he would follow me with his big boy legs, I slipped away toward the front. I caught my breath as I hid behind a red curtain.

"Hey, come back. Where are you?" His large feet clomped past me toward the front of the church.

The voice of the other boy said, "Where is she? You lost her? You dumb ox."

"Where is the priest?"

I prayed my anxious heart would silence.

"I looked for him. He might tell my master at the shop I missed Mass for the last few Sundays."

"You never found him?"

I heard a punch, flesh meeting flesh, then another. The two boys battled each other and knocked against something that broke. They cursed each other and although I could not see them, it sounded as though they were rolling on the floor bumping into the benches. I crept along the wall and ran out the door. Their ugly faces beseeched my stocking feet all the way home, through muddy puddles, past creaky mule wagons and worn families returning from the processional. I was merely a child racing by in tears.

My grandparents, pacing when I returned, hugged me to them. My grandmother began to cry, pounding her chest with a fist.

"Thank God," she repeated over and over. "Come. You must drink."

"But the *matzo* is broken," I hugged her skirts. "And I lost my shoes." I held up a foot, the stocking ripped, the sole bloody.

"Anything can be replaced. You cannot," said *mi abuelo.*

We sat in the kitchen, Aunt Grazia listening, as I told them what happened, embellishing where the big black bird relieved itself on the boys' heads.

My grandfather sat back. "You saw ravens near the church?"

I nodded yes.

"They saved you."

"Hermando, what do you mean?" My grandmother placed warm stew in front of me. Grazia had opened the bag with the *matzo* and was placing the broken pieces on a plate, her expression dour.

"Two sacred ravens keep vigil in the tower over the boat that brought Saint Vincent's relics to this shore. Lisbon put the raven on her coat-of-arms. It represents liberation from the Muslims. Descendants of those birds live in the towers. Your protection, my child. They saved you twice today." He reached out and touched my nose.

I turned my head toward the fire, a flutter whispering by my ear.

"Never mind about the *matzo.* It doesn't matter. God will still bless us as we celebrate the Jews being led out of Egypt."

My grandfather reached for my hand, I reached for Grazia's and she held my grandmother's. Together we looked into each other's eyes and recited the *shema,* "Hear O Israel, The Lord Our God, the Lord is One."

Chapter Fifteen

Bellina

25 Sivan 5267 (15 June 1507)

Six months have passed as I set down this record in an effort to recall my childhood. I sink deeper into sadness, a true motherless child, who weeps with abandonment. Aunt Grazia, my protector, comforts me, although at times I sense her resentment.

Our unfortunate fate, tied to the evil queen who "banished all Jews of both sexes forever from the precincts of our realm," forced us to Portugal where we were once again pawns. Soon after our arrival King Joao died in 1494. My grandfather wailed in protest. Now what would happen to us? Many vied for his kingdom, but his cousin, Manoel, desired power and a solidification of his bid for the crown. After rumors we might be expelled again, Manoel agreed to marry Princess Isabel, daughter of Ferdinand and Isabella. The evil queen so hated us that she forced Manoel to agree to our banishment. In a dilemma, he agreed to the terms of our expulsion when he signed the marriage decree on November 30, 1496. My grandparents were bereft, anguished, beyond despair.

"What more can they do to us except take our lives?" my grandmother cried.

After the Edict of Expulsion in October, 1497, five years after our settling in Lisbon, my grandfather decided we would not leave like the rest of our brethren. Most were headed for the Ottoman Empire where Sulieman the Magnificent, known for his aqueducts and culture, welcomed us, our wealth, our skills. Some were allowed to stay behind, *conversos* like us who were personal physicians to cardinals and dukes or textile merchants of silk and cotton like my grandfather or manufacturers of paper and tobacco like one of our neighbors.

My grandfather did not want to move again. He also did not want to stay.

"What will happen now?" I asked.

"We are doomed."

"Why?"

He shrugged his shoulders, his rheumy eyes weighted with bags.

"Are we Jews or not? We converted, yes?" I peppered him with endless questions and sometimes he did not know the answers, switching identities like his cloaks.

Impatient with my questions, he told me, "Be like Grazia and accept our fate. We do what we have to do to survive."

Was it worth it to hold onto the faith of his forefathers in the light of danger? The manners and traditions passed from generation to generation had one purpose: to conceal the truth. Even I learned to be an actor. We were part of a clandestine society, players on a stage of hidden truths.

The Portuguese called us *Nação*, people of the nation, but our own Hebrew speakers had other names: anusim, for those forced to convert, *meshumadim* to identify those who converted willingly, and *goyim gemorim* for those accepted as full gentiles.

Almost overnight our temples, rabbis, cantors, torahs, prayer books and *mikvahs*, the ritual bath I enjoyed so much, disappeared. All the symbols of our faith had to be hidden: mezuzahs that graced our doors were removed, *menorahs* hidden, Stars of David buried. To read was a giveaway. In a very short time most of the prayers save a few blessings, were forgotten.

The circle of friends and family we relied upon, kept our faith alive. We had secret signs to identify each other. My grandmother used to speak of peacocks to another she thought might be one of us, a symbol as important as our tree of life, because they signified superior status. Or, slipping a small bag from her sleeve, the elegant birds embroidered on one side, she would wait for a flash of recognition in her co-conspirator's eyes.

At any rate, we stayed behind as our compatriots packed and moved on again. We remained because the fabrics and cloaks my grandfather made were desired by the aristocracy: plush velvet dresses, cloaks trimmed in fur and closed with a gem at the neck and silk doublets that graced the bodies of the elite.

Once, when I went with *mi abuelo* to deliver a capelet to a wealthy patron in her salon, the white-haired woman said with a knowing eye and nod of her head, "Senhor Guzman, you do fine work. Leave your old ways behind and you will succeed. Your kind often do." He sighed.

My grandfather refused to be degraded by a yellow circle the size of a hand Jews were required to wear when traveling. He resented that others were heavily fined if caught without it.

"So Christians and non-Christians cannot plead ignorance of the other's faith and marry. The Lateran Council in 1215 ordered it. I must also wear the Christian hat when I leave the house, something not yellow."

My grandfather traveled and traded with others from Lombardy, Greece, Spain, France and England. He brought my grandmother pearls and other gems, tales of picturesque towns and of course, stories of peril. His search for a living drove him from shore to shore along the Barbary Coast of West Africa through secret networks of other *conversos*. Not even the danger of storms or pirates could keep him from his textile world.

When he arrived home, tired and sometimes frightened, he would hold my grandmother tight and say, "Come, Estrella, let us prepare for the Sabbath so that I may be who I truly am."

Chapter Sixteen

Alegra

September 23, 1998

"Hal, I'm upset about the kidnapped children," I say, slapping the manuscript down on his desk. "How could the Church justify such a thing? Are you sure it's true?" I munch dry crackers and sip an Orangina.

His hair, wet in the front, another attempt to get it under control, is parted unevenly. He picks up a small bag of tobacco, rolls back his chair and looks at me over the top of his glasses. "When I researched this years ago I had nightmares. I didn't write it as bad as it was—parents smothering their babies, families renouncing each other, people throwing themselves down wells rather than give in to apostasy."

"You use that word a lot, but I'm still not sure what it means. At least not in this context." I press my lips around the straw of my drink.

"It's a renunciation of faith." He waits while that sinks in. "And to Jews that's heresy. They've never believed in proselytizing so what the Church tried to do was abhorrent." He stares at me, eyes hard. "The Jewish people have been willing to die for their beliefs for five thousand years. Maybe I can't prove to you the passion burning within Grazia and Bellina, but I know it's there." He stands up, pulls a pipe out of the holder and picks up a file.

I don't say anything while I finish the soda. Why so much controversy?

He continues. "Of course there are always those who converted to make their lives easier, unwilling to be persecuted and hounded and who can blame them? People don't learn. The irony is that the ones who did that in the late 1930s and early 40s didn't escape. Hitler got them anyway." He strolls toward the patio with its magnificent view of the white-capped Sierra Nevadas. This time of day the sun is high in the sky, the mountains carved in shades of lilac and mauve. I follow him outside, a trail of cracker crumbs in my wake. Irma may be right. There's something to be said for maid service.

"Why were the *conversos* afraid to give in? I mean, if my family was threatened, I'd just say okay, sprinkle the water on my head." This is bothering me.

"No, you wouldn't." The Professor sets the file next to him, stretches out on the lounge chair and slips off his loafers. He pinches tobacco into the bowl of his pipe and tamps it down. A cherry aroma sneaks into the air as he lights it pursing his lips, clenching his teeth, sucking in his cheeks. It takes forever to get it lit.

His presumptive attitude annoys me. "How do you know?"

"Because you have strength of character." He leans his head back, puffing with satisfaction.

I step back. "You don't know me that well."

"I know you were willing to leave your sisters and Saul to take a chance on working for an eccentric, cranky professor." He smiles, a bit embarrassed.

"I still don't understand why they didn't just accept Jesus." I'm persistent because I can't get my head around why these people were so obstinate. I'm never like that.

"Ever have someone want you to do something and the more they ask the stronger you resist?"

"Hmm. Sure. Irma trying to give me a make-over. Saul's mother bugging me about cutting my hair." I know I'm being flip but I'm frustrated. This topic is nothing I would have pursued on my own, but now that I'm involved I feel nagging guilt and anger.

"Something in the depths of their soul connected them to their heritage and God. The power of self wouldn't let them give way to another belief system." The Professor looks out at the mountains, lifting his hand to block the light. He motions me. "Stand at the end here so I can see you and the sun's not in my eyes."

I let his comments sink in for a minute. He must have that same commitment to pursue this with such passion. "How can you bear this painful history?"

"Because the story must be told. Maybe if the Jews had had better knowledge of the Inquisition more could have been saved during the Holocaust."

"How do you know all your information is accurate?" It's not that I doubt this happened or that the Professor isn't a good scholar. It's just that who knows what happened 500 years ago? My puzzled look prompts a reply.

"We have documented records of the children's names. The Catholic Church kept accurate logs. Recently, the relatives of the kidnapped children held a celebration on São Tomé in acknowledgement of their Jewish ancestry on the 500 year anniversary. It's a close-knit community." I felt chagrined. He's always so smart. "Besides all the scholarly journals and historical reviews, there are eye-witness accounts. The Inquisition recorded all the trials. Oh, they were very efficient. In the case of the children of São Tomé, Bishop Coutinho wrote down what happened thirty years later."

The professor reaches for his file and rustles through the papers, balancing the pipe between two fingers. He rattles a paper at me and then reads, "He said, *'The anguish of families calling out to God and their wish to die together in the Law of Moses will forever be with me.'* Here, I quote, *'Yet more terrible things that were done with them did I witness, with my own eyes.'* He looks up at me, his eyes in a watery movement behind his glasses. "Moslem children were included in the edict, too, but they were left untouched. The authorities confessed that the Crescent was prominent in certain regions and they were afraid of reprisals." He looks at me, thumping his finger on the file. "Things haven't changed much."

"But why did they believe the authorities? Why didn't they just run? It's bad enough the Jews were led like sheep into trains in Europe. Why would they trust the Church with their children after everything that had happened in Spain prior to that? The forced conversions had been going on for years."

He shook his head in disbelief. "Alegra, there's a part of you that is so naïve. It is hard for the human spirit to accept horror, more difficult for the imagination to acknowledge evil. True, the *conversos* had been persecuted for a long time, but they never gave up hope they could live openly and in peace. If I didn't think most people were good, I couldn't go on. It is my obligation and duty to share our history with people who are ignorant."

"Are you referring to me?" My hand holds my chest in mock horror, my voice hitting a higher pitch.

"Well, you're not one who has educated yourself in the customs and history of your faith." He takes a long drag on his pipe, holding it in his teeth.

This steams me up. "I'm empathetic about what happened to these people but I'm not Jewish."

"Don't be so sure."

I'm quiet, thinking about the times my mother prepared large dinners for our family and Cuban neighbors before Easter. She said she was re-creating the Last Supper. She never went to church, but I assumed she was a lapsed Catholic because she was always lighting candles for some relative's death or on. . .Friday. . .nights. . .How could I not have noticed? I mean, my sisters and I joked that Mama must have thought she was Jewish because she was always cooking or shopping, but. . . I haven't thought about this in years.

Wait a minute. This can't be my fault. I'm angry. "Listen, I can't be feeling guilty about the Jews all the time. This has nothing to do with me. I have to live my life now." I bite into a cracker, a few crumbs falling on his feet. He doesn't notice.

"Don't you feel a connection to the people who suffered before you?"

I turn away from him. "Please. You sound Catholic."

I stomp to my room, sandals flopping on the terra cotta tile floor. I grab my fanny pack and pull a visor low to my eyebrows. I am not coming back to eat dinner with this stubborn man who makes me feel responsible for the ills of the world. It's time for a walk. I head toward the front of the villa. I slam the door with satisfaction even though he's on the patio and can't hear.

Maybe I've been cooped up too long with this guy. *Or maybe he's struck a chord in me.* Or maybe I'm connected to Grazia and Bellina emotionally more than I am to my own sisters. These women trapped in the fifteenth century occupy my thoughts day and night. What would it be like to live in an era without power or choices, to be threatened at every turn? I've always thought I had no history. Just a blank past. But maybe Hal's right. There's a lot I don't know.

I hike toward the main city of Granada, about two kilometers. Small adobe houses dot the landscape. The paved road is surrounded by alfa grass, the kind used for tightly-woven baskets in the market. Beyond that, some scrub brush serves as scraggly ground cover. In the distance I can see the Alhambra high above the city, its parapets majestic above the tree tops. Siesta time is quiet except for a few flies buzzing around my head.

It's pretty safe for a woman alone in Granada. I put my thumb out when a car rumbles behind me. It doesn't stop and I'm left covered in dust that sticks to my damp arms and legs. I search through my fanny pack for a shredded tissue. I wipe my brow and swipe my dirty arms. I could give up and go back. But that would be like giving in and I'm not going to do that. This professor thinks he's so smart. I trudge harder, my sandals sticking to the melting asphalt. The sun, a fiery globe, bakes me, its relentless rays shimmering on the blacktop. Not a cloud in the sky. I am not going back.

But I'm getting very thirsty. Why didn't I grab a bottle of water? In Miami I have one with me wherever I go. I stumble down an embankment, stop under an apple tree and sit down, desperate for shade. My body's sweaty, aching for mercy from this heat. Gnats zoom around the rotten fruit that litters the ground, a noxious smell rising. I bang my heel and squash a spoiled apple. Worms crawl out from the underside and I gag. All I can think about is cool, clear water.

When the roar of another engine sounds in the distance, I contemplate jumping up and running back to the road, but I can't. I hate to complain like my sister Marta, but I think I have heat stroke. I touch my cheeks with the back of my hand and they're hot. Very hot.

My eyes flutter. Maybe a nap will make me feel better. Damn professor and his dogmatic ideas. The red pick-up truck chugs closer. A small tornado of dust kicks up as it pulls off to the side.

"Honk, honnnkkk." The owner of the vehicle must have his elbow on the horn. Using the heel of my hand to get up, I squish my fingers into a mushy apple. I stumble toward the truck and lean into the passenger side.

"Can I get a ride to town?" I try not to pant.

"Only if you let me buy you a cold beer."

I pull my head back. Who is this masher? And then, I get a lovely surprise: my Antonio Banderas from the restaurant.

Suddenly I'm self-conscious of my sweaty, smelly self. I wipe the rest of the yellowed apple slime from my fingers on the back of my shorts. "Oh, hi."

"*Hola*," he says, reaching over to open the passenger door. "Remember me? Le Bistro? You were with an older guy."

I nod.

"I'm Marco." I see my reflection in his mirrored sun glasses and it's not good.

I hesitate for a second, glancing at his pecs in a tight white T-shirt, and climb in. He picks up a starched white shirt on a wire hanger, black bowtie wrapped around the neck, and hands it to me. I know it's his uniform so I try not to wrinkle it. With a shift of the gears, he guns the engine and we take off.

I feel better already. I look toward the craggy mountains, stately and strong. With the breeze blowing in my face, the radio blaring words of *amor* and Marco's white dress shirt flapping in the breeze, I'm revived.

My Latin heartthrob parks in the rear of the restaurant where the professor and I had dinner. The back of Le Bistro isn't as sexy as the interior with overflowing garbage cans, cardboard boxes and a few broken crates on the ground. In halting English Marco explains he has to get ready for the dinner hour, but he wants me to come inside. He looks relieved when I tell him I speak Spanish.

He seats me, his hand grazing my back, at a table under a spinning fan and brings me a cold beer, the bottle wet with condensation. After a long drink I hold the bottle against my cheeks. Marco returns in the white shirt, his black bowtie not yet tied around his neck. He moves with efficiency in the restaurant, setting tables, fluffing napkins, placing salt and pepper shakers just so.

Finally, he pulls out a chair and sits next to me. He's even better looking in the light of day, white teeth flashing, dark hair thick and shiny. His eyes are second-day coffee brown, that deep warm color that makes people look serious even if they're not.

We banter back and forth a few minutes. I'm awkward with male attention. I don't know how to flirt. I've watched Irma do it enough times, snaring a guy with a look and an implied promise, but it doesn't feel comfortable for me.

"So, *Señorita*, I have a bit of time before the dinner rush at eight. Have you seen the Alhambra Palace in the fading light?" He aims his megawatt smile at me.

Señorita? Sensing a come-on, I say, "Certainly I've toured it during the day. The high-domed ceiling in the Hall of Ambassadors is quite impressive." Oh dear. Why did I mention that? I'm such a nerd. Irma would kill me.

"*Señorita*, it's the extraordinary view of Granada from those windows that I speak of."

His formal way of speaking and his Castilian accent seem so elegant to my *Cubana* rattle.

"What's so special about it?"

The professor must be getting to me. History weighs on me. All I can think of is the evil Isabella signing the document that expelled the Jews in that very room. Of course she also put her signature on the document for

Columbus to sail to the Americas there, too. I decide not to dazzle him with my intellectual footwork. My head feels a bit woozy from the beer on an empty stomach and the earlier heat.

"Say, Marco, do you think I could get a little something to eat?"

"Of course." He stands up, takes my arm and escorts me toward the back of the restaurant. "Come. I have something special to show you."

"But what about your job?"

"I'm the head waiter. Flavio will cover for me. I want you to see something." He pushes through a door with a large glass window.

We cut through the kitchen where a chef in a sauce-speckled white jacket is chopping greens. Marco whispers something to him, reaches for a piece of tinfoil and transfers shrimp skewers with chicken and peppers into the silvery paper. He also takes two cold beers from the huge gunmetal gray refrigerator in the corner of the room and puts them in a bag.

Marco dazzles me with a smile, guides me through the back exit and holds open the passenger door of his truck. His hand grazes mine. On purpose? It must be. I feel so adventurous that I've forgotten why I was upset with the professor and walked half-way to town.

"Where are we going?" I ask, butterflies in my stomach. I'm aware that I could be taken somewhere against my will. I glance at his profile, the cut of his jaw, the Roman nose, his olive skin. Could I be so lucky?

"Somewhere special."

Uh-oh. Not only am I basically a good girl, I'm afraid I won't pass the sniff test. I pull down the visor desperate for a mirror. No luck. I've never been one of those women who's obsessive about her weight, but suddenly I'm convinced I look very fat. Obese even. My thighs are so huge they melt into the blue towels that cover the red vinyl seats and then turn into oozing purple. I'm spreading out like a fat lady in the circus.

"So many visitors never see what I am going to show you. I want you to experience the full flavor of the Alhambra," says Marco.

"Uh-huh." I can't seem to make any conversation.

The truck cranks into the next gear as we climb through a labyrinth of quaint, narrow streets, higher and higher above the city to a hill. The temperature has cooled down and I take a deep breath of the fresh air. My momentary insanity flies out the window.

"Look," he says as he stops at the Alhambra Palace on a plateau that spreads out onto green plains. I take in the magnificent view, the shadows settling over the high walls, a single bird floating through the sky. It looks so different than when I was here before. Few tourists, the unusual light of a fading sun, everything is heightened.

"Come." Marco takes my hand, flashes a card at the guard, who responds with a wink, and walks with purpose. My hand feels sweaty in his and my elbow begins to hurt because I've tensed my arm. "The Hall of Ambassadors is closed this late in the day, but I have something else I want you to see."

I follow him into the entry court of the Moorish military fortress. The walled site is set on acres and acres of land with red brick fountains, watchtowers and gardens filled with blooming flowers. Twelve enormous statues of lions surround us, roaring in my head. The Medina, a town built for craftsmen, perches above us. Most of all, there's the constant sound of dripping water, flowing, gushing, tinkling around us.

Marco walks past the Water Stairs to the Romantic Mirador. The signs are posted in Spanish and English. He picks a spot near the edge of one of the courtyards. We perch on the ledge of a stone fountain, the bag of goodies between us. He opens our appetizers. A nightingale begins its evening song.

"This is the time to see our city," says Marco, offering the food and beer.

And, indeed, he is right. Granada fans out below us. The colors of the sky blend lilac, rose, aquamarine and dusty-gold into the most exquisite sunset I've ever seen. We watch in silence, sharing the moment.

Of course I think about my sisters and Saul and how out of character it is for me to be here with this Adonis at a spontaneous picnic. I used to plan everything before I lost my mind and came on this odyssey. The professor and I view the sunsets. He would appreciate this one.

Marco reaches for my hand. I don't pull away but it's awkward. We sit in silence. He moves the debris between us and slides closer.

"*Señorita*, you are very lovely."

"Oh, I don't know. I don't think I'm very lovely right now." I look down at my lap so I won't have to look at him. My other hand pushes a piece of hair behind my ear.

Marco turns my chin toward him. I can barely breathe. His lashes are longer and darker than mine. They disappear as he sinks his lips closer to me, melting my resistance. Chills shudder through my body and I feel myself wash away. I've never been kissed like this before. Suddenly, I feel so out of control that I pull away. Have I really kissed this gorgeous man? I glance around with a nervous notion that someone is watching but no one is there.

Marco holds my arm and looks at my watch. "It's time for me to get back." His eyes linger on me. He takes our debris and tosses it into a receptacle, leading me to the exit through Oleander Alley. Raspberry and white blossoms spray our path.

I urge him to drop me at one of the hotels so I can get a taxi. He avoids the motorway ring road, the main access around the city, and in a few minutes stops in front of the Andalucia. A doorman in white shirtsleeves and an open collar grabs for my door.

"When can I see you again?" Marco asks.

Oh dear. This could get complicated. What would the professor say if he came to pick me up for a date? On the other hand, it just might make him take notice.

"Uh, I don't know. I don't think this will work out."

He pulls back, hurt. "Why not?"

"My position with the professor doesn't give me much time off and. . ."

"Yes?" He looks so expectant, his eyes blinking with hope.

"You're a bit younger." I stop because I'm so uncomfortable, picking at my nails and not looking at him. "I appreciated the view. That was very special but I just don't see how. . ."

He moves across the seat and kisses me again, this time a bit rough with his hand on my neck. I haven't kissed anyone but Saul on the lips in years. Marco's are soft and urgent, sending chills up my spine.

"*Basta!*" brings me back. "You're holding up traffic," says the witness to our embrace.

"Your number?" asks Marco.

"No! I'll stop by to see you."

Marco plays his finger down my arm. "I do want to see you again."

I don't know what makes my heart start fluttering, nerves or maybe fear, but I jump out so fast the blue towel sticks to my thighs. Embarrassed, I toss it back into the truck. Our eyes catch for a minute.

"Taxi, *por favor*," I say.

The doorman sounds his whistle.

Chapter Seventeen

Grazia

5 Shevat 5267 (28 January 1507)
Lisbon, Portugal

When the *conversos* first trailed into the outskirts of Lisbon in 1492, King Joao welcomed us. He was preparing for war against the Moors and the New Christians had expertise in making weapons. We paid 100 *cruzados* to establish ourselves with speed. My mother told us our Catholicism was a temporary state, the rules changed often.

Although our family knew nothing of weapons my mother and father were in demand. The aristocracy from the Barrio Alto wanted my father's exquisite textiles. With my sewing skills and my mother's charm at creating the design and their desire for fine garments, we worked long hours filling orders.

The rest of the 100,000 poor souls, who only paid eight *cruzados* to enter the country, lived in a shanty town below the Barrio Alto, shoved into rat-infested wooden barracks. Wild dogs roamed the streets depositing their dung on the cobblestones, their piss on the walls. Approximately twenty thousand refugees resided in Little Jerusalem at the bend of the Tagus River. Plague broke out and the city council banished them outside the city gates of Saint Vincent's. The chaos and despair of these unfortunates driven from their meager homes, belongings scattered in the street, moaning about their *azango*, Portuguese for bad luck, traumatized all of us. After eight months they were allowed to return, the debris of their lives mended with scraps of hidden faith, only to find that King Joao declared they had lost their liberty and were to be his slaves.

My father was right. In nine months a monster had been born. Although our ancestors converted after the riots of 1391, we knew our status was not secure. Our hearts were as heavy as bricks dropping to a bottomless pond. King Joao died in 1494 and his cousin Manuel came to the throne. Rumors circulated that the new king would change his mind about us. What would he do without all our commerce? Our hearts ebbed and flowed with panic and relief dozens of times.

On Friday, the 10th of Adar 5257 or 21 February, 1497 according to the Gregorian calendar they forced us to use, I huddled in my bed, the crisp morning air transmitting chills through me. I arose with dread, a sinking feeling inside my chest. My mother believed our textile business would protect us and refused to listen to my father's gloom. "Perhaps King Manuel will change his mind, or Isabella, the wicked queen, will show mercy. After all, the court still has to be well-dressed."

My father, his eyesight fading, had prescient thoughts about our hopeful future. How many times did I hear him say, 'Estrella, they will never leave us alone as long as we believe in an ever-present God who resides in our soul.' Yet, he doubled his inventory, buying a shipment of fine Merino wool in crimson, marigold and lapis lazuli.

Through an edict read at Mass and a parchment posted on the church doors, our people were told to arrive early in the morning at the courtyard of *Os Estaos*, a palace used for diplomatic receptions where foreign ambassadors came to pay their respects to the king.

That morning I was finishing my toilette when a hysterical neighbor pounded on our door crying, "Hermando! Estrella! Open the door. They have taken little Rosario from me. Help! Help me!"

Our neighbor's frightened wails coursed through my body and I doubled over, my stomach cramped in fear. I sat on my pot, images rolling in front of me--, the kidnapped children, neighbors turning in friends to be rewarded with half of their belongings, the *pinga*, a torture of boiling wax where they made designs of the cross or their savior on the chest of the Judaizer until a confession or conversion was obtained. I prayed every day I would never have to wear the penitential habit or witness my loved ones burned at the stake, a requirement of the church for heresy. They required us to bring green branches to the pyre because they burned more slowly. The smell of bodies lingered for days.

I shuddered, straightened myself and covered the pot. My monthly rags were sticky between my legs.

My mother opened the door with caution until she saw who it was. Then it flew against the wall, banging with intensity. Señora Ezrati screamed, her eyes wild, "Our children are being taken from us." Sobbing and coughing, her mangled words inspired terror. Bellina, petrified, hid in the corner where we stored the brooms.

"What? What is it?" My mother held the Señora's arms and shook her.

The horror of the scene I witnessed near the fountain, babies torn from their mother's breasts, heartbroken families divided from their progeny in the street. Was it to be repeated? I gasped. We had been on guard for months. "My Rosario." The woman let out a wounded animal moan and collapsed in my mother's arms. "My Rosario," she repeated over and over again. My mother and I slid her onto the floor and propped her against the wall. She ceased her noises, eyeballs rolling back, the whites left as abandoned bird eggs in her slackened face.

"Grazia, get Señora Ezrati water," my mother ordered me as she took her Sabbath head scarf from a shelf. She began to put figs, dates, dried apricots, and pomegranates in it, tying the ends in a knot. "Take Bellina."

Where was I to go? Where can a child be hidden in a small house? It was no use.

My mother moved with deliberation, but her voice expressed the panic she felt. She pushed aside the small rug with her foot, bent down and lifted the board where we hid our ritual objects: Sabbath candles, a clay pot, forbidden prayer books with their vellum covers. She slipped her hands over our coveted treasure, a rare printed edition of the Old Testament produced by Eliezer Toledano, with its lacy border on the cover.

"No, Mama." I saw what she was doing. I poured water from a pitcher into a clay cup for Señora Ezrati. She leaned her head against the wall, eyes closed, gulping air like a fish slapping against the bottom of a boat.

"Hush," my mother said, looking at me with stoic eyes. "Only my sapphires." She hid a small velvet bag into her bosom.

Without warning two of the King's guards flung open the door to our front room and marched into our kitchen. One was fat with large pockets of flesh under his eyes. The other was thin, his cheeks slack, teeth rotted when he opened his lipless mouth, grinning with delight at his catch. The events fractured in my mind—uniforms flashing gold and red, the glint of a sword, my mother's hands fluttering, the hollow wails of Señora Ezrati, the glassy eyes of Bellina and my heart beating, frantic, trapped, willing to sacrifice anything to be free. Bellina, terrified, flung herself at my mother, clinging to her skirts as the men's hands reached for her. She dragged her feet as they pulled her toward the door, her ungodly sounds worse than a dog choking on a split bone.

"Walk," the soldiers ordered. My mother whispered something in the child's ear and Bellina stood taller.

"Sirs, I beg of you, come for us later. My husband travels and–"

"Walk," the corpulent one bellowed. "Heathen Christ-killers," he mumbled to the one with rotten teeth. "Think the ability to read the Bible gives them power."

My mother glanced at me, lifted the Señora to her feet and we filed out without water or supplies, our precious goods and remnants of faith left behind. I spotted her Sabbath scarf with its meager supplies left on the table, but was afraid to reach for it.

We waited to fall in line behind flagellants with leather scourges, naked backs raw with blood, followed by friars carrying blue and yellow pennons, triangular flags attached to lances that slapped in the breeze and, finally, the rest of us herded along like cattle. Beggars lined the streets, their cracked hands asking for coins to rescue relatives from Purgatory. "We are poor sinners," they repeated in a litany. Others sold small wooden likenesses of the saints and fake relics. Everyone had a sliver of wood from Saint Antony's boat.

I trailed behind with our moaning neighbor, incoherent in her grief. Another group of older boys pushed and shoved us down the street, keeping us in line with large wooden sticks. Again, my mother tried to explain my father's absence to a priest she recognized, but he ignored her plea, waving her on. We continued down the familiar cobblestones, past buildings casting shadows. At our backs young men with newly purchased firearms made sure no one escaped. Physicians and tax collectors, some in fine silk clothes with gilded swords at their sides, as well as humble shopkeepers and fishmongers, even women in nightclothes, all mulled together in despair. We were goats led to a biblical sacrifice.

"So this is our royal protection?" my mother said as we stumbled along. Her hair had come undone, whipping wildly about her face, cheeks flushed high with color. Her shawl hung on her shoulders; a blue vein pulsed on her ivory swan-like neck. I was without words. Bellina clutched my hand. Señora Ezrati melted into another group of inconsolable mothers. "Where are they taking us? Why are there guards? I crossed my arms in defiance. Bellina copied me.

We passed a corner familiar to us, three streets, Rua de Sao Pedro, Temple Street and Rua de Sinagoga. Then we crossed the Rossio district and reached the limestone courtyard of *Os Estaos.* I rubbed my eyes. One more body could not be squeezed inside the high walls. The chaos of guards insisting on order and the acrid smells of so many people, animals and goods, crowded together, filled every space. Dizzying flies buzzed around my head. I slapped them away. I looked up for the merciful God and found only a gray blanket sky.

"How will Grandfather find us?" Bellina asked, pulling on my sleeve.

"I hope he does not," my mother said under her breath. Her sleeve had ripped and she looked as though she had been dipped in dust, unkempt and unsmiling.

We found a spot and sat down. The best places in the shade of the walls were taken. Our view of the front was blocked by bodies. We waited hours. My mouth grew parched. Bellina slept with her head in my lap while my mother begged those around us for a small hand-out of any nourishment. Some, thinking they were about to board ships to Morocco or Salonika, had hampers of carrots and garbanzos and wine. Where was my father? And what would he think returning to an empty house? An empty street? A city empty of Jews?

Information was passed to us by families from the front. "We are being organized for the caravels." Then, "The Queen wants us to return," and then finally, "Hush. Hush. An announcement," murmured through the assembly.

Shell horns and drums sounded. I could not see the person speaking, but I heard a deep, commanding voice. "Many of you have arrived voluntarily for your departure to new lands. How many for the Ottoman Empire? Africa?" Hands went up and down.

Weak with hunger and thirst I did my best to catch the message. The blurry sun moved across the sky. Maybe this would be over soon. My mother returned from her wanderings looking for my father and sat beside me. Up until now there had been the constant raucous cries of bewildered children, whining animals and voices of the afflicted, but now even the babies fell silent.

With measured words amplifying the announcement, the speech of authority began. If someone tried to talk, the others shushed them into silence. A donkey brayed. "It is with sad regret that I inform you your departure has been cancelled. There are no caravels." Murmurs turned to cries, wails, shrieks of disbelief, moans climbing toward the sky. "Your only salvation is to join us in Jesus Christ."

"Those devils. They tricked us," said a man with shoulder-length hair standing next to me, two slumbering babies in his arms. His wife, red-faced and fat, pushed herself to her feet and screamed, "King Manuel has sold us to win the hand of Princess Isabel." The crowd cheered. A guard approached, grabbing her shoulders. She leapt at him, clawing his face. He touched the blood, examining the stain on his fingers. As another soldier rushed to his aid, panting, eyes fierce, I thought of a falcon swooping down on prey. Her mutiny was silenced with a swift hand, her body pulled toward the gate. Her husband handed the babies to another and tried to follow but was killed. I swallowed and looked away. I vowed to remain strong.

My mother hugged herself, silent in grief. Her eyes, once a clear green, watered with dark tears. The flush in her face evaporated and she looked whiter than a hen's breast. Bellina looked back and forth at us, as though we had a solution to our predicament.

Priests and apostate Jews began to harangue parents to bring their children to the baptismal font. "Bring your youth to accept Jesus, the Savior of us all. Jews, forget Issac, Abraham and Jacob. Where is your God now? Join us in the Holy Trinity of the Father, the Son and the Holy Ghost. You will avoid hell and damnation like these souls who have made the choice to follow us into glory."

The father of a nearby family stood and announced in a hoarse voice, "We are condemning our children if we do not join them." With that he herded his group together. A few people spit on them as they made their way to the front.

Another man in his twenties with a saffron turban and a jet-black beard engaged in a dialogue. "I will always believe in the Law of Moses. You want to keep your people ignorant so the priests have power. We do not need intermediaries to speak to God."

At first the priests made an effort to convert his mind, citing biblical texts, but soon they motioned for guards to take him away. The authorities banged their staff and called for order.

Hours passed. My stomach growled like a hungry dog. Puffs of dust swirled every time someone shifted near us. I wiped my eyes. My mother,

her face brooding, sat looking at the solemn sky.

Levi ben Shem-tob, a well-known collaborator of the King, strutted through the weakening crowd, his gait confident. A giant of a man with a large head and an enormous belly, the gold buttons of his vest caught glints of light. He walked among us, urging us to act with haste. An ancient man near me, his countenance wrinkled with years, said under his breath, "I do not believe in hell, but he will burn there." Then he turned his back to Levi and toward the east, swaying in prayer.

Levi ben-Shem-Tob raised his hands in an embrace to the crowd. "Fellow Jews, it is time to leave the Laws of Moses behind. Let us unify behind Christ. Great wealth and peace of mind await you once you come to the truth and light. Let us embrace the Trinity together."

The elderly man vomited. I turned away from the stench. My mother, who, only a few weeks ago, hand-delivered the fine boucle vest and silk collar our tormentor wore, the seams of which she had sewn herself with black silk thread, leaped at him, her hands grasping his sleeve. A shadow eclipsed her eyes, a penumbra of inky black.

"Levi, how can you walk among us as a traitor?" she screamed. Guards in tunics and leggings appeared on either side of her and hauled her back, securing each of her arms. Her ruby shawl fell to the ground and Bellina's small hands grabbed for it, clutching it to her face.

Levi ben Shem-tob looked my mother up and down. I held my breath. "Let her go. She is among the stiff-necked," he said to the men. "Estrella Guzman, for a beautiful woman you are very stupid. You do not have to believe in your heart. That can come later. Accept the Messiah." He leaned in closer, his moon-face seeming wider with sweat, "Do not be a fool. Save yourself and your family. Use your Judaism internally. Join us now to see the advantages, the joy of success."

"I would never leave the faith and beliefs of my people," said my mother, lips set with resolve. Her spine straightened as though an iron rod lifted her. She brushed hair away from her face, jaw quivering.

Levi lifted his head in superiority. "The lack of struggle and resistance will set you free. What is the point of being stubborn as a mule? The church is all powerful."

My mother, defiant, stared at him with hatred, her fists clenched.

His mouth twisted in disgust. "Your fate is sealed." He moved on and

I stood to hug my mother. With our arms around one another, I cried, my tears wetting her breast. Bellina circled her arms around us, too. After no more tears came, we let go of one another and I wiped my face with a handkerchief hidden in my bosom.

We continued to hear Levi ben Shem-tob's endless harangue as he strutted through the crowd, urging others to join him. "What is wrong with you? We offer you prosperity and you turn away? With your knowledge as *marranos* you can become powerful within the hierarchy of the church. We have rabbis who are priests, followers of the Torah who are monks. What is the point of holding onto a philosophy of learning that cannot work for the masses?"

A mother and father next to us kneeled, their hands on their children's shoulders, tears streaming down their faces, whispering last words of encouragement. Royal bailiffs pulled families apart and dragged them, their feet leaving furrows in the earth, prayers tumbling from their lips, to the baptismal font.

A priest standing on a platform announced, hands cupped around his mouth, "Those of you who do not join us in Christ will forfeit your freedom and become slaves."

The crowd began to scream, hurling curses. A woman beat her breast, yelling, "Slaves? You want us to be slaves after Moses led us out of Egypt? May the devil force plagues on all of you." She threw a piece of rotten fruit toward the priest.

A scream caused us all to turn and look in the direction of the noise. The silent Señora Ezrahti was now spewing blasphemous curses at the priests. I glanced at the altar. A priest dressed in white robes spoke to soldiers behind him through a shell horn. "Silence her."

In moments two guards ran toward the Señora, dragging her to the font, a captured wild woman belligerent and protesting. A third guard met them and in moments they had her on the ground holding her limbs. When I saw them bring a hot poker, orange-red with heat, toward her I knew they were going to mark her forehead with the sign of the cross. My mother's fist came up to stifle a scream. I clutched for her and buried my face in her arm. All sound ceased except my neighbor's piercing shriek, one that halted my flow of blood, ringing in my ears. My mother grabbed for Bellina's head and pulled it into her skirt. Drums began pounding, their steady rhythm a heartbeat of doom.

Afterward, a few more succumbed and stumbled forward to be anointed with water. Some cheered and greeted them as though it was a celebration. We waited under guard in the back. As more people arrived our bodies pushed forward. Finally, my mother said, "Go. Be baptized with Bellina. You care for her." The child began to draw circles in the dirt with her finger.

"No, Mama." I was so bereft I thought I heard my father's voice.

"Estrella, Estrella, where are you? Do not do it. Do not give up the law of our fathers. Say the *shema*." Our protector was nearby!

We all turned toward him. "Hermando, my husband! I am here!" My mother waved her arms in the air but could not reach him.

A flash of recognition softened his face. He called back over the crowd, "Resist, Estrella. Do not give in."

Three guards surrounded him. In moments my father, attacked with their flashing knives, fell to his knees, crimson spreading over his velvet *jubba*, his shouts silenced forever.

"Oh my God." My mother's hand clutched her chest. She began to cry, sobbing her words, "Hermando. They have killed Hermando." She repeated his name a dozen times, her fists balled into her eyes. Without warning she lifted her head and stumbled over people toward him. A few tried to stop her. A goat squealed as she tripped over it.

The young man who had protested our situation earlier grabbed her arms and held her. The older of the two said, "What's the use? Do you want to die too?"

Tears stained her face. "I love him. So brave, strong."

Shocked, I could not cry. My mother, hysterical, her face red, struggled to be free. In moments she was limp. What would become of us without my father? The young man brought her back to me, settling her on the ground. Someone nearby passed a jug with wine. I put some on my finger and touched her lips. She looked at me as if she could crawl into my eyes, took the cask from me, threw back her head and took a long swallow.

Over-zealous fanatics began to drag people to the baptismal font, a giant bird-bath made of stone. Their screams incited dogs to start barking. Simon Maimi, the chief rabbi, our last *arraby mor*, urged us to thwart the infidels. He was one of the few who held out until the end.

Bellina clung to my mother's skirt. My mother's face altered from anguish to calm, devoid of expression, a sea erasing footprints in the sand. She stood, removing Bellina's small fists, touching my arm. "Open your hand." She passed me the small velvet bag with sapphires. I stuffed it in my stocking. "Watch over Bellina." She kissed her grandchild on the head and pushed my niece toward me.

"If there are no more volunteers we will sprinkle holy water over everyone. Please fall to your knees in supplication."

I knelt down, Bellina's body tucked next to mine. I put my arm over her head. A child does not always know the difference between real and pretend. Maybe she would think this was a nightmare, one from which we would all awaken. My mother remained standing, shoulders squared in perfect posture. When I saw the guard's leather boots come closer, I pulled on her garment.

"*Shema Isroel, Adonai eliheynu, Adonai el hod*, Hear, O Israel, the Lord our God, the Lord is One." My mother steadily repeated the ancient prayer twice, once in Hebrew and once in Spanish, her voice low and solid. People around us stopped talking. Children ceased playing. All sounds became hollow. A shudder rocked me, a lightning bolt through my body.

With her head held high, a twig of hair drifting across her cheek, my mother pulled her kosher butcher knife, the one she used to slaughter animals, from inside her sleeve. In a swift slice she slit her own throat, a movement I had watched her do many times to squawking chickens or bleating sheep. A thin crimson line stained the white of her neck then gushed over her chest. I covered Bellina's eyes by nestling her head in my bosom, her whimpers wounding me, as I watched.

The elegant, much-envied Señora Estrella Guzman collapsed as the King's men reached her, blood staining her clothes, the ground, me. I gasped as she fell into a heap, not unlike the piles of fabric that lay in our sewing corner at home, as though a person was no longer there, had never inhabited them.

They pulled my mother's body away with haste, the trail of blood staining the earth. With one finger I reached out, touched it and smeared the inside of my hem.

In an afternoon of fate I lost my mother and my father, my hopes and dreams. Now, responsible for my young niece, my life would take a different course. And so, on that treacherous day, King Manuel rid his kingdom of all its Jews.

An unfamiliar song rose from the lips of a few who had succumbed earlier. Most of us sat in stunned silence. I felt drops of water on the back of my head. I sat up while Bellina remained supine. A priest announced, "You are all declared Christians now and forever. You are members in good standing of the Catholic Church. Let us pray."

Chapter Eighteen

Alegra

November 19, 1998

I agree to stay and see the Professor's project through. One afternoon after siesta he sits at his desk, feet up, staring into space while the haunting songs of Sarah Aroeste drift through the house. She's a singer who blends *Ladino* and lyrics adapted from five-hundred-year-old poems. The translations in the CD notes are contemporary. People dispersed throughout the Iberian peninsula knew heartbreak, too.

I stand in front of his desk. "Professor Guzman?" He's a thinker and I can tell he's flying in outer space. "I found more information about the *conversos* after the day of forced conversions in Portugal."

He looks at me over his half-glasses. "Call me Hal." He takes his well-worn sneakers down from the desk and sits up, brushing off a few pieces of pipe tobacco. He drums a yellow legal pad.

"I've been thinking," I tell him.

"Uh-oh."

"You really should think about using the computer for your novel."

"Why? I like the feel of pen and paper. Computers are for email."

"But it's so easy to edit and paste."

"Not for me."

"Professor Guzman, you don't realize—"

"Call me Hal. Anything but Professor Guzman. Yes?" He raises his brows in anticipation of my fascinating revelation.

"It's not professional." He makes a snorting sound of disgust. And it's awkward. After all, I've always had a boss.

The music seems to get louder and a strange instrument plays an interlude. I point to the stereo, imagining a spinning dancer. The professor says, "That's an Arabic instrument called a *qanan* with eighty-one strings. Like our zither." He taps his fingers. "That's how they get that metallic, shifting melody to sound ancient."

Nodding and self-conscious, I brush hair back from my face. "In the research I found only a small fraction of the population left after the day of conversion at *Os Esatos*. About seven or eight people were badly beaten and refused to change their faith. Some accounts say there were deaths. The rest stayed in Portugal and labeled themselves 'New Christians.' Of course they were never trusted, but here's the interesting part."

The Professor settles back into his chair, rolls backward to the wall and puts his fingers into a steeple. I have his full attention. "Go ahead."

"They had to disguise their Jewish origins to reduce prejudice so they took names of places or trees. If you look in the Portugal phonebook today, there's lots of Oliveiras for olive trees, Perieras for pear trees and Lisboas for Lisbon." I hold papers to my chest, proud of my discovery.

The professor stares at me in silence, his expression thoughtful. Sarah Aroetse wails a love song. I catch a few words about sleeping without worry or sorrow, something that escapes me.

"Listen to this," I say, continuing. I assume his lack of response means he's impressed. "Belmonte, a town built around the hilltop castle northeast of Lisbon? They put small stones on gravesites when they visit them. People still observe the Sabbath on Saturday after five hundred years. Of course they also attend Mass with their Catholic neighbors on Sunday. But they've held onto their religion for centuries." I search my notes. "Mainly because they're cut off by the--"

"The Serra de Estrela mountains. Very isolated. It was the home of Pedro Alvres Cabral, the explorer who discovered Brazil." He nods his head gently. "Yes, I know about that."

The Professor's knowledge doesn't deflate me. "This is unbelievable," I say with the enthusiasm of a new learner. "None of the men are circumcised, but the women have held onto practical details and remember the prayers. Even lighting the candles."

He leans in, elbows on the desk. "The Jews weren't given legal status in Portugal until 1921," says the professor, ever the scholar.

"That doesn't seem fair. How did they get away with banishing a religion, a people, for centuries? Were the monarchy and church that powerful?" I pull over a wicker chair and sit down, frustrated. There's so clearly good guys and bad guys in this scenario. Some nights I lie in bed and get angry thinking about it all. Digging into my pocket for a small box with pieces of *mazapan* I bought in town, I open it and offer him the almond-fruity confection. Nothing dampens my appetite.

He puts his hand up in refusal and answers me. "How did the Nazis get away with it sixty years ago? Anti-Semitism is pervasive. You should be asking why you weren't taught this in school." His expression is so serious. He combs his fingers through his hair in a nervous gesture.

"Professor, I mean Hal, this is getting to me. At first I was just doing research with an objective eye. Now I'm emotional when I read what these people went through." I hesitate for a moment, licking my lips. "The stories of Grazia and Bellina are haunting me."

"Really?" He looks at me with more interest, eyes wide, maybe a bit flattered.

"I feel connected to these people. Please don't think it's silly, but I dream of them and their family. Sometimes I wake up in a sweat as though I've spent time with them, a play thing in their world. They wait until I sink into the lower levels of consciousness. I can see what they look like: Grazia, short, a bit plain, and Bellina, a beauty with green eyes. I catch glimpses of them disappearing around a corner, exchanging looks, sneaking something from their pockets, whispering. I'm grief-stricken about what happened to their family. Like the Inquisition is looking for me. Then I can't go back to sleep."

The professor contemplates me, unblinking. Suddenly, I feel foolish, like those people on TV who say aliens kidnapped them for sexual pleasure.

"Do I sound silly?" I ask, furrowing my brow.

He puffs up a little, flattered at my interest. "Not at all. I believe a collective consciousness or a genetic pool stays with us. I want to captivate people, affect their thoughts, connect them to what came before. It's a story that has to be told, especially for young people."

"But what's going to happen to them?"

"Ah, you'll have to follow the story."

"Is it written yet?" I thought about how awful it would be if he left me hanging. I want it to go on forever like my steamy *telenovela*, *Velo de Novia*, the Spanish version of *Days of Our Lives*, which I hope my sisters are taping for me.

"No. I can't work on it in Miami. I–I plan to stay here until next May to finish. This is my sabbatical year."

"You're staying? Why didn't you mention this to me before?" His matter-of-fact attitude shocks me. Did he expect me to stay, too? I'm a little ticked off. After all, I'm with him every day. He could've said something. My foot starts a swinging rhythm as the music fills up our silence, the crazy Arabic instrument hitting a solo and expanding into the room.

He speaks first. "I thought you'd do the research for me and then go home after three months." He hesitates, fumbling in his pencil drawer, taking out scissors, trying them.

His eyes disappear in the glare of his glasses. I'm more curious than annoyed now. What is he thinking?

He looks up, puts the scissors back, removes his glasses and gives me a sly smile. Shutting the drawer, he gets up and moves to the front corner of the desk. I can see his eyes clearly now. I also smell a pine scent. Is he wearing aftershave? He's missing the few days growth of beard he normally sports.

"Uh, but, now I see I'm going to need your assistance longer than I thought."

I raise my eyebrows and lean toward him. What does he have in mind?

He continues, emboldened. "In fact, I want us to visit some of the ancient sites in Lisbon, especially the Alfama district near the sailors' quarters and Rossio Square, even look for some of the *mikvahs*."

"You're going to Portugal?"

This guy is a surprise a minute. First, he wants me to stay and now he wants me to accompany him on a side trip? Is he thinking hanky-panky?

I must look like a blinking frog, eyes bulging, because he adds, "The *mikvahs*, the ritual baths, were an important part of women's cleansing, often hidden down secret stairs. They needed fresh water for them. Even kept records about who visited them." He slows down, picks up a pencil, tapping it against his desk to the music, confident in his intellectual domain. "Ironically, the Inquisition's Edicts of Grace were a great resource."

"What are they?" I'm perplexed at how fast his mind races around.

"When the Inquisition started in Andalucia in 1478 they called an assembly that all *conversos* and Jews had to attend to read a proclamation that included detailed lists of customs so people could recognize their Jewish neighbors."

"And turn them in."

Yes, he's distracted me with his fancy footwork, but I haven't forgotten he's suggested a trip together. I'm intrigued. Let's face it, Saul never took me anywhere. Has my new colorful wardrobe made me more appealing? I adjust the elastic on the neckline of my blouse.

He squints a bit, straightens his body to lean forward, not lecturing me, but speaking with emphasis.

"Almost overnight everything went underground. They buried their prayer books wrapped in burlap or, if they were more daring, hid them behind Christian covers. A few copies of the Old Testament circulated, but for the most part Hebrew prayers were forgotten quickly. Secret possessions set up a moral dilemma, destroying the foundations of human trust. The 1480s and 90s were the worst. Mass arrests, public burnings, torture. Yet, they were passionate that they could only be saved by the Law of Moses."

I shake my head in disbelief. "I don't understand why they just didn't give up. Why? What was driving them? I mean, after a while, if you're being persecuted through generations, why not let it go? Why were these people so obstinate?"

"Some gave up, but there was a core who held onto three tenets." His thumb pops up. A belief in one God, a radical idea for that time." He unfolds a second finger. "That the Messiah hadn't come," and with the third finger, "A belief in the Laws of Moses."

I wait, relaxing into my chair, adjusting a pillow into the small of my back.

Slowly and with deliberation, he says, "My ancestors were some of them." He waits for me to respond.

I'm quiet, emotional. I swallow to fight tears and look at my hands in my lap. Voices call from the past, suffering souls, an ancestral family reaching out from an abyss of struggle.

The injustice of it clutches me, sweat dampening my body. This history means something to me. All the flights in the search of freedom, the terror and persecutions, a resolve to cling to a faith that must have offered them solace. I feel so alone.

Sarah Aroeste's songs remind me of the sweet tunes my mother sang, ones she learned from her family in Cuba. The memories blend into the lyrics of *A la Una, In the Beginning*. I look at the professor's serious expression and his concern for me. Is it the past or the potential of a new present gripping me along a new path?

At one I was born
At two I grew up
At three I took a lover
At four I married into the world
Soul, life and heart.

Tell me where do you come from
Because I want to get to know you
If you have no lover
I will defend you as mine
Soul, life and heart.

Going off into the world
I throw kisses into the air
One is for my mother
The other is for you
Soul, life and heart.

"How 'bout a glass of wine on the patio?" he asks, getting up from where he's perched himself on the desk.

I'm numb with my jumbled thoughts of the past and how I got to this point. Do I have a future? I feel disconnected from Saul, wondering if it was ever a valid relationship. In his last email he didn't even ask what I was doing. With a sigh I stand up and head toward the kitchen. "I'll get the *tapas*."

Overwhelmed, I stand in the blue-and-white tiled kitchen next to Manuelita's saran-wrapped platter, a pink hibiscus on top. I stroke a velvety petal. All I have to do is pick up the *tapas* and go outside.

I turn and lean my belly against the counter, my head touching the cool cabinets. I have to acknowledge where my family and I have come from, what my future holds and, even more confusing, how I feel about the professor. I smile, wetting my lips with my tongue. Maybe I'll have to use the name Hal to his face, but internally, he's The Professor to me.

"What are you thinking?" He stands beside me, a glass of wine in each hand. I turn to face him and for a split second I can see him as a young man, his hair darker and not out of control, the studious eyes, his shoulders squared in the same blue batiste cotton shirt, glasses hanging on the front.

"I'm just bewildered by some of my feelings right now. The music is getting to me." I pick up the appetizers and turn to leave the kitchen.

He sets the wine glasses on the counter. "Can I help? I'm a good listener. Watching a sunset play light off the hills can cure lots of worries."

On a particularly glorious sunset a few days ago when we lingered over a second glass of wine, I shared my fading relationship with Saul, guilty that I didn't even miss him.

"No, you don't understand." Tears well up in my eyes again. "I'm very emotional right now." A tear creeps down my face.

He steps toward me, takes the platter from my hands and places it on the counter. Then he reaches for me, his arms solid as they wrap around me, pulling me toward him. I succumb and lean my head onto his shoulder and a warm, comforting feeling slides over me.

Soul, life and heart.

Chapter Nineteen

Grazia

11 Adar 5257 (22 February 1497)
Lisbon

By nightfall Bellina and I were released from the site of the coerced conversions to make our way home. Distraught families choked the narrow streets, shoulders hunched in misery like black crows huddled for comfort.

In the incessant downpour I heard cries of trauma, dismayed murmurs and the slow shuffling of feet drowned by joyous church bells ringing throughout the kingdom. We passed renovated structures with Gothic arches and elaborate Manueline stone work sanctioned by our new king. And we, fragmented and shattered, shards of pottery that could not be melded together again, marched toward emptiness.

Nothing waited for us. The familiar creaky hinge, one left un-oiled by my father to warn us of strangers, unnerved me as I opened the door. No Mama and her bustle calling to me. No Papa and his textiles. Nothing simmering in the copper pot. Orphans. How would we eat? Pay for our needs? Follow the Laws of Moses?

The first night Bellina and I curled up in Mama's comfortable bed, one she stuffed with her own hand from chicken feathers she had plucked. The linen ticking was rough to the touch. My mother's fragrance enveloped me in dreams of safety. We slept from exhaustion, or maybe it was an escape into a netherworld.

Bellina's damp body clung to mine, the stain of my mother's blood on our hems. Sometimes she cried out. I did my best to comfort her, stroking her hair, cooing soft words, useless gestures. Who was going to absolve me?

By the next afternoon we were hungry and had to relieve ourselves. I brought water from the cistern outside and poured it into a washbasin to clean our faces. Then I undid Bellina's hair and re-braided it.

Bellina did not speak. She mimicked my moves, following me, sometimes stepping on my heels, a scared shadow. I had no desire to start a fire. We ate brown bread, cashews and apricots my mother had left behind. At the table, empty chairs an overwhelming reminder, I broke down. I covered my weeping eyes with my hands. When I looked up, wiping my wet face with my sleeve, the child was staring at me, her small chest heaving in terror, green eyes dulled to a dark grey.

I calmed myself and we finished our meager nourishment. I felt an urge to follow our routine and sweep the floor. I stood there for a moment, broom in hand, waiting for my mother to take it from me.

Instead, Bellina reached for it, and although she could not do a thorough job, she followed our faith by sweeping the dirt toward the center of the room so it could be gathered and disposed of outside.

My mother never swept past the front door out of respect for the *mezuzah,* the sacred talisman carved into our ancestors' doorposts, but not ours. My father hid the few lines of sacred scripture between stones near the top of our well.

A fly buzzed, trapped in a corner, accompanied by the sound of our swishing skirts. We moved, wordless. My mother's claret velvet cloak hung near the door, empty of her body and soul. I took it, closing the mother-of-pearl clasp at the neck, covered our heads with caps trimmed in lace and grabbed Bellina's hand, venturing into the street.

I could hear my mother's voice saying, 'Grazia, hold your head high. We are a proud people,' as the latch on the gate clicked. I had a mission.

A road of twisted alleys and narrow steps in front of our house led downward toward the church. It was cluttered with debris from the forced processional—broken dishes, lost shoes, rotten food, human waste. Drainage ran down the middle. A small cat floated by, feet frozen in the air. I smelled the filth and gagged, steering Bellina around the garbage. A mangy dog scavenged in front of us. A pall hovered over our community, and as in the past, people stayed behind their closed doors.

I wanted proper burials with crested tombstones inscribed with Hebrew letters for my parents, similar to the ones for my grandparents. "Dedicated to the Señora Dona Estiline Guzman, daughter of R. Solomon ben Abigal, who died of the plague. 'Let her rest in peace,' Daniel 12. So be it. Amen. 5037."

The Hebrew date instead of the Christian calendar always reminded me how long our people were struggling not to be oppressed. Maybe the elders would object to a proper burial because my mother committed suicide, a terrible sin with our belief in the sanctity of life.

The only exception was to rescue a Torah, our sacred book. I longed to order a fine limestone tomb from Barcelona or maybe one of marble from Leon, a tribute to both of them. They loved each other. I wanted them to be side-by-side for eternity.

I planned to inquire at the *Iglesia de Maria* about receiving their bodies. I also desired another sapphire necklace my mother had hidden in her dress. My good fortune had her ruby one of butterflies and the star of our faith around my neck.

As I entered the cavernous structure it took a few minutes for my eyes to adjust to the somber light. Streaks of red and blue from the stained glass painted designs on the floor. The smell of burning incense wafted past me.

A few women dressed in black sat on the floor sobbing, one banging her head against the stone wall. I recognized the tall, corpulent priest with slack jowls and silver hair, as he approached me, his hands out, voice lofty. He was a *marrano* himself from an important family, one we were told to go to if forced to make a Confession. His Hebrew name had been Issac but now he went by the Old Christian name, John.

"What can I do for you, my child?" he asked, folding his hands across his chest. My father cursed him in our home, but at the same time envied his family because they were granted certain protections and favors.

Bellina clung to my cloak, fidgeting and maneuvering the velvet through her fingers.

I stood straighter, trying to ignore the wails of the women. "I want to claim the bodies of Señor Hermando Guzman and his wife, Estrella Guzman." I spoke in a forthright manner although my insides cried and cramped at speaking my beloved parents' names.

"And you are related to the deceased?" he asked, narrowing his eyes.

I felt a resolve to retrieve them from this evil place, these people who imposed their will. "Yes, I am their daughter." I lifted my chin and looked at him, repeating my request.

He cast his eyes away from me. "I am sorry, my child, it is not possible."

Insistent, defiant, chin in the air, my voice filled with fortitude. "Their souls must be at rest. I want my parents' bodies."

According to the laws of our faith a body required preparation before burial–cleansing, white linen, a fresh pine box. I wanted to scratch his face, to fight him with the ferocity of a wet cat, to protest the Church's righteousness.

"Precisely why we do not give them to you. They died resisting our Lord Jesus. We object to the mumbling of blasphemous prayers over them."

Bellina clung to my cloak, face hidden in my back. "What are you doing?" I asked, annoyed at the interruption.

A small voice answered, "I do not want to see him." I sighed.

I leaned in toward the priest, examining his face, searching his cold blue eyes. I had no fear. I knew confronting him was dangerous but I did not care.

"My family deserves a proper burial." I waited and softened my voice, "Monsignor, you once were of our faith. Have mercy," I begged, lowering my eyes.

"Your parents defiled church law and you are bordering on heresy. If you value your life and the child's, leave, and I will forget this encounter."

I looked up, my mouth hardened into a grimace.

He shook a finger at me. "I expect to see you at Mass taking communion on Sunday. Your people have to learn to leave the old ways behind. We are all Christians now." He crossed himself and proceeded toward the font, his frock sweeping the stone floor, a puff of dust following him.

"But what of my mother's sapphire necklace?"

He turned with haste, his words biting. "It belongs to the church now. Forget what happened and accept Christ into your heart." He waved me away.

"Not as long as I have breath in my body," I whispered. Bellina crawled out from under the cloak and slipped her small hand in mine.

Afterward, I learned they burned my parents' bodies. I grieved for them. Others who died on the same day were buried with last rites. Levi ben Shem-tob, the traitor, presided at their funerals.

The fact that we could not say *kaddish*, the prayer for the dead, made my heart ache and my mind played tricks on me. Was that my father pacing the courtyard, stroking his beard? Sometimes I thought I saw my mother slip to the end of the bed, a ghost in a dream. 'Go,' she said, 'Go.' How could their souls find peace?

I sat with my neighbors for a week to observe their tragic deaths, unable to get food past my lips. I sipped only water. Señora Ezrati, whose daughter was still missing, lost her ability to speak. She sat for hours in silence, her stricken husband spoon-feeding her nourishment.

For a time I sold off inventory, made clothes for others, ransomed my mother's jewelry including the ruby necklace of butterflies. I kissed it as I exchanged it for *maravedis*, the wealthy patron snickering at my attachment.

We ate with neighbors, clung to each other and finally, with most of our resources depleted, moved out of our home on *Beco do Espirito Santo* in the Alfama district. I cursed the mighty and imposing castle that towered over our neighborhood. I buried the prayer books in the back under an olive tree and wrapped the candlesticks in sheaths of fabric to take with me.

Wealthy *conversos* took me in. Señor Torres, the man with the misshapen foot who accompanied us on our voyage from Spain, and his wife, Orlinda, a stout woman with a sharp tongue and an abundance of flatulence, employed me as a servant. They understood I could not be separated from the child. We said the blessings with them, cautious that no one could hear. I repeated *kaddish* for my parents, whispering it close to Bellina's ear so that she could learn it, too.

The community paced through their days, a caul over us, steady but slow, furtive yet resigned, trudging to the Christian church, fearful of the Sabbath, our holiest day.

The Torres family had us sew and assist with food preparation. There was no pay, just a meal and a place to sleep. My seamstress skills proved to be valuable and I spent long nights repairing and mending the family's clothes, even fashioning new ones for them. The señora took my mother's claret velvet cloak from me, strutting proudly in the streets, a sacrilege that made me cry myself to sleep.

Bellina did her best to help by picking lettuce from the garden, playing with their grandchildren and staying out from under foot, but her physicality was a distraction. With budding breasts high and firm and her uncommon face, the señor stared as she moved in languid motion, dreamy eyes cast downward. The señora delighted in humiliating her, making her wash a floor twice or firing off so many tasks she could not remember any.

One night, after we had been there more than the passing of two Rosh

Hashanahs, I overheard their conversation from our pallet along the wall in the kitchen. The fading fire threw some warmth into the room. Bellina's thin body curled around mine, her ebony hair under a nightcap, the embers lighting her sweet mouth and long lashes.

"Paulo, they can't stay here forever. How many mouths can a chicken feed?"

It was true our community was suffering with so many restrictions on trade. Señora Olinda tolerated us, never looking me directly in the eye. We were an obligation sanctioned by the rabbis, who lived in an undercover world moving from house to house, doing their best to minister to our wounded people, keeping traditions alive. Our kind could not be left out in the cold.

"I have to help them. I promised Señor Guzman to watch out for his family when he traveled. He was good to me, a religious man with integrity. He gave me an entire trade route from Girona to the south of France when his eyes were failing."

"It is not important to me. He and that showy wife of his are gone. Why do we have to be responsible for their children? The older one can take care of herself. We have our own needs."

"You will have to learn to do without. With the many prejudices against New Christians, we have to be clever to survive." There was a silence. Then he began again. I shifted my ear to the cool wall to hear more. "Guzman was right. We will never be accepted. I want to leave."

"What? Leave? I can not move again. Where do you think we can go? The authorities will look for us everywhere." Her tone mellowed. "My husband, please do not uproot us from here." She pleaded, "Let us raise our grandchildren as Catholics and forget the past. No matter what we do we will be *marranos*, but maybe our children will not be known as swine. Send the orphans away. We have fulfilled our obligation."

My heart beat faster with the idea that the señora wanted to be rid of us. Where would we go? I had seen women of the street, a frightening thought.

"I want us to go far away, a place where we can worship without fear of being caught," said Señor Torres.

"What about them? The older one is helpful, but the young one is lazy. A beauty who thinks she can get by with a smile. I want them out." The señora's voice filled with resentment.

Many found Bellina's remarkable face disconcerting.

"A group of families is leaving for Brazil. Enrique is already there in a small colony. The land is cheap and sugar fields are available with free slaves to tend them. We can have an enclave to worship whatever we want in the wilderness." The señor's voice sounded firm, controlled.

"Are you serious? Am I a feather drifting across the world? We cannot start again."

His voice was more muffled. "Move or die. I cannot give up the faith of my fathers. They will never let us live in peace. Look how some of us have lost our minds like Señora Ezrati. Never trust the Church or our capricious rulers. Who knows what they will invoke next?"

Señora Torres began to wail. Her fists banged the wall and I clutched the coverings under my chin. I put my ear back on the cool bricks when her cries subsided.

"Shush. Begin again. It will be fine. There are exotic butterflies and birds called parrots that fly through jungles with yellow and blue feathers."

I imagined him holding her, smoothing her hair.

Her sobs became louder. Bellina stirred.

"Auntie, what is wrong?" she asked with wide eyes.

"Ssh. Nothing. Go back to sleep."

A dark curl drifted across her cheek and I twirled it around my finger. What about us? Where would we go?

Señora Torres began to shout, her voice hoarse. "What about the orphans? Get rid of them, especially the beguiling younger sister. Tell me it is done."

I did not hear the master's answer, only muffled weeping. I turned away from the wall, silent tears staining my face.

Bellina asked, "Do we have to leave? Where will we go? Why?"

I whispered, "Bellina, our future is uncertain. The señora wants us to leave. Avoid her, obey her every wish. Pray to God we can stay."

I felt an obligation to protect Bellina. She had become my charge and although she burdened me at times, I loved her. Not for a day did I forget that she was the blood of Hanna, my only sister, all that was left of my family.

I thought about my sister daily when I looked at Bellina's unusual eyes, how Hanna's passion led her to defy my father. Was she in a sacred state of being now? Did she wonder about us? About her daughter? Sometimes I considered that my parents' death was the punishment of a vengeful God for banishing her. I did not know. I knew my fate was not secure.

When I returned from the market the next day, our belongings were packed, waiting outside the door.

Chapter Twenty

Alegra

December 12, 1998
Lisbon, Portugal

Hal and I embark on a quick flight to Lisbon, the Paris of Portugal. We're staying at a pension, a former monastery renovated to accommodate tourists. More prison than former sanctuary, it's not friendly.

Behind a monolithic wooden desk stands an unsmiling host, hair combed forward Caesar-style, dressed as a monk in a brown dress and rope belt. He passes us a leather-bound yellowed guest book to sign. The lobby, dimly-lit with low-ceilings, has stucco walls, wooden benches, a few well-worn velvet chairs, and an abundance of hanging crucifixes.

Our pseudo-monk hands us over-sized keys attached to small wooden paddles. "There is no bellman service. We lock the front doors at eleven. Please do not leave the premises with our keys." His English is heavily accented.

"How could we?" I ask The Professor, trying to manipulate the key with its wooden guard dog in my hands. "Why did you pick this place?"

"Great location. Reasonable, too." He gives me a weak smile.

And, yes, we have separate rooms.

When Hal first brought up this trip, I felt uncomfortable. After all, our kitchen hug and a few glasses of wine hardly constituted a relationship. I wasn't sure how I felt about him. Grappling with my identity crisis has preoccupied me. However, that's all changed since the water shortage.

I trudge down a dim hallway lit by fake candles, my rolling suitcase bumping over uneven terra cotta tiles. I follow The Professor until he stops. The number on the door doesn't correspond to the one on my key.

"Look at this archway," he says pointing above us. Good example of Manueline architecture. Even has an armillary."

"Huh?"

"The King's personal symbol. He used it everywhere. See the carved globe with rings of stars at the top?" The professor responds to my silence. "A device used by sailors to locate where they were in relation to the heavens."

"Uh-huh." I shift my suitcase to the other hand. Sometimes his information is fascinating and sometimes I just want to get on with it.

Finally, we find our rooms. I open the door. Our rooms are next to each other. Dated, but large. Pretty tiled floors. Shutters that open above the street. Balconies across the way burst with pink bougainvillea and planters of lavender.

I pick the room on the right, wheeling my bag into a corner and closing the shutters. It paints the room in soft light that's perfect for a nap. I fall on the bed, arm over my eyes, and doze off.

The first afternoon we ride vintage trolleys that shake and shudder as they climb narrow streets. They're crowded with the aroma of too many bodies. It's hot so I'm relieved when we get off to tour *the Se*, a Romanesque cathedral built in the twelfth century after the Christians took Lisbon back from the Moors.

The Professor carries a notebook to jot down details, craning his neck to see and read everything from his guidebook. He explains that this fortress of God is home to Saint Vincent whose remains were brought here guarded by two sacred black ravens, symbols of the city.

"Is this where they held mass conversions?" I ask looking up at the enormous towers and a rose window nestled between them.

"Yes, some, although many were held at the courtyard in the palace that housed the Inquisition. It's still used for diplomatic receptions. Others were forcibly baptized at the Church of São Domingo."

I try to absorb it all.

Hal in khaki cargo shorts with lots of pockets, socks and sandals and a camera around his neck looks so touristy. Am I as shallow as my over-glamorized sister, Irma, because I'm embarrassed by what he's wearing?

On the other hand, maybe I don't look great either. In this warm weather I've got my hair in a ponytail with a visor hiding my eyes from the intense sun. Whew! I thought Miami was hot. At least the Portuguese are blessed with cool breezes from the Tagus, the wide river that flows through the city to the sea.

I'm exhausted and sticky. Hal drags me around the São Jorge Castle with its grand view, the highest point of the city. It was first built by the Moors in the eighth century and stands in ruins, its parapets high and wide.

Afterward, we're lost in tangled streets and confusing alleys, some so narrow we walk single file. The Professor tells me that they were built this way to foil the invaders so they couldn't find the castle.

Well, I give up. It feels like we've been walking for hours by the same stone houses with their laundry hanging from windows and balconies. Why would anyone want to display their underwear, especially old lady bloomers, for everyone to see? All I want is a place to pee in this maze.

The hardest part about Portuguese is you think you can understand it because it resembles Spanish, but you can't. Everything's off, like that Rod Serling story where life changes just a little because someone went back in time and stepped on a bug. I can make out a few Portuguese words, but the rest is impossible.

Hal makes a few bold attempts to ask about a public restroom for me as we wander the labyrinth of streets. Two men shrug their shoulders and a widow dressed in black missing her front teeth responds with something that sounds like wet carpeting. We laugh.

Finally, as I hop from foot to foot, we enter a small shop that sells statues of saints. I examine a plaster-of-Paris Teresa that's been badly painted, the eyeball missing the mark of the indentations, red mouth partially on her chin. The Professor inquires for me.

He repeats his question in a loud voice and points to the phrase in our guidebook.

The female proprietor holds a smelly sardine sandwich in her hand. A slimy silver fish falls onto the counter. She keeps repeating one phrase that sounds familiar.

"What is she saying?" I ask, sidling up to the Professor to look over his shoulder at the book.

He sounds exasperated. "Wet carpets."

"Wait a minute. You're asking about a bathroom and she's saying wet carpets?"

He begins to search his shirt pocket for his pipe, patting himself down like a cop searching a perp. When he locates it he sucks deeply even though there's no tobacco. He repeats, "Wet carpets," through clenched teeth.

I'm about to give up. What if I let it dribble down my leg? It'll fade into the stone floor. A tourist with a florid face and a baseball-cap arrives, fanning himself with one of their useless maps. He surveys the scene and approaches us, hand held out.

"Sam Spade, that's right, just like the famous detective. From Lubbock, Texas." He pumps The Professor's hand.

"Say, you don't know where we can find a bathroom, do you?" asks Hal.

For God-only-knows-what-reason the fake detective speaks Portuguese.

After an exchange that includes hand gestures and squatting between the sardine lady and Sam the Man where I almost faint from squeezing so hard, my rescuer turns to explain to us.

"Ya gotta look for the hanging wet carpets cause that means there's a laundromat in the neighborhood and they all have public restrooms. Not many places have bathrooms. Seems that's why the young people are movin' on."

I would, too, if I could only pee once a day. I nod in thanks. Never underestimate a Texan in a Hawaiian shirt.

"Hey, where y'all staying? How 'bout a drink later with me and the missus?" I hobble to the door, glancing at the cock-eyed Saint Teresa with a mental thank you. With mincing steps on the cobblestones I look for iron balconies with wet, dripping carpets.

"I think not," Hal mutters to himself.

The Professor trails behind me mumbling about the poor translations in the book and being bested by Sam Spade. A drop of water falls on my head. I look up to see soggy Turkish rugs hanging over my head, strange red and blue fruit.

With frantic abandon I look around and, desperate as only a full bladder can make you, I ask the first person who approaches, a young kid with dragging pants and his underwear exposed, evidence the hip-hop invasion has found this corner of the world.

"*Casa de banho?*" I ask.

With simplicity he points to a storefront across the street where women are exiting with bags, carts and plastic bins filled with colorful, clean folded laundry. I dash across traffic to the other side. It's amazing how life can come down to a bodily function. Saint Teresa with the drooping eye and lopsided lips has blessed me.

The Professor gives me discourses on what we're seeing or working on, but he saves the evenings to discuss his novel and characters. I feel very much a part of it, more of a collaborator than an assistant. He asks me questions about how women react and feel in certain situations. I get uncomfortable when it turns personal. What makes me cry? What triggers jealousy with my sisters? What happens when I'm scared?

I do my best to answer truthfully, but I don't always know how to express myself. I've never been in therapy to analyze why I do the things I do. I simply react.

He sets up situations for me like: if you saw someone close to you being harmed, what would you do? Would you try to rescue them? Save your own life?

I don't really know what I'd do. I cover my eyes in the scary parts of movies. Or: what if your sister revealed a shocking secret? Would you still accept her? My first reaction is: nothing either of them does shocks me, but my best answer is, I don't know.

The afternoon of the second day, early in the evening with an orange sun fading into a lavender sky, we sit on the patio of the Alfama Grill, sipping sherry, enjoying the cooler air.

The proprietor, a slight man who speaks English he learned in Canada, has left us olives, oil, cheese, salmon paté and my favorite in this city, hard-crusted warm rolls that break open in a white explosion of fragrance sending my salivary glands into apoplexy.

Our view overlooks the centuries old sailors' quarter, bustling at the end of the street, a picturesque scene.

The professor points his finger over the landscape. "The exact spot where many of the *conversos* left for other ports."

I imagine Grazia and Bellina waiting for a ship as I grasp the present. Plastic bags filled with water hang out of windows, supposedly to keep away flies. Shabby buildings lean into each other. There are stalls with women in black or young men with sculpted faces selling fresh, raw seafood on ice–clams, fish, shrimp. Couples stroll by doorways crowned with images of Saint Peter, protector of fishermen, while wrinkled men with wizened faces mend nets on small stools. A few families gather to set tables for a communal dinner in the street, the backdrop of their blue-and-white tiled houses shimmering in the light.

The professor leans back in his chair, arms behind his head, squinting into the sun and sighs. "The next chapter I'm working on is difficult for me."

"Why?" I offer suggestions where it's appropriate.

"I have to work the history of how powerful the Church was without being too didactic and contrast the differences between Spain and Portugal in terms of the *conversos*."

A chameleon on a nearby hibiscus puffs up his throat, changing colors. First he's brown, then green, the red-orange ball on his neck expanding and deflating.

"Like what?" I ask, reaching for my glass.

"The Spanish Jews didn't have much time. Isabella decided she wanted them out and it was done. The Portuguese Jews had twenty maybe thirty years to practice their religion in secret before the Inquisition came down hard on them. Their crypto-Judaism had deep roots as they searched for a new country to practice their religion."

I'm struck by how long these people held onto a faith as it became more and more difficult and dangerous. Would I have been able to do that?

"Not that they treated them any differently. The Portuguese *conversos* were still tortured and burned at the stake if found Judaizing. Many historians agree that the purpose of the Inquisition was not so much a hatred of Jews as it was an opportunity to fill church coffers."

"Why wasn't I taught any of this in school? I mean, I learned the Spanish were brutal in their South American conquests. My history teacher barely mentioned the Inquisition. Now that I think about it, she skipped almost everything unpleasant. We mostly learned about the tenets and threats of communism, the Cold War and the domino theory."

"Some historical perspective." Hal lights his pipe.

I sigh and pull my feet under me. A lot of things were lacking in my *cubanidad* experience. On a small stage musicians begin to set up their instruments, tapping the microphone, strumming a note or two.

"I have to show in the book how far reaching Isabella's power was that it crossed borders and secondly, why the Church supported the Age of Discovery. Many of the expeditions were funded by the Order of the Cross utilizing monks who were also soldiers."

"Monks in the military?"

"Their mission was to bring Christianity to the world, no matter what the indigenous people believed." His expression, serious yet relaxed remains confident with disclosure.

I give him a puzzled look, sinking deeper in my chair.

"You're my private tutor."

He acknowledges me with a *harrumping* sound. "I'll give you an example. If you go to Chichicastenango in Guatemala the Church has incense and idols so they can cater to the Indians. The Church had to stop slaughtering the natives and incorporate their gods."

I shift in my chair, searching for something positive in this sad history. My mouth feels dry and I swallow.

"It's upsetting that people are not allowed to worship whatever they want, free from religious persecution." I reach for my glass and as I take a sip of the sweet liquid, the sun splays orange-pink fingers through the sky. I turn my face toward the Professor.

"What happened to King Manuel?"

The musicians begin a ballad in the *fado* tradition, one of fate, a folk music of the people. They play it in a minor key that begins with a moan on the *guitarra*, an instrument rounded like a mandolin. A young man perched on a stool, black hair falling over his eyes, strums and sings the sad melody in English and Portuguese, one of the sea and lost loves.

What's my fate? Am I destined to remain single? Or go back to what's-his-name?

Hal waves to the waiter to re-fill our glasses. The professor's relaxed, different than when I first met him.

"Ah, that's where Manuel became creative and as evil as the queen. He didn't want to lose the taxes or skills of the *conversos*, who were by that time also iron workers, experts at making muskets. War with the Moors was imminent."

"What did he do?"

He sips his sherry, looks at my expectant face and sets down the glass. The music fills up the background drowning out other voices.

"You're quite tantalizing in this light."

The next part is difficult to share, one, because it happened so quickly, so naturally that I look back and still get goose bumps, and two, it aroused me in a new way.

We walk back to our rooms, me a bit tipsy from the sherry and he, a bit verbose. We say good night. It's awkward at the door while I manipulate the small key on the wooden stick, dropping it twice. Finally I get into my room, giggling at my clumsiness.

"Good night," says the Professor. "Wear your walking shoes tomorrow. We're touring the Cloisters and I want to examine Rossio Square, the site of a brutal massacre in 1507 where four thousand were murdered." Then he hesitates, looks me in the eye and says, "I enjoy your company." Embarrassment floods his face.

I know he isn't adept at social skills and neither am I, but I manage to say, "I learn so much when I'm with you," before I add, "You're the most interesting person I know," bursting through the door, the slam final.

I imagine him looking down, grinning that smile of his, the one when he's pleased, a smile of satisfaction. I lean against the back of the door.

What possessed me to say that, even if it's true? Will he think I'm attracted to him? Am I? I peel off my damp T-shirt, roll down my long skirt, drop my bra and underwear on the floor and head for the shower. I need warm water to wash off the grime of the day.

As I'm about to step into the blue-and-white tiled bathtub, a bit chipped and mottled, I examine myself in the mirror. I lift my hair off my neck, massaging my scalp. My hair feels dirty, too.

I face the mirror straight-on. A bit lumpy in places but nice full boobies. I cup one in each hand. Could be higher. Big bush. My sisters always made fun of me because of it. I swipe my hand across my belly as I inhale. Do I have sex appeal? I close my eyes, the haunting *fado* music, soulful blues, sweeping by me. I dance in my lover's arms. I open my eyes, blinking. I can't believe I'm thinking about him.

I turn on the hot water, wait a few minutes and test it with my hand. Icy cold. I have never liked cold water and as a kid refused swimming lessons at the Venetian pool in Coral Gables because of the sub-zero water. I adjust the knob, wait and try again. I wrap a towel around me and call the desk.

"No hot water? What? Some rooms? A few days? Expect loud clanking?" He's got to be kidding.

Why do the simplest matters of bodily function and hygiene have to be a crisis for me?

I debate with my neurotic self for a few minutes. Should I call Hal? Maybe he has hot water. What if he thinks it's a ploy, a come-on? What if he doesn't have hot water and we're both ripe? I smell my armpit. Forget what he thinks. I need a shower. I pick up the old-fashioned black telephone with a dial.

"Uh, Hal, do you have hot water?" I wait for a moment.

"Nice and toasty here. Just took a shower myself."

"Would you mind if I took a shower in your room? I mean, if it wouldn't inconvenience you." I add, "I don't have hot water."

"By all means, come over."

I stand outside his door in my robe and rubber thongs. No way was I going to get dressed again. I mean, we share the same house. Why am I nervous? What's the big deal I keep asking myself? No one has ever said I was tantalizing.

He answers the door wearing his striped robe, silver hair slicked back and no glasses, blue eyes bright with surprise. He's freshly shaven, too. I can tell because he has about as much skill as I do in that department. A few pinpricks of red sprinkle his neck and he has one small piece of toilet paper on his chin.

"Come in, come in," he says. Opened shutters waft a slight sea breeze across the room. Sounds of the street—kids laughing, a tapping horn, radio music—fade away.

"I'm really sorry to disturb you. I can't stand cold water, especially to wash my hair—"

"It's okay. Go ahead. The mirror may still be a bit fogged up, but I don't think I used up all the hot water."

I enter the bathroom and know it will be awkward if I make the clicking sound to lock the door. Like I don't trust him or something.

He's been honorable up until now. I don't know why I'm getting so obsessed about a semi-naked man sitting outside the door where I'm showering.

I leave the door unlocked and step into the tub, pulling the curtain closed. The warm-to-hot water feels refreshing and I stick my head under it to wet down my hair. Shit. I forgot shampoo. I look for some and there isn't any. I turn off the water, wrap a towel around me, open the door and stick my head out.

"Prof–, I mean Hal, do you have any shampoo I can borrow?" He's sitting up in bed, glasses perched low on his nose, reading his manuscript.

"Do you think Grazia should find romance?" he asks.

"Huh?"

He repeats the question and adds, "But with whom? She doesn't have access to a dowry."

Fado music drifts in from the street. "I think I'll tell you after you tell me where the shampoo is hidden."

"Oh, sorry. He reaches into his bathrobe pocket and holds out a travel-size of Paul Mitchell.

I open the door, a bit self-conscious, and approach the bed with my hand out. "Conditioner?"

Chagrined, he reaches into his other pocket and hands me another small bottle.

I take them, one hand gripping the front of my towel, and march to the shower. Why was he playing games with the shampoo?

I exit in my robe, wet hair in a terry turban. Hal sits on a chair near the open window.

"Alegra, sit down. I have something to ask you."

Is it another of his questions about female quirks and motivations? I notice his glasses are on the nightstand. He looks handsome in the light, more assured than usual. I settle onto the edge of the bed. His fingers drum his knee.

He clears his throat. "This may come as a surprise to you." He pauses, uncomfortably, now spreading his fingers on his legs. "I'm a solo sort, not prone to much company."

Uh-oh. Am I being fired? I love this job. Learning, exploring the past, being with someone interesting, traveling. Shit. Every time things get good, something goes bad.

He continues, concentrating, oblivious to my internal dialogue, his voice softer. "The question of attraction is an important one. I know how I feel but I don't want you to feel obligated."

I'm sure I look puzzled. Where is he going with this? Shower droplets trickle down my neck. I lean forward to hear him better. He stands, approaches me and offers his hands to lift me from the bed.

Without hesitation he asks, "Would you consider marrying me?"

Chapter Twenty-one

Grazia

15 Nissan 5267 (7 April 1507)
Lisbon

Bellina and I wandered for days, sleeping here and there, begging food from vendors who remembered the elegant Doña Estrella Guzman and her husband's textiles. They offered cabbage and fava beans.

My father had told me the Torah required farmers to leave a small amount of olives, grapes or fruit on branches to be gathered by widows and orphans. I searched orchards and found oranges, taking them without guilt.

In our meager belongings I carried our silver candlesticks, painted black, to hide their value and our Bible. I knew it was dangerous but I could not leave it behind. Although my faith had dimmed without a home in which to be observant, I prayed to the Almighty Father to rescue us so we could continue our lives in the religion of our ancestors.

I also cursed Señora Torres and her weak-willed husband for turning us out before Passover. Without a confrontation I rehearsed invectives to the vile woman who abandoned us. *You selfish bitch, you donkey's arse, you–*

It was of no importance. When Bellina looked at me, hungry face smudged with dirt, shabby clothes in need of repair, I could not waste energy on anger. Without coins I had to be clever.

We sat leaning against a brick wall on the Rua Nova d'El Rei, the busiest street in Lisbon, watching the parade of people, our bundles beneath us, baskets at our side. Filled with aggressive peddlers and beggars the sounds were deafening. Church bells almost drown out their calls.

"Wooden birdcages! Keep an exotic pet! Look at my fabrics in glowing colors made from worms! Ceramic cups, mirrors, and mother-of-pearl combs for your lady's hair! Goats! Goats for you! Fresh milk every day! Sandals! Leather sandals with the finest cork soles!"

The sandal-maker, his goods tied together and slung over his shoulder, was followed by an old man in rags pushing a wheelbarrow filled with cork. My sister and I used to peel the bark from that tree until it bled red. A phalanx of the King's soldiers, chain-mesh shirts molded to their bodies, marched by with muskets pushing the sandal-maker out of the way. He cried out in protest.

Well-dressed men from the shipping industry strolled by deep in conversation, content in their success, oblivious to our stares, unaware of the Africans who stood across the street with leg irons standing against a wall, eyes burning with hatred. Explorers kidnapped the poor souls from the coast to work in the mines. My fate was not much better than theirs, but I had the ability to hide. Their ebony faces, worn with work, sealed their fate.

I drifted back to an afternoon when my father and I lingered after a delivery at the docks in Belem. Caravels bounced in the clear blue water, lateen sails slapping in a yielding wind. An enthusiast about the Age of Discovery, he told me with awe, "Portugal is the most powerful nation in the world. Such possibilities."

We even stopped at a stall where he pointed out globes and magnetic compasses, hourglasses and charts, all instruments of navigation. "Prince Henry the Navigator spawns these ships, yet rarely goes to sea himself. He has the vision of other worlds." He turned to me, his hand on my shoulder. "Someday we will be on a ship again, one that takes us to a place of safety." My eyes flushed with tears at the thought.

Bellina interrupted my reverie. "Auntie, I am ill." At fifteen, she was a woman at a marriageable age, but without a dowry, even her extraordinary beauty would not bring a prospect.

I turned to her and touched her forehead with my lips. She felt warm. "What is it?"

Bellina shook her head back and forth, bending over and holding her middle. Our terrible diet this last week probably clogged her. My mother used to administer an enema of linseed oil for relief or a cup of verbena tea also used for headaches, but I had no access to such remedies.

In a few hours darkness would fall, a dangerous time for us. I had to find a place to sleep. I pulled her up, loaded our belongings on my back, baskets on our arms, pushing through beggars asking for alms, their filthy hands pulling at our skirts, and began our journey through the city gates.

We walked until I found a small *finca* where a farmer's wife, a short,

round woman missing teeth, teased us with warm bread, which we refused
with longing. Even in hunger I could not break the laws of Passover. She
offered a casserole of Swiss chard, eggplant and cheese that we devoured
on her back steps, and afterward, cups of cow's milk. Bellina's thirst must
have been stronger than her pain. She drank hers with such haste she spilled
a bit on her chin and dress.

"You can only stay one night. My husband refuses to feed your kind. You
must be gone tomorrow." She directed us to an ancient wooden shed used
for tools where we made a bed of hay among the scythes and hoes.

Did she know we were New Christians? Maybe. We were taller than the
Portuguese and our refusal of bread might have been a hint. I ached because
we had no *matzo*. For Bellina I repeated the story about the Jews expulsion
from Egypt, the Pharaoh's oppression, the terrible plagues and our flight.
"Next year in Jerusalem," I whispered over her sleeping body.

In the morning I left to scrounge for more food, begging some spoiled
lettuce and celery from a peddler resting along the side of the road. I
hurried back to bring it to Bellina, still ill, her face white and sweaty, brow
hot with fever.

I waited until the sun's fallen crest left a sliver of light to see us back into
the city. I knew many families would be having secret seders and I longed
for my family, the warmth of our fire, the sweetness of the apples and wine. I
had no plan other than where we could rest for one more night. What would
my parents think if they knew we were wandering on a Sabbath eve?

My niece, too tired to continue, huddled in a doorway with our
belongings. In the moonlight I searched for a safe space to sleep. Avoiding
the wealthy Barrio Alto that overlooked the city and our old neighborhood
in the Alfama district, I kept to the lower parts near Rossio Square, a shanty
town of wooden barracks.

At the end of a row of houses I discovered a small odiferous stable with
an empty stall and cleared it of debris and waste with a shovel. I gagged at
the pungent smell, but could not be particular.

I hurried back to retrieve Bellina, leading her to the barn. I pushed the hay
back with my foot in our abandoned stable and placed some of our clothes on
the bare spot. We settled down, covering ourselves with the straw for warmth
and wrapping our arms around one another. The horses neighed, snorting at
intruders. After a time it gave me comfort. In my mind I lit the Sabbath candles

and said prayers, soon drifting into an exhausted sleep.

I woke to horrible screams, cries for help and the clamor of terror. Bellina did not move. In only my dress, without protective garb for my hair or a cloak, I stumbled into the street.

Older boys with axes and men with swords rushed by me, grim expressions on their faces. I shrank back into an alley, petrified, my panicked heart wild with fear.

I did not want to think about what this meant. An old woman in widow's black passed me with measured steps. She hunched forward on a twisted spine, the basket she carried swaying with determination. I glanced around and saw no one else.

I rushed to her. "Tell me. What has happened?" She did not answer me or alter her pace. I put my hand on her arm. "Please, tell me."

Her face, wrinkled as an old grape, did not change. She shook her head and said, "The Jews."

And then I knew. Another pogrom had started.

I ran back to our hiding place to tell Bellina that we could not venture out. Out of breath, I held her, putting my hands over her ears to muffle the tortured screams.

The day passed as we cried together for our family, friends. Who would they murder this time? We had no food and relieved ourselves in a corner filled with hay. In our cupped hands we drank the dirty water from the horses' trough.

On Saturday morning my nostrils burned with an acrid smell. The fires had started. Even though we were hungry I was afraid to leave our safe space. We drank more foul water meant for the animals. Bellina, weak with fever, slept most of the time. When she was awake, she was frightened.

She sat up, delirious, eyes wide in terror. "Grazia, do not leave me. Will I die? *Mi abuela*? I want her."

"Shush. *Yie tov.* It will turn out all right. I must leave to look for food."

"No, do not leave me. What will they do if they find me?" She gasped a breath I thought might be her last.

"Bellina, talk to me." I shook her shoulders.

The screams intensified, horrible shrieks of pain and despair so loud that she put her hands over her ears and fell back into the hay.

With eyes closed and a hushed voice, she said, "Let me die." And then she sobbed with the wails and howls of wolves on the plains, a sorrow so deep I could not touch it.

By Sunday I had to venture out to find nourishment. I dressed in dark colors and covered my hair. My hope was to find a friend to help us, although most had turned us away before, not so much out of meanness but their own survival.

I crept toward Rossio Square where crowds gathered outside Magdelena Church. Pulling a scarf close around my face, I made my way through the people, some raucous with rage, others somber and downcast. No one would know me here.

Squeezing inside the church, a monk passed me, swinging a silver *censer*, passing the worshipers. I stood in the shadows of one of the side chapels near the confessionals.

A priest in the front encouraged the men and women to do evil deeds. "The non-believers are the cause of your ills. Your children know hunger because others take their food. Those who speak blasphemy must burn in the fires of Hell. Avenge our Savior's death."

I did not understand every word but I knew it was said to incite. He cursed the Jews in Latin, a somber language that made the threats more frightening.

One man punched his fist into the air. "We must kill the non-believers!" A group of inspired men followed him as he ran outside.

I blended with them cautiously, hiding my face. In minutes a crowd of what must have been a hundred peasants and farmers with picks, axes, hoes and scythes gathered.

The first man repeated the priest's words, louder, angrier, his yellowed teeth monster-like as he spit out the words. An unsuspecting co-religionist walked by with his family.

A shabby man with a swarthy face and purple lips called out, "The cobbler does not work on certain days. He is not a true Christian." Another yelled, "I know this man. The cross does not hang in his shop."

They confronted him, his petrified wife and three small children. I witnessed their terror.

The first man asked, "Why are you walking on a Sunday? You do not set foot outside on a Saturday." Young hooligans grabbed his beard. I saw him urge his family to run but they were stopped. The youngest child, a boy with light ringlets, began to cry.

I turned my head away. I cannot bear to see people in pain, feeling it myself in some way. The sounds–horrible beyond belief—torn flesh, curses, an ungodly curdle, screams of death, and finally, glee and rejoicing from the perpetrators as they danced around the remains. The men crossed themselves, heads thrown back in glory, blood of the innocent on the walls of the church.

"More," they shouted, running from the square as other men brought a group of terrified New Christians. With only escape on my mind I fled the Rossio, hurrying through the Moorish Quarter toward the Alfama district, a place that was familiar.

Doors were closed and windows shuttered tight. I banged on a former neighbor's door. "Let me in. I am Guzman's daughter, Grazia."

No response. I tried a few times at other people's doors. Ignored.

Desperate, I ventured to the Torres family even though they cast us out. Cruel, yes, but maybe they would feel guilt and let me in. They did not answer.

Rua de São Pedro was so quiet the squeak of a door would have echoed. Again, no response. Finally, I went to Señora Ezrahti's home. I stood outside banging, crying in frustration, my fists aching against the hard wood. A small movement opened an upstairs shutter a crack.

"Go away. You will get us all killed," said a female voice.

I banged harder. A trickle of crimson curled around my wrist in a bracelet of blood. "You have to let me in. Do you remember my mother helped you?" I picked up a rock and slammed it against the door. "I will not go away. I cannot go away. You must let me in."

Suddenly, it opened.

"Stop the racket," said Señor Ezrahti as he glanced up and down the street. Then he pulled me inside, his clothes awry, normally well-groomed silver hair hanging in limp strands.

The room, dark except for a few candles, had the leather blinds closed. When my eyes adjusted I saw many of our former neighbors crouched on the floor, including Señor Torres who cast his eyes away from me. The women sat on the floor at the perimeter of the room weeping. Señora Ezrahti whose glassy eyes stared in an unchanged mask, sat in a corner. I took a small stool behind the men.

"The Dominicans are making the pyres to burn Jewish flesh. We can see the smoke from the roof," said a man with urgency. I knew him as Moishe Cardoza whose Christian name was Daniel. He had a long face with a bushy beard and his eyes blinked rapidly in the dim light. His wife sat behind him nursing a baby.

"Do not panic," said a coarse-faced man with a large head whom I did not know. "If we stay still, this will blow over."

"Issak is right. Let us stay inside for a few days and mind our own business. They will forget why they hate us," said another.

A few murmured in agreement.

I stood and stepped forward, an interruption. A woman gasped at my insolence. "You are fools! I was there. The barbarians chased people shouting, 'Kill the Jews, kill them all.'" I began to sob. "I saw a man, his family pulled apart." I could no longer hold back my sorrow. Tears flowed, speeding currents in the Tagus River.

A few people moaned.

"How many did they get?" Señor Cardoza asked.

"Thousands," I murmured. "Maybe more."

"We are fools to stay. We must go," said Señor Ezrahti with urgency.

"How do you propose we execute an escape with mobs searching for us?" asked another gentleman in an amethyst-colored cloak, a Señor Carbajal known to be of great wealth and a benefactor to our community.

"Why? Oh why?" wailed one of the wives on the perimeter of the room, her head thrown back in grief. A few women joined her.

"Who started it?" another asked me.

"The Dominicans," I said with eyes burning and a dry throat. I began to cough and one of the men ordered a woman to bring me water.

My father used to say the deep hatred came from the Old Christians who were jealous because we read the Bible. The church thought it heresy that we spoke directly to God without a priest as an intermediary. We published books and passed them among ourselves. The Church would lose control if the masses read. Did not the teachings of their Savior who was a Jew offer tolerance? Was kindness a Christian virtue?

"Maybe King Manuel will help." offered Señor Ezrahti without hope in his voice.

"You are a fool to think that. How can he? The followers of Nazarene will call for his head," said Issak, the shadow of his fist dancing on the wall. "We will always be known as People of the Book." He spit out these words.

"The riot has to burn itself out. Soon these beasts will want to go home and eat, have sex with their wives and hit their own children," said Señor Cardoza.

"What happened to our rabbi?" asked a chubby gentleman who had not spoken before.

"He took some families outside the city gates to Sobral," offered Moishe Cardoza. In a hushed silence he added, "He said we should flee, that the monster will return."

"If we survive this I think we should all study Turkish and leave for Salonika," said Señor Ezrahti slapping his hands on his knees.

"Are you crazy?" asked Señor Carbajal. "The Muslims hate us, too." Sweat beaded on his forehead.

Smoke from the candles made the room close in and I felt dizzy.

"No, their king welcomes us and our mercantile skills," he replied.

"How do you know?" asked another while two different men shouted at each other about the level of tolerance in the Ottoman Empire. An odor, not unlike animals about to be slaughtered, permeated the room.

A few argued among themselves, voices rising in fear.

They had no plan, only panic and hearsay. These people could not guide me. I stood up and slipped to the back of the room, searching their faces one last time. A dark-eyed woman with full lips caught my eye. She reached inside her shawl and motioned to me. With caution I approached her.

She handed me a package of food that I slipped inside my sleeve, nodding in acknowledgement. Then I opened the door with discretion, viewed an empty street and hurried away.

On my return to our hiding place I passed a quiet Rossio Square. I huddled in a doorway to whisper *kaddish* for the poor souls who had not escaped, muttering the forbidden words. They offered little comfort.

I saw bent women, carob wood crosses hanging away from their chests, picking up Jewish teeth, bony fingers reaching between cracks in the cobblestones. One, with a face like a turnip, placed a few in her bosom, "Good protection from the plague," she said to no one in particular.

I bowed my head and hurried toward Bellina, saying a silent prayer that she was still alive.

Chapter Twenty-two

Grazia

22 Nissan 5267 (April 14 1507)
Lisbon

Twenty thousand souls resided in Little Jerusalem, the *Judaria Pequena*, at the mouth of the Tagus River. I had been there many times with my father to buy and sell textiles. Perhaps we could find refuge there.

A few days passed with Bellina sleeping, never waking, moaning in a private world, her shallow breath gasping for air. Her waxen face became thin, the fullness of her cheeks melting away.

I never left her side, lifting her head to help her drink the soiled water, although she barely took any, bathing her feverish forehead with a rag. Finally, in the morning light of the fourth day when I no longer heard any mobs, her eyes fluttered. I put my lips to her forehead. Cool. I ate some of the cheese, bread and figs the brown-eyed woman had given me, but I also saved some for Bellina.

She woke ravenous, stuffing the food into her mouth, barely chewing as she swallowed.

At last, she spoke.

"Auntie, what has happened?" She glanced around, her eyes filled with confusion. "Where are we?"

I explained what had transpired. "Do you feel well enough to travel?"

She stood, her legs shaky as a colt, a hand reaching out for the stable wall. Heading to a far corner, she lifted her skirts and relieved herself. Almost unrecognizable from the beauteous child of a few weeks before, she appeared as a person of the streets–unwashed, without color, her clothes covered with stains and hay.

"Ready yourself. I am going to make arrangements for us," I told her, wrapping a shawl around my shoulders. I had no idea what I would do, but

I had to save us.

Outside, I headed toward the Tagus. If only I could find a ship to take us to a foreign shore. Once inside the *Judaria Pequena*, I spotted the old synagogue built in 1374 that stood on a small hill. I hurried toward it, not fast enough to draw attention to myself but moving with purpose.

Maybe some of my co-religionists could help. My disappointment overwhelmed me as I stood in front of a shuttered and abandoned building, one that could no longer provide solace to people.

Nothing stirred, not a leaf or a soul. I wandered, not sure where to go or what to do. I prayed God's guidance would show me the way to a better place. My hunger and the aroma of life drove me to the market.

Grieving Jews, many who had not been out for a week since the tragedy at Rossio Square, shopped with starved frenzy. Many women had chopped off their hair in sorrow. With a nomadic rambling they stumbled through the crowd, repeating their lost loved one's names, incoherent with grief.

A group of men in mourning clothes swayed in rhythmic prayer behind a low stone wall. I guessed that they no longer cared about being *conversos*. My stomach gurgled with hunger pangs.

A young man with curly black hair, a comely face and soulful eyes, his mustache barely visible, stood behind a nearby stall and stared. I believed him to be younger than me. I had no chances of marriage. That opportunity passed.

I touched my throat with self-consciousness. The baskets he guarded were laden with fresh fruit—apricots, dates, some small rosy apples. Could I steal a few pieces and run back to Bellina? Stealing was wrong.

I pondered the idea. Could I be quick enough? If caught, the crowd would surely kill me. Instead, I approached him, emboldened by my hunger.

"What is your pleasure?" he asked, his welcoming soft eyes glancing at me.

"I would love to purchase some fruit, but I have no *suelos*."

The young man, neck skinny as a stalk, looked uncomfortable and sounded apologetic. "My mother does not allow me to give charity until the end of the day. The spoiled pieces. Perhaps if you–"

A commotion ensued and I lost his words as someone bumped into me. I stumbled.

Turning, I saw clusters of families pushing full wheelbarrows and carts that rattled on the cobblestones. A foot protruded from one and I knew it was a dead body. They knocked against some the stalls, causing goods to fall. Women beat their breasts and screamed obscenities echoing the names of their loved ones over and over.

"What is it?" I asked.

"No one is left to help prepare the bodies, sit *shiva* or make coffins. They have to bury their dead in white shrouds in open fields."

At least they are burying them, I thought with bitterness.

An idea came to me.

"I have not eaten in days. My parents were killed at the mass conversion. I was wondering if–" With that I allowed my knees to buckle and I crumbled into the street. The young man rushed to me and did his best to pull me up.

I remained limp.

"Help, help," he called to others passing by, struggling with me, his hands under my arms, but no one came to his aid. People preoccupied with their own miseries ignored us. After a few minutes I fluttered my eyes.

"Thank Goodness, you are well," he said, his face so close to mine I could taste his sweet breath.

"Water, water."

He seemed to dance about me in confusion, unsure of what to do. He ran to the next stall that overflowed with baskets of heather and black wool.

I opened my eyes a slit.

"Please. Watch my stall," he told the corpulent woman guarding her wares.

"Where is your mother?" she asked with skepticism and a frown.

"Helping with the dead. Please."

The vendor hesitated.

"This woman fainted. I must take her to rest. Take a few of our best plums."

She gave him a nod with her second chin jiggling. "All right, go. But be back quickly. I am busy today."

He guided me to an alley and in a short time we climbed down steps to a small room. It took a few minutes for my eyes to adjust. It was plain but more than we had. I took a deep breath.

Observing me, nervous sweat dotting his brow, he shifted his feet on a woven rug. I sat on a chair drinking water from a ceramic cup. My eyes searched the dim room.

The area where we sat had benches and a table, not the fine furnishings I knew from my parent's home. An expensive candelabrum sat on the table with a wooden bowl of fresh fruit, the floor covering made from sheared wool, rustic yet soft.

I became the aggressor although I did not know my way.

"Have you been with a woman?" I asked picking up my head and looking him straight in the eye.

He shook his head in the negative.

"Would you like to touch me?" My power shocked me. I was taught to be chaste until marriage.

He was young, an innocent, but anxious to release himself.

He stood, stepping toward me. Waiting for permission, his thin fingers tweaked the sides of his garment.

"First I want a piece of fruit."

He reached for a pomegranate in the bowl and held it out. I shook my head knowing the skin was too tough and reached around him for a plum instead. I bit into it, my sharp teeth breaking the skin. I devoured it. The delicious juice dribbled onto my chin. I wiped it away with my hand.

He swallowed, his neck apple, bobbing. In the distance I could hear the sounds of the market and wailings of mourners. Shuttered light streamed across the floor. We stared at each other.

I began to unbutton the top of my dress with trembling fingers, pushing Mama's harsh words out of my mind. My breasts lifted over the top, succulent pink berries tantalizing him. I stroked myself and felt aroused.

He fell to his knees and reached for me, his hands crushing my breasts with urgency. He buried his face in me, his lips searching my nipples like a hungry baby.

The rest happened quickly when he pulled me to the rug—the movement of skirts, a dropping of pants, the lifting of hips, a thrust of his member, a moment of searing pain, a cry of pleasure from him and it was done.

And so, in a dank room with a skinny stranger, I gave myself for a few pieces of fruit.

We lay there for a moment, our chests heaving.

I spoke first in a whisper. "Are you staying?"

I felt his shrug. "No, my family is leaving. We are closing the stall and our store and giving up on this place."

"Where will you go?" It made a difference to have means, a way to make things happen.

"Belem, where the caravels leave for the New World."

"Can I come?"

"You need *reales* for passage."

My heart fell. *Reales* were more than *maravedies* and I did not have either.

"What if I worked? I am clever. I can sew, mend, clean."

"Meet us at the São Lourenco Gate in Belem. It is not too far from where the Africans are building a monastery for the king. I will see what I can do."

Before he hurried back to his stall he pressed a few more pieces of fruit into my hand.

When Bellina and I arrived at the dock I could not find my fruit benefactor in the crush of people exiting for Constantinople and Africa. The ships, heavy with their loads sat low in the water.

I waited on a stone bench watching them pull from the harbor, sails plump with a light wind. Bereft of ideas of what to do next, Bellina clung to me still weak from hunger, her fever subsided.

I hesitated to call out to a pimpled boatswain who strolled by lest he think me one of the loose women who frequented the docks. A vision of me on the floor with the young man slid into my mind. I grabbed his shirttail.

"Sir, any ships with space setting sail today or tomorrow?" I could not take us back to the filthy stable. Bellina would not survive without food and clean water.

He stopped, his eyes captured by Bellina's face, her head on my shoulder. "Yes, at the end of the dock there is a small *taforeia*." He pointed.

"What is that? I straightened my spine to get a look.

"A transport vessel that carries horses and other goods. We sail tonight."

"Where is it going?"

"A new place called Brazil."

Chapter Twenty-three

Alegra

February 7, 1999
Granada

I slap the latest chapter of Hal's novel on the patio table next to me. "I don't want to read about something bad happening to Bellina on that ship."

Hal, lying next to me on a cushioned lounge chair, semi-dozing to catch a few rays, grunts. I glace at the international newspaper spread across his lap with the headline, *Aging Society: Japan Suicide Rate for Elderly Women Second Highest in the World.*

"Look," I say, pointing at the paper.

He grunts again.

Gathering dark clouds to the west begin to erase our sunshine. It's been a relaxing Sunday with a morning walk to town for breakfast, bells tolling, and then a leisurely stroll home, but now I'm discontented.

Emphatic and anxious to get his attention, I add, "I'm sick and tired of women being victims."

Eyes still closed, he responds. "I'm not making Bellina a victim. Women were vulnerable in those days. Especially a beautiful one."

"Women are prey now," I snap, "but that doesn't mean you have to set them up to be taken advantage of."

"Listen, it's very likely that with Bellina's ravishing beauty and her aunt's desperation, she was traded for food." Hal opens his eyes and begins to fold up the papers, a breeze rustling the edges.

"What? I refuse to believe her aunt would do that." Of course my own sisters would trade me if someone paid them. This was different.

"Are you kidding? Grazia sold her own body for a few pieces of fruit." Hal's professorial tone seeps back into his voice.

I was a student challenging him. "It's not the same thing," I say, retreating into a complaint.

"Why? Since when did you get so judgmental? Tell me why that situation isn't parallel. If you're hungry, you're hungry. Besides, she did it to save Bellina." He sits forward and plants his sandals on the tile and looks at me, elbows on his knees. "Every ship had a hierarchy of power not unlike prisons today. Rape, violence--all part of it."

"I don't think it belongs in the story."

A light drizzle scatters drops on his newspaper with a tapping sound. I stand up, my sister's letter in hand and take the manuscript. A few drops splatter his glasses and he wipes them with his finger.

"Wait a minute. Who's writing this?" he asks, his voice irritated by my insolence.

"You are. But I'm the research assistant and I say women don't want to read that crap."

"Oh?" he says, dripping sarcasm.

I clutch the papers to my chest and move inside as the rain beats down.

"Who says my audience is only women?" Hal calls after me. I turn to him, half-way inside the patio door. "Because women buy more books than men and your protagonist is a woman. It's a woman's story of survival."

"Right. And I'm not going to leave out what she's surviving." Hal can't resist a challenge. Upright, he picks up the newspaper and marches inside. Drops spot his shoulders as the steady sound of rain floods the patio. With a plop he drops the papers on a table, removes his glasses and tosses them on his desk. He says, "I am writing this story and you are not going to direct my characters. It's bad enough you direct me."

As if the words don't sting enough, he points to his chest with his thumb for emphasis.

I step forward to get closer to his face. "Hold on. I am not trying to control you. I thought you said we were partners and you were going to give me credit." I feel flushed on my face and neck.

He looks away for a moment, maybe to re-evaluate the situation and takes a deep breath. Voice quieter but still annoyed, he says, "I am. For your research." In an effort to distract me, he adds, "By the way, I can use the stuff about Columbus bringing the sugar cane plants to Santo Domingo from the Canary Islands and I'm sure I can work in about the kings begging Portugal to stop importing slaves to the West Indies. The Pope sanctioned it. The information you found on peanuts coming from the Bantu word, *guba*. . ."

"Forget peanuts. Stop blaming the Pope! I don't care about your stupid book," I scream. Hal looks horrified, his bushy brows raised in surprise. I have hurt him. I catch my breath. "That's not true. I didn't mean that. I do care." My eyes water and I'm embarrassed. I look down.

Hal lifts my chin with his finger. "Alegra, we're partners but you can't pick the plot points in my novel."

"Real partners?" I ask. I struck a nerve because he turns away from me.

Marriage, not mentioned since his impulsive proposal in Portugal, has not come up. I didn't say a firm yes and he hasn't offered a ring. It's too awkward for me to bring up. I want him to feel he can't live without me. We're in engagement limbo, the story of my life.

For the most part we get along, even though we're together all day every day. Except for his occasional tennis games and my forays to the market, we stay attached. But it's times like this that his obstinate streak, coupled with absent-mindedness and a bout of misogynistic fervor, drives me crazy. And, then there's the matter of sex.

We had a clumsy liaison on the night of my hair washing in Lisbon. And that's the best of our attempts. Every day I think about my robe falling away as Hal's thumb followed the depression of my collarbone. When I touched his chest we tumbled onto the bed. I wasn't satisfied although he was a gentle lover. He had a few problems, which made him begin a few times and rush to a hurried conclusion. Was it his age?

Oh God. I can't believe I'm thinking about this. I'm not terribly practiced myself. With Saul it was so rare, an event that could only happen if his aunt kept his mother entertained for a few hours away from home. I'd almost forgotten how. Besides, I wasn't a bombshell like Marta. But I could ask her advice. A few weeks ago I wrote to her. ". . . and please send your comments back, pretending it's a synopsis about Rosario on our *telenovela*."

She wrote back. "... so Rosario bought some Viagra to enhance Marco's staying power and that satisfied his young Americano wife."

Great idea but I didn't know how to get any let alone bring it up.

Hal paces around the sofa. "Alegra, I don't want to mix our lives with my book." His voice sounds less agitated. "This could work. Between you and me." He stops to look at me, his eyes sad, blinking.

I feel stronger. Maybe this is my chance. "You mentioned our partnership. And, if you want to know, I'm not happy." I fold my arms across my chest. Now or never.

"You're not happy? This isn't about Bellina on the ship, is it?"

Hands on hips I square my body toward him. "Yes and no. What about my fulfillment?" Oh God. I'm sorry the minute it comes out. His face crashes. I have no choice but to continue. "Sex has to be part of it. Otherwise, I'm an employee. Besides, you haven't made clear your intentions. Are you serious about us?" I figure as long as I'm clomping through forbidden territory I might as well slog into the Okafanokee swamp.

Lips pale, his eyes dart with an internal struggle and indignity. He walks toward me and puts his hands on my upper arms. They feel cool. "I've been worried about that and I don't want to lose you. Look," he says, fumbling in his pocket. He shakes a small yellow vial. A surprise crack of thunder from the storm makes me jump. Lights flicker and the room is dark. We've lost power again.

"I'll have to get the candles," I say.

He turns his back to me and I see his shoulders slump. I have crushed him.

He turns back to me rattling the little bottle.

"What is it?" I ask squinting.

"Cialis. The French call it 'the weekender.'"

Oh dear. I hang my head in embarrassment. He lifts my chin with a finger. With twinkling eyes he says, "It lasts thirty-six hours."

I can't say anything I'm so humiliated.

"What do you think? Want to give it a try?" he asks.

When I don't answer he drops his hand. "Alegra, this is awkward for me, but. . ." he stops. "I want you."

"Oh, Hal," I reach out to hug him. "I'm sorry. I didn't mean to..."

He takes me in his arms. "No. It's okay. Say, I took one earlier if you think..."

I pull away, grab his hand and lead him into the bedroom. Gingerly, we undress each other in the semi-darkness, our garments falling into a heap. I grab the colorful striped bedspread and yellow sheet and strip them down to the end of the bed. We sprawl out on the clean sheets. The rain pounds a rhythm above us. Ah, the marvels of science.

In his arms after a second round, my head on his chest, he says, "Okay. You win. Bellina will be threatened on board but no harm will come to her."

I get up on my elbow to look at him, his hair disheveled, arm behind his head. He squints without his glasses. "Does Grazia save her?" I ask with the tone of a fan who wants her heroine to triumph.

"You'll see," he tells me caressing my back.

"Oh." I say drifting into satisfying dreams, but not before I ask myself, *Would he have told me about the pill if I hadn't brought it up?*

Chapter Twenty-four

Bellina

30 Tammuz 5267 (21 July 1507)

My fifteenth saint's day, one in honor of the parents of the Virgin Mary, Joachim and Anne, passed without notice on board a rocking vessel that stank of horses. Slaves shoveled manure overboard, the stench invading our dresses, hair and what little food I could eat. The neighing, whinnying and snorting kept us up at night. Grazia told me we needed to be grateful to be alive. This as I vomited over the side.

My grandmother's face, full of courage and defiance, flashed before me. I could not eat. I screamed for her, hoping she could hear me in the vast known world and rescue me. In and out of delirium I heard snatches of her voice singing forbidden prayers. I remember little of the voyage. Only that I survived. Grazia said some of the men leered at me, but my puking allowed no one near me.

Finally, we reached the South American shore less five horses that perished at sea and were thrown overboard. The magnificent creatures' heads bobbed in the water for a few minutes, then sank into the abyss. They belonged to a grieving family of *conversos* who promised us employment. They had purchased the animals to work on a sugar plantation they owned carved out of the jungle.

The Palumbos told us very little. And really, what choice did we have? The adventure, an ocean voyage, the freedom to worship, sounded better than staying in Portugal fearing we would be discovered. Every day the Inquisition had new horrors to inflict—even on people who said they were believers.

Here, the possibility was no one would look for us in this God-forsaken place. We remained cautious. The Inquisition wanted apostates everywhere. It was to be a Catholic world.

The family, Senhor and Senhora Palumbo had a son of twenty, Alfonso, who traveled with them. They also had two married daughters and small grandchildren waiting for them on the plantation.

A rickety, lop-sided wagon met our group. The horses would be delivered later. After a two-day ride that jostled us like rolling sacks of potatoes, we arrived at the edge of a clearing located in an area known as Pernambuco.

We followed a wagon track road until we pulled up to the front of a low plantation building. Grazia steeled herself, sighing. Not the grand structure we expected, but merely a large sprawling primitive home in need of repair. I looked away in despair, tears flooding my eyes, and held my aunt's arm.

We were shown our quarters on the side of the house by an imposing African woman who did not speak. I collapsed on the small bed in our barren room, my face to the wall and cried. We traveled for weeks on the ocean for this? Grazia did her best to comfort me saying, "We are safe, Bellina, we are safe." But I did not feel any safer. Just more alone.

From the first day I did my best to please Senhora Olivia as she asked me to call her. I cleaned and polished wood furniture made from strange trees that grew in the jungle. I also helped in the kitchen. The cook, Antiga, had me wash, peel and dice native fruits: *jatobas*, *garibobas*, and *marmelo-de-cachooros* for chutneys and salads. Some were bitter, others sweet and sticky, all had unusual fragrances. I tasted a few when she turned her back.

Grazia and I were not paid for our labor. We had a clean place to sleep and food to eat but no remuneration, no way to save a few coins and buy our way out of here. Yet, we were treated with more respect than the Africans, poor stray dogs, fear in their eyes, trust vanished. Their families fended for themselves in shacks fashioned from mud and palm fronds, sad dwellings that melted away in the monsoons. We had a dry bed.

Midnight-dark slaves with white teeth and pale palms worked in the sugar cane fields. Abused with the lash they also had little to eat. And not all were African. Native Indians, tan with short straight black hair and pointed cheekbones hacked at the grass with machetes. When it was ripe they were driven to exhaustion, yelling among themselves in a concoction of languages, indigenous tongues mixed with Portuguese. At night they turned to song, melodies and tribal beats that echoed through the valleys.

I overheard the plantation manager, a swarthy Portuguese named Zachariah Sellam, explaining to Senhor at breakfast one morning as I served a strong coffee made from local beans. "A worthless crop if we wait. Cut too late, cane dries out, juices sour."

"Drive them," said Senhor Palumbo, sitting back in his chair.

The slaves were pushed with frenzied panic to get the cane to the mill, an engenho. Heated in vats and forced through heavy machinery, the sugar cane liquefied, resulting in crystals, a valuable commodity.

The processed cane resulted in blistered palms and fingers from the intense heat of those who were forced to labor. I turned away from the poor souls when they arrived at the back door from the fields, cut and bleeding hands staining their ragged clothes.

Stringy stalks, sweet to suck, were sharp to touch. The plantation already had its share of child cripples wandering around with lost digits or limbs from swinging machetes. This horrible, brutal place made me sick.

Grazia went about her work polishing the floors with oily rags on her feet and a hum under her breath. Sometimes I saw her stop to stare out a window. Once, when she swept the porch that wrapped itself around the perimeter of the house, she took the broom and danced for a few minutes.

We did not mix with the Africans except Antiga, the cook. We helped her with meal preparation, washing and chopping vegetables from the garden, setting the table. Relieved not to be involved in the slaughter of animals, which Senhor Palombo and his brother did according to our laws, I was grateful for food.

On the eve of the Sabbath we joined the family for the lighting of candles and recitation of prayers. Afterward, we retreated to the kitchen to eat our meal. Often, Alfonso stared at me. Once, I glanced back and the Senhora reminded me of my place.

"You are a servant in this house, Bellina. Nothing more." I nodded and left the room. One of the male servers, an elderly man with grey curly hair and red-veined eyes smirked at me, enjoying my scolding.

The women, except for Antiga, were quiet, obedient, bowed heads wrapped in colorful scarves. One, a tall woman named Ruth with smooth golden skin and large feet, expelled her baby squatting in the fields, without privacy, barely hidden between rows of white-green stalks. The men shifted away if we were near, their lean bodies sculpted in blue-blackness often marred by scars from the lash.

Rupert, Antiga's son, frightened me. Broad-shouldered and fierce-looking, his angry eyes flashed like bolts of lightning on a starless night. One evening he waited outside the back door, hands splayed against the wall behind him, signaling his mother with a whistle.

I was a few feet away, gathering dry sticks from the pile to enhance the fire. I stopped. Antiga slipped him a package. I imagined a cold potato, a sliver of meat, the heel of bread that the owners left on their plates. She touched his arm and went back inside. With a nod he tucked the food into his waistband, glared at me, and leapt into a run, daring me to tell.

On a particular Friday afternoon I assisted with Senhora's bath, carrying the heated water from the kitchen fireplace, helping her into the tub, washing her back. Mint leaves made the air fragrant. A burst of frustration escaped my lips. "Pooh. I forgot Antiga's lye soap," I muttered to myself.

"Hurry and bring it," she said, sinking up to her neck in the water, tendrils of dark hair framing her face.

"I will be back in a moment, Senhora."

I scampered to the empty kitchen and bent down to open a pantry bin. *Antiga must be in the garden* I thought to myself. My hurried fingers searched until I touched the soap that had been cooked in a vat on the open fire during the full moon. My duty was to cut the hard squares after they cooled. I held a piece to my chest, my nails chipping a few slivers that fell to the floor. The strong aroma teased a sneeze from me. A buzz of voices stopped that I had not noticed. In a rush to return I slammed the bin back into place with my foot. Voices. I froze.

"Is someone near?"

"Hush."

"No sounds now."

A muffled laugh.

Muted noises from the cold storage closet next door, one where valuable food was stored, sounded familiar. I approached, placing my ear against the door. The padlock was missing. A man and woman. Sounds of pleasure. The laugh–Grazia's. And she was with someone! Who? I looked around to make sure no one was nearby. With caution I pressed the handle. The door squeaked and cool air rushed my face.

"Grazia?" I could not see in the darkness.

A gasp. "Go away."

"Grazia, what are you doing? If they catch you with the meat you will be punished."

Her firm grip came out of nowhere and turned me around toward the light, pushing me out.

"Who is there with you? I heard voices."

"Go." She shut the door with finality.

Without a way to peer inside I turned away. Later, as I scrubbed the Senhora's back, the tendrils damp on her neck, I thought about the low moan from behind the closed door.

That night, as Grazia and I curled into our bed, unbound hair covering our faces, I asked, "Who was with you?"

She answered with a hoarse whisper, "Since when are you so direct?" After a pause she said, "Mind yourself. Senhora Olivia does not like people who snoop."

"But I heard you speaking to someone."

"Harrump. Imagining things. The ghost of your grandmother maybe." She snapped the covers around her and smoothed her nightclothes.

Adamant, I persisted. I am not a fool. "I am not imagining anything. I know your voice. And there was another, too."

"It is of no importance." With that she turned her back to me and pretended to sleep.

But I did not forget. I spied on her. In time I learned her secret. Grazia had been good to me. I would not have survived without her, but a wedge drove us apart.

After two years the plantation became our danger zone. The slaves, mistreated and filled with unrest, lost their docility. In recent weeks they banged their frustration on drums at night, hollow sounds reverberating against the stone walls of the house. Rumors of rebellions at other plantations haunted us, horrors whispered. No one told me anything definitive but I knew. Even Grazia remained stoic.

One evening after I tucked the grandchildren into their beds, I checked on the Senhora. "Close the windows," she instructed me as she sat with embroidery near the fire. She squinted at her stitches, a frown crossing her face. I poured a glass of sherry and placed it next to her, moving to the window, my curiosity aroused. "I do not want to hear their sounds." Fires blazed and native rhythms echoed with urgency as I closed the wooden shutters and latched them.

Chapter Twenty-five

Bellina

Grazia and I awoke late on the Day of Atonement, the holiest day of the year, ready to fast for our sins. We washed from a ceramic blue bowl. With a dripping face Grazia repeated a verse from Levictus, "For on this day shall atonement be made for you, to cleanse you from all your sins shall ye be clean before the Lord." We dressed with haste.

We had been released from our duties and instructed to assist Antiga who planned a feast for the Palumbos. We would share the evening meal and dress later in bleached white linen. My hair was caught in a handkerchief and I wiped my brow with the back of my hand as I chopped vegetables for Antiga.

Grazia stood next to me chopping cane into small cubes for the Senhora's tea, her long faded skirt tucked up in the kitchen heat. The Senhora and her daughters lazed in the main room while Senhor and his son, both unshaven, rode their property.

Except for my grumbling stomach the day passed with ease. Grazia and I washed dishes, utensils and linens, sorted spices, picked and arranged flowers. We spoke little, honoring the solemnity of the day. She did whisper to me that when the shofar was sounded the Bible wanted people to release their slaves. I shrugged my shoulders. That would not happen here.

The sun, a crimson orb, fell low in the sky. The first stars appeared. I anticipated our meal as I polished a silver pitcher, my hand repetitive over a stubborn spot, perched on one foot like an absent-minded crane.

A calf had been slaughtered the day before, its blood drained, the meat marinating in a savory sauce. Antiga prepared a stew of tomatoes, corn and beans, adding spices with care.

An old native woman responsible for the garden had taught her the differences between plants and medicinal uses of herbs. She claimed her knowledge from the native peoples and showed us how she used papaya leaves for cuts, chewed amaranth leaves for strength and the benefit of gluing bark to the soles of our sandals with plum tree resin.

Now her firm dark hand stirred a simmering concoction in an iron pot. She also cooked ugly wild yams, brown skin cleaned of dirt, the orange meat inside simmering and steaming with flavor. My mouth watered, the fast weakening me.

We had been instructed to wear white for the evening meal, avoiding leather slippers in honor of our traditions. I counted the short hour until sundown. We worked rhythmically, Grazia humming as we finished our tasks.

Without warning the door slammed open with a thrust. I reached for my aunt. In the flutter of a butterfly's wing she grabbed my hand, the silver and cane abandoned, and pulled me under the large table in the center of the room. My thumping heart pumped almost outside my chest.

"Quick, the rebellion has begun," she said, her voice tinged with excitement. Rebellion? We heard rumors of discontent at other plantations where the slaves were punished, the instigators tortured and killed. But rebellion? Was there not enough cruelty?

Antiga's son, Rupert, and his friend, Jamba, stormed the room. Rupert stared at us as we cowered under the table. Without sustenance all day my breath was foul. I huddled next to Grazia. I had seen Jamba before, a huge black man with lash marks and a shaved head. Jamba's eyes darted around the room before settling on us. "They die," he said with a growl.

I gasped for air and pee let loose wetting my skirts. Embarrassed, the acid odor burned my nostrils. No, no. I cried a soft whimper, bending my head toward my knees. If he was going to kill me, let it be swift, the white of my neck an offering to God.

"Leave the women alone, Jamba," Antiga told him. "They are slaves like us." I tried to swallow. Dryness sawed my throat.

"Mama, the rebellion has started. We will escape."

"Where will you go? To the jungle to live in a tree?" Antiga's feet were filthy and the hem of her dress dragged on the dirt floor. She sounded angry. "Are you going to drip blood in my cook house?" Then she turned to face Jamba. "Who are you slaughtering? Goats? My boy is not like you. He will not kill anyone."

Jamba, with his shaved head and intimidating size, spit out words in a native language that I did not understand. The vicious tone sent chills up my spine.

Grazia's breathing steadied and I could feel her sweat through my clothes. She held my hand.

"White women die now," repeated Jamba. I crept forward and lifted my eyes. He swung a machete back and forth, blade red with blood, slicing the air, his nostrils wide, grasping for air.

Rupert stood next to him and grabbed his arm to quiet him. "Mama, we need supplies, food, water."

Antiga held fast, hands on hips, feet apart. I could not see her face but heard her clucking sounds. "I help you, I die anyway."

"Then we take what we want," said her son.

Grazia put her arm around my waist and pulled my trembling body closer. *Why have I been allowed to come this far in life's journey?* I cried softly.

"Shush, *yie tov*. It will be all right," Grazia told me, a finger to her lips. No longer afraid, something had steeled her.

I thought of the Lisbon courtyard where my grandparents died. Our desire to survive drove us to this new country. My grandfather's voice echoed about how grand the universe was, how just God's plan. Is this my end? Will I perish without a trace in a strange land? Or will the ancestors protect me from evil?

Jamba slapped the machete against his leg, his impatience palpable in the room. "Time is short. They will be looking for us. Take what you want, Rupert."

Antiga hovered near the fire. She pleaded with her son in their native language, guttural and harsh, her face distorted in the light. She inched closer to her pot of stew, her words gnawing at him.

Rupert, with white straight teeth, was anxious. His eyes, rimmed with red, darted nervously. He moved toward the open fire placing his machete on the table over our heads. Perhaps he wanted one last meal from his mother's hand or he desired the pot for their travels. I do not know.

Rupert's pink palms and Antiga's large dark hands, both impervious to the hot handle, battled for the stew. Taller and stronger, emitting grunts, he pulled it from the iron stand. Twisting it away from his mother, he loosened her grip, swinging it toward himself, the hot steel burning the flesh of his stomach. When he screamed, Antiga tipped the heavy pot away from him. White chicken meat nuggets lay limp among ripe, crimson tomatoes, yellow maize, jack beans, spices and broth. All seeped away in front of us, wasted on the dirt floor. Rupert fell, hands on his stomach, howling in pain.

"Look what you have done," said Antiga, voice filled with rage, eyes seeping tears. She bent on her knees to gather the pieces of chicken. Rupert, crumpled on the floor, was eye level with us. He glanced at Grazia and she lowered her eyes.

Antiga, her girth forcing her to her knees to rise, placed the empty pot back into its iron stand. She rummaged in a small tin and came over to Rupert with a piece of lard. "Here, son," she said. "For the burn."

"Come out," said Jamba motioning to us. "Come out from under the table."

I did not move, shaking my head no, clutching Grazia's hand. Sweat beaded on my forehead. I prayed to the God we worshiped in secret, the Father of Abraham, Isaac and Jacob to save me. I pleaded with Mother Mary. I repeated a litany of *save me, save me, save me.* What cruel God takes a child from its mother and sets her adrift with barbarians?

I took a deep breath, ready for my fate. Calmness drizzled over me. Maybe it was the thought of my grandmother who died with dignity, perhaps Grazia's strength, but I no longer felt fear. If I could survive crazed Africans whose sole desire was to chop off my head, I could face anything with strength and determination by dedicating my life to God.

"Jamba, Jamba. Rupert, you there?" Voices outside the cook house called for the men. Dark legs gathered in the doorway. The men urged one another in their native tongue, strange words and energetic sounds expressed in different tones.

A tall, bare-chested young man with scars patterned on his face was rumored to be the son of a warrior. He entered and surveyed the room. Jamba stood near us with his machete.

"They are looking for us. Our time for safety is short," he told Rupert and Jamba. He reached for Rupert's arm, lifting him as he grimaced in pain. Rupert straightened his shoulders, pulling himself to his full height.

A shot rang through the room. Jamba crumbled to the floor, crimson streaming out of his back. I screamed into my hand, horrified to witness such brutality.

Two Portuguese entered the room, one the plantation manager, Zachariah, known for his bad temper, and the other, his brother, Carlos, olive-skinned and short with thick black hair swept to the side. Their powerful stocky bodies moved with a swagger. His face impassive, Zachariah stepped over Jamba as blood pooled under his body.

I wanted to turn away, but could not. My body shook with sobs, a hollow rawness in my soul. Rupert moved to the wall near the door in the confusion, his glistening weapon in his hand. Fierce, he held the machete over his head.

"Stop. Everyone halt," said Zachariah. He pointed his pistol at Rupert.

I could not breathe in the stifling space, the sweet, sickening smell of body fluids putrid in the air.

"Antiga, leave," said Carlos, urging her with a movement of his iron musket, the type soldiers carried in Portugal. Her dark eyes swept the room and without turning her back she inched toward the door. Had we been forgotten? Left to stare at a blood-soaked man on the floor?

With his mother gone, Rupert sprang at the two men, his muscular body poised in the air, a panther pursuing prey. The tip of the machete flashed. Blood splashed onto my skirt. I hugged Grazia, her eyes wide with terror. The firearm exploded and cries ripped the air. Carlos fell to the ground with a deadening groan, shot by his brother. Rupert stared at Zachariah for a moment, dismayed, then vanished through the door, Antiga's fragrant stew forgotten in a mess on the floor.

Chapter Twenty-six

Bellina

11 Tishrei 5270 (5 October 1509)
Pernambuco, Brazil

utside, in the not-so-still night, a chirping insect played a razor-sharp song in a cadence of woe. Next to me Grazia turned onto her side. Asleep, mouth slightly opened, her breath came in measured paces, absent of the anguish I felt. Unable to get yesterday's events out of my mind, I could not slumber. The violence in the kitchen haunted me– Rupert's anger, harsh voices, shots and blood everywhere. How could Grazia rest? Why were we in this dangerous place?

My fingers spread out on the coarse sheets, a reminder of my grandmother's soft linens and finery, the velvet cape that Grazia wore for a time, extravagant scraps I played with as a child at my grandfather's feet, his kiss on my forehead after Sabbath dinner. When I was small their love seemed endless. It filled the gap in me, the hollow crevasse a motherless child always feels.

Now, with an uncertain future, anxiety seared me. I turned away from Grazia but my mind would not rest. Shrieks from monkeys and parrots rang out; this *fazenda* had been carved out of a dense jungle.

The bedcovers slipped and I stole to the window, careful not to wake my aunt. I opened the shutters with care, squeaky joints of the rusty hinges whining. The first puff of chilled air in my face carried a burning scent that singed my nostrils.

My view from our quarters in the main house showed fires everywhere--bonfires blazing with scraps from the cane scum, the men's torches as they traipsed through the fields searching for the insurgents and to my right, open fires of slaves cooking a meager meal. My eyes watered. Caustic air or my trembling sadness?

I watched the dawn rise without sleep. I turned away. Grazia stretched her arms and washed her mouth with water, scrubbing her teeth with a root, a habit learned from Antiga. She urged me to meet her behind the slave shanties, a pathetic group of lean-tos made from scrap wood and mud and covered with tin roofs, some with giant leaves perched on top like precarious bird's nests.

"Hurry to finish your chores," she told me, patting her mouth dry. I saw her hands shaking. *Perhaps from the recent events? I thought.*

"Senhora Olivia has told us to stay inside," I said, twisting my hair behind my ears and into a linen cap.

She dismissed me with a wave of her hand. "Act as though everything is normal."

"Normal?" I hissed. "We are in the middle of a slave rebellion. Jamba's dead as well as the manager's brother. Men were out all night searching for Rupert and the others. God knows what they will do when they find them." I stared at her in anger. I blamed her for this predicament. I began to sweat despite the chilled air in the room.

Grazia grabbed me and shook my shoulders. "Listen, be careful. Meet me. Wait a bit. Do not let the Senhora see you leave. I have something to tell you." With that she seized her apron and left.

What? A plan to get us out of here? Where could we go? We were trapped in this God-forsaken jungle, prisoners in a different way than we existed in Portugal. No mad priests looking for us, but could we survive more?

I left to serve the Senhora her tea and bread for breakfast in the parlor. She waited, vacuous eyes, rosy lips pinched into a grim line. Perched on a settee, white linen doilies covering the arms, her back leaned into plump azure pillows, a doll without expression. A fine wood cabinet displayed vases and porcelain figures while brass lanterns from Portugal graced the walls. Much of the polished wood floor was covered with thick woven silk rugs that displayed tapestries of hunting scenes and pastoral pictures.

The whiteness of her bosom set off emeralds, green as fresh leaves after a rain. The upsweep of her hair revealed a long neck and haughty chin. There were not many women in Brazil. Most of the *conversos* who came--landowners, explorers, physicians, slave traders, historians and poets—followed their hearts and pockets, leaving their families behind. Senhora Olivia looked lonely.

She acknowledged me with an aristocratic nod. On a normal day she did not speak to me except about my duties. If my grandparents were alive we would have been equal members of the gentry, part of the merchant class attending the same secret synagogue. I would have been a possibility as a bride for her son, but instead of discussing servants, I was one.

Today, dressed in her finest like a queen, she forbade me to leave the premises. "Be careful. Savages can attack anyone, especially a woman," she said, her hands fidgeting. Odd that she would care since she merely tolerated me.

She continued, "Set the mahogany table for dinner. I expect company." She shifted her gaze out the window to the savanna, eyes vacant. "In Venice the aristocracy has so much money they make sculptures from our spun sugar–delicate silverware and plates for confections."

And so she sat, hours passing, tea and bread untouched, embroidery on her lap, weeping, sponging her eyes with a piece of silk, waiting for the men to return.

I excused myself, hurrying to arrange white bougainvillea branches in vases. When I re-entered the parlor to collect Senhora Palumbo's dishes, she waved me away. She rose with a sigh and went to her bed chamber.

What did Grazia want? Posses of armed men searched the surrounding land. Beyond the plantation fields stretched with wheat grass, jungle grew thick with giant trees, dense vines and plants with leaves the size of a child. Luxuriant ground cover carpeted the surrounding area as far as I could see in brilliant green.

Grazia said they would never find them without the help of the native Indians, expert road and bridge builders I might add, who resented the intrusion of the plantation owners and saw them as enemies.

As I swept the rooms I dwelt on Grazia. What was her plan? Who kept her company in the store room? Little pieces of hay left a soft trail as I worked gathering debris—mud tracked in, bits of grass, shards of cane, a few dead bugs. I returned the broom to the kitchen.

Antiga, glum, stood with her back to me, preparing marmalade from red zapotes, a fleshy sweet fruit. She had been questioned about her son earlier in the day. "I know nothing," she muttered to herself over and over. "The boy is no good," she repeated with a shake of her head.

I sneaked away.

Grazia waited for me behind the wooden shacks where the machetes and other tools were stored, a short distance from the shanties, eerily quiet as I passed. No slaves worked the fields today even though it was harvest. Cane had to get to the mill before the stalks fermented. Lack of production was chancy.

Slaves who had not run off with Rupert's group sat on low benches fidgeting, waiting for punishment, the women and children plaiting hair and mending worn clothes. A small boy with a missing hand chased a black and orange grasshopper.

Grazia, impatient, glared at me, pensive eyes shaded by her hand. She urged me to hurry as she scrambled to her feet, took my hand and led me toward the fields.

"Auntie, is it safe to be here?"

"Why do you worry so much?"

With bowed heads Grazia and I walked in silence through the rows carefully planted on flat land. Jagged sugar cane fragments from stalks cut low for the sweetest part, bled syrup. I stuck my finger out for some and sucked it. Sliced green leaves, slippery under our feet, were left to protect the roots through the winter, a silent peril. I followed her strong back, the adversity of our years and her sacrifices for me apparent on her squared shoulders, sturdy calves and threadbare blue dress. Rigid uncut stalks from a harvest interrupted became a fence. As we headed toward them I bent down to pick up a small piece of sugar cane that had been hacked off, forgotten. I pressed it between my lips.

Grazia cleared her throat. Her pace had quickened and I was a few steps behind her. In a few minutes she turned to face me, a slight twitch pulling at the corner of her mouth. "Bellina." She took my hands in hers, both of ours rough from housework.

I contemplated my aunt, her plain face almost pretty in the late sun, tears welling up in her eyes. A bee buzzed near us and she shook her head to scare it away.

"I have done my best to care for you."

"I know, Auntie."

"Tomorrow is a holiday, Sukkot, the festival to thank God for his protection when he led us out of Egypt. We are supposed to build a temporary hut covered by loose branches." She grabbed one of the cane stalks and shook it.

"Grazia, with the turmoil of the uprising, do not worry if there is not a celebration. God will forgive us."

"We are supposed to take four branches and shake them together—the citron, the palm, the myrtle and the willow—to symbolize the Jewish people from the learned and pious to the less fortunate."

"I will think of the holiday in my heart."

"Sukkot is to remind us we are all one people, to be respectful of one another."

What is she trying to tell me? I am impatient. I suck hard on the piece of cane and sweetness explodes in my mouth.

"I promised my parents on our sacred Torah that I would always care for you."

"And you have, Grazia. What is it? Tell me. I will always love you." I bent down for another piece and sucked the stringy end of the cane fragment, taking a breath. "You have protected me."

Sharp veins throbbed on Grazia's neck. Her breasts heaved as she blurted out her words, "I am leaving with Rupert." Her shoulders slumped in relief at her confession. "We have no future here. Our choice is to run away."

My hand went to my chest in shock. "You know where he is? They will kill you."

"Rupert has plans for us to disappear into the city of Bahia."

"My aunt, that is impossible. The jungle?"

"Others will help us, people who will no longer tolerate Africans being worked to death." She raised her chin in defiance.

"No one will assist you. They will be killed, too." I began to cry. She had lost reason.

"Before we came the Indians lived off the land, ate strange papayas and plums, played with blue and yellow parrots, chased the jaguars, fished the seas. Now they feel a kinship with dark strangers brought in shackles from Angola and Mozambique."

I composed myself. "So you are leaving? With an African?"

"Yes." Her eyes widened.

My surprise was so great I could no longer speak. My mouth fell open, the gnawed pieces of cane falling to the ground.

Grazia, her tone resentful, said, "He is not the sullen, angry person you see. He loves me."

"But our family? Our faith?"

"I am teaching him to read. He has intelligence. I have to please myself. You would not deny me happiness, would you?"

"Grazia, where will I go?" I shook with anxiety.

"You will be safe here. The Palumbos will not let anything happen to you. Maybe their son. . . ."

The sugary taste left in my mouth turned sour. I was her burden. I turned and ran before she could answer–between stalks, breaking the leaves with my hands, avoiding the well-worn path next to the endless rows of peeling cane waiting to be culled, cutting my hands, heart pounding with breathlessness. *I will find a way to leave, too*, I thought. *I will find a way. Away, far away from this terrible place.*

Chapter Twenty-seven

Bellina

21 Tishrei 5270 (15 October 1509)
Pernambuco, Brazil

Smoke and the aroma of beeswax wafted through the room when Grazia extinguished our candle. My aunt, dressed in onion layers, crawled into bed. I wanted to sleep and not think about her plan to abandon me. She struggled with skirts and bedclothes moving closer, warm breath and nervous fingers palpating my back. I did not respond. She leaned over me, tense, expectant in the murky light, stroking my hair, humming. I turned away from her.

"Bellina, please. Our last moments together cannot be ones of frustration. Come to me. Let me hold you." I pulled away, not interested in her soothing. I was being left behind. For a time she was quiet. Then she tried a different way. "You must not tell Senhora Palumbo I have gone." Her voice sounded husky with excitement, words rushing together. "She will know I am missing by mid-morning, but by then I will be far away. Besides, they cannot do anything to me. I do not belong to them."

I turned around to spit out my words. "You are helping a slave escape. Punishable by death."

Grazia flung herself onto her back. "I would rather die than give up Rupert."

I was shocked to hear my aunt speak this way. The realization that they meant more to each other, that he meant more than me, was incomprehensible. "How can you leave me after what we have shared?"

"Bellina, my beautiful niece, you mean a great deal to me." She sighed.

I could not be pacified by flattery. I cried, tears flowing. She reached to hold me and I jerked away. It remained quiet for a time.

"What of your obligation to the Palumbos? They took us in." I dried my tears on the bedclothes. I was still hopeful that I could convince her to change her plans.

"Obligation? I have fulfilled the duties of my servitude many times over. As much as I despise them they will be kind to you. If I had known this would be my fate, I. . ." She was going to follow her heart no matter what.

"Where will you go?" I swallowed hard at the reality.

She exhaled, speaking with confidence. "The jungle until they stop looking for us. After that I do not know. Rupert and the others know their way. Preparations have been made. I will be safe."

My chest split with rocking pain. I clutched my aunt's arm. "How can you leave me? What about your promise to *mi abuelas*?" I began to sob for all my losses—mother, grandparents, and now my aunt.

Grazia wiped my tears with her coarse fingertips. She cooed to me as I had heard mothers to babies. "Dear Bellina, I love you. You will be safe here. It hurts me to leave you but I have to find my happiness. Life has been unkind to me in many ways—my plain face, the absence of companionship. If this is my lot, so be it." She stopped for a breath and renewed her speech with more passion. "But I believe the Almighty meant for me to have more. Much more. Life's adventures wait for me. Rupert will show me."

I had no vision of my aunt as an adventurer, a destiny for explorers and pirates filled with bravado and finery. How could this plump woman in faded skirts forge into the unknown with nothing save a few bags of food? She had planned her escape with a slave, a man with whom she was casting her fate, one who would be hunted for the rest of his days.

"Rupert?" I sputtered. "A runaway. What has happened to your logic? Reasoning? Ach, you are a crazed fool. You could be eaten by wild animals."

She stared at the ceiling. "I am not afraid of animals. Humans do worse things to one another."

Her whisper choked back emotion. She pulled me to her and began to cry, her tears wetting my shoulder.

"Maybe I am making a mistake abandoning all, but Bellina. . ." She held me away and contemplated my face. "I do not expect you to understand, but when he touches me, flames race through my body."

I opened my eyes wide and gasped, realizing she was no longer pure. My own flesh and blood. Nothing I said would change the mind of a wanton woman. "Grazia."

"Do not judge me. My decisions have kept us alive through the worst of circumstances."

What would my life be without her? "Please do not leave me." I begged her with the soulfulness of a lamb led to slaughter. "You have been my protector."

"Shush, shush." She held me tight, hugging me close to her bosom as she did when I was a child. I smelled Antiga's lye soap on her scrubbed neck.

"I will never see you again." I cried.

She pushed aside the bedcovers and stood looking down at me. "Follow your heart and believe in God. Learn. We are People of the Book. The candlesticks are yours now. I will think of you every day. When you see the stars, remember me. Good night, sweet Bellina." She leaned down and kissed my forehead. I turned to hide under the quilts, my aloneness palpable.

The shutter opened and I knew she was gone. A prickly exhaustion rained over me. Bereft, I wept and wept and finally, slipping into an exhausted sleep, I dreamed of fires. When I awakened, a forsaken soul, Grazia had slipped away, her few belongings pushed into a faded drawstring bag, the pattern of her life forever altered.

Chapter Twenty-eight

Bellina

23 Adar 5270 (15 March 1510)
Pernambuco, Brazil

I waited in front of the Senhora, dressed in my shabby shift, worn felt slippers on my feet, weight tipped into my heels. She wore a rose taffeta gown, ivory lace at the neck and sleeves, her décolletage emitting the fragrance of perfume. The lace, tattered in a few places, had not been mended since Grazia's exit five months before. Her jewelry, earrings with sapphires and a necklace of intricate gold set with rubies, glittered. On her elongated fingers with groomed nails, she wore a ring with a large new stone the color of the sun, its facets cut to reflect light. Topaz she called it. Her black hair, held in place by pearl combs, was swept from her nape in an elaborate style, a few loose curls emphasizing her long neck.

A delicate embroidered cloth covered the table next to her. It had been one she worked on for months, red, green and purple threads woven into vines of grapes and cherries. On the far wall a massive fireplace glowed with logs, pushing heat through the room. A small slave boy known as Ebony, dressed in white and wearing a dark velvet vest, played a mandolin near Senhora's feet, his childish, high voice alive with a fisherman's song.

Outside, the fields stretched, dark slave heads laboring in the cane fields. Life went on after the rebellion, the punishments harsh on those who remained, freedom elusive for those not yet caught.

"Bellina, sit down." She motioned toward a brocade chair across from her. "Ebony." She dismissed his song with a wave, turning to me, her face serious with displeasure. *My work. It is less than satisfactory.* Without my aunt to remind me of dusty corners and polished gleam I was lax, flooded with melancholy. Or perhaps it was another warning to ignore any advances from her son. I was not good enough for him. "It is almost Passover. Time has passed since the rebellion. Have you had word from Grazia, dishonorable as she is?"

I bowed my head with anxiousness, staring at my folded hands. She wanted information. "No, Senhora Olivia, I have not."

"Ungrateful whore running off with a slave. If not for us you both would have starved. Or worse." Her words bit with resentment at my aunt's betrayal.

Her accusation that my aunt was a woman of the streets wounded me. It was not the first time she had tortured me with spurious remarks. I cast my eyes downward unable to defend Grazia's actions. I was angry, too. Questioned repeatedly at her initial disappearance I refused to help. Besides, what I knew was vague. Had she even survived the treacherous jungle with its poisonous snakes and insects?

"My husband has men who continue to look for Rupert. The dogs lost his scent but they will find him. I am sure Grazia will be nearby." She paused to stare at Ebony lost in a dream of childish slumber, his eyelids twitching. "Punishment will be swift when they are found." She adjusted the folds in her skirt, staring hard at me. Will she dismiss me because of Grazia?

The Senhora's words pinched me. I felt cold and ran my hands up and down my arms. If they were caught it would be horrible. As upset as I was at Grazia's abandonment, I did not want her or Rupert to be harmed. *Run*, I thought, *run. Make a life.*

"Ebony?" She urged the young boy with her foot to wake him. The child opened his eyes, lids droopy with sleep. "Go." He scampered to his feet, mandolin in hand and scurried, barefooted, toward the door.

She rustled a piece of paper on her lap. It shook in her hand as she began to read. My heart beat in anticipation. Perhaps a missive from my aunt?

Tishrei, 5268 (October, 1509)
Amsterdam, Netherlands

To My Dearest Senhor and Senhora Palumbo,
Allow me to introduce myself. My name is Arlindo Mar-
celino, a diamond merchant of renown with roots in Spain
and Portugal, a descendant of the Mendes' and Marcelino line
from Madrid. With great sadness and relief a group of our
countryman have found refuge in Amsterdam after search-
ing for a safe place to conduct business. Our small congrega-

tion has been welcomed with caution. With respect for our forefathers we have built a secret synagogue of adequate size with Dutch co-religionists. Our prayer is that some day we may be able to practice our faith with impunity.

At a recent meeting of elite gentry we gathered to discuss trade and importation of products from East India, diamonds and pearls in particular, but also Brazil, Portugal's newest conquest. Sugarcane and its byproducts, paper made from bulk and exotic woods, have great appeal in Europe. We understand the expansion in São Paolo has landowners flooded with wealth, including a few whose soiled garments arrive here to be cleaned and sent back.

As conversos who survived the Spanish and Portuguese expulsions, we also lost whole families in the terrors. I, myself lost a wife and child in an auto de fe as I traveled.

We are faced with decisions. Some are reluctant to give up lives free of commitment. Others, whose days are filled with ambivalence, consider existing in their dual nether world of our true faith and Catholicism, the two religions not blended but adversarial inside and outside the home. Matched with different names and identities it makes for a sad confusion.

Others, like me, take this as an opportunity to follow the faith of our fathers, to keep the Laws of Moses alive. We wish to establish families, to keep the line unbroken from Biblical times until now, to have children who will forever keep the future from being lost.

So, it is to this I address our situation. Many of us are bachelors, widowers, men alone who have forged ahead without wives. It is our understanding young women of pure Sephardic blood escaped to your shores, some without families or means. When the fine Palumbo name was brought to our attention, we learned that you have two young women in your employ who fit our needs. Others might also be available in your area. Our charitable dowry society, Santa Com-

panhia de Dotar Orphans e Donzellas, has great interest in
bringing ones of marriageable age to join us.

For those between the years of fourteen and eighteen, we of-
fer passage and forgive any advancement of a dowry. We do
not have interest in those older than eighteen. Acknowledging
that many may not remember prayers or synagogue rituals,
arrangements will be made to teach them. A boat and chaper-
one, Senhora Angelina Solomon, will leave from the shores of
Recife in the weeks preceding the Festival of Lights.

With Kindest Regards and Sincerity,
Arlindo Marcelino
Representative, B'nai Isroel

With a slip of the wrist the Senhora slid the letter into her sleeve. I froze. A log in the fire fell, crackling, the air alive with sparks. Her head sank back into the settee, the white of her neck exposed. She closed her eyes. When she opened them, they were glassy, the dark pupils blending into the outer circles.

In an even voice, lips tight, she said, "Bellina, you must go. My own daughters are married and not in need of such an opportunity. An orphan like you can use her beauty. Your background is not of importance."

"Senhora, I do not want to leave. My aunt. . ."

"Can never return. This is right for you—a chance to change your fate and obey your grandparents faith. We can no longer keep you here. It is a favor to send you away. For the best."

I could not breathe.

In the days after the reading of the letter I barely slept. I tossed and turned at night, sweat plastering hair to my brow. I lived in fear of what lay ahead and what would happen to me if I stayed behind. I was more alone than ever.

I desired a place of peace, one where all had not been lost—our family and its traditions, our faith, and, most of all, my beloved Grazia.

It would have been easy to forsake our stiff-necked beliefs—not just in God but an entire religion's inability to protect us. Where were the kings and prophets of the Bible to lead our group of loyal followers? Resolute in my convictions, I remained steadfast, snippets of psalms and prayers clogged in my mind, even though I knew they could bring damnation to me and future generations. After reciting the *shema* I often repeated two lines from the 137th Psalm.

"If I forget thee, O Jeruselam
May my right hand fail me."

Was God listening?

As for Grazia, I prayed that she was not gone from me forever, that she once again survived the insurmountable challenges laid before her. I harbored a secret delight when the posses came back empty-handed, dogs panting, tongues lolling, men, dogs and horses exhausted from the futile search.

Grazia. I whispered her name in the night, my eyes closed, wishing she would turn to me, perhaps a bit irritated and ask me my need. I regretted her flight but I knew this new opportunity for me to find a husband would not have helped her dreams of romance. She was too old. They wanted youth. She would have pushed me to leave her behind, to take the opportunity to name children after my grandparents so their souls could live on. I wondered where she was, if she had survived the jungle and the rocky landscape of the *sãrtao*. It was rumored some runaways were starting new lives in Olinda, a coastal city north of Recife controlled by the Hollanders. I heard that besides convicts and opportunists, New Christians settled around the churches and forts being built.

Was Grazia happy with her choices? Would Rupert care for her and be kind? Was the duty of her affection another chore to be carried out? When I was small I amused her, perhaps allowing her to forget I was a niece instead of a daughter. But, in the end, I became an obstacle, one that kept her from a life of her own.

I dreamt of her in the jungle with her dark lover, arms entwined on a rug of thick vines, her hair wild, his back sweaty, rope-like muscles glistening. The echo of their moans from the cold storage closet resonated in my head and woke me. My blurry imagination could go no farther.

I repeated the *shema* in an effort to cleanse my thoughts. Anxiety roiled me, waves of excitement about a new life and dread, too, for an extended journey through dangerous waters. I vowed to look forward now and never behind me, images of a sea voyage and serpents of change dancing across my mind.

Chapter Twenty-nine

Bellina

14 Kislev 5271 (26 November 1510)
En route from Brazil to Amsterdam

We left when the Senhora's garden bloomed with rare white and purple orchids, embracing the air with a lingering fragrance. My voyage back to the continent took place within six months after the letter arrived.

Just past eighteen, I joined a dozen other young women at the docks on the designated departure day. Most were orphans like me, bedraggled, worn from being servants and surely not comely enough to think any of us could be brides. Our hair lacked shine above our sallow skin. This was our fate. Among three groups of sisters who clung to one another, I made my place. I glanced at my sailing companions, their eyes, sad with upheavals endured, more stories of displacement and death, revealed slivers of hope barely visible.

I was to marry in my faith which is what my grandparents wanted, what they sacrificed their lives for. The church authorities wanted our beliefs to perish. I was the last link in my family to *Ley de Muysen*, the Laws of Moses. Ah, I sighed, no one to guide me except a stranger who awaited me.

In a small expedition of three ships, ours christened The Isabella for the evil queen who still followed us, we set sail from Recife filled with goods, especially bags and bags of sugar from the New World.

Most adventurers wanted to travel away from tyranny, wars and an iron-handed Catholic Church. Only a few had the desire to leave a continent that promised great wealth for generations to come from nature itself.

There were no other passengers on board save the orphaned brides-to-be, a curious fact because sometimes priests, fortune hunters and slave traders sailed back to Europe, their resources from the New World a valuable commodity. I felt relief no African slaves were among us. Sometimes they were returned to Europe in trade. I could never bear to look into their lost eyes, a reminder of our own bondage in Egypt and those I knew, especially Antiga.

As I surveyed our meager quarters I remembered the warning that in a storm a passenger's belongings might be thrown overboard to lighten the load. I leaned against a wall. Our sad group had nothing, save the clothes on our backs and our chaperone's personal trunk.

The voyage began calmly enough. Each end of the deck was stacked with supplies, barrels of water and logs. On top of it all, tied down, sat numerous cages with exotic blue-tailed parrots, their squawks filling the air, and monkeys, many monkeys, with white faces and miniature pink hands reaching between slats.

The carrack, a long, low ship with three sails, lacked railings in the middle so the sea could sweep across and wash the decks, a preventive measure to keep us from sinking. We huddled together for warmth in the belly of the boat, candlelight illuminating our faces, young, expectant and somewhat fearful of the changes ahead.

Our chaperone, a Senhora Angelina Solomon whose honey-colored hair wound in coils around her head, was sent to shepherd us. With apple cheeks and porcelain skin, she was a large woman with stout hips that quivered when she walked and a tongue that searched for moisture on her lips. Her brother, Senhor Saul Solomon, was one of the bachelors awaiting our arrival.

The Senhora's teachings were knowledgeable and dire. She taught us prayers and rituals, reciting the psalms daily with solid cadence. I began to fill in missing pieces of my education as we rocked and swayed with the ship's movement. She reminded us that the women were the ones to bring the traditions to the family, God willing.

"You must go to the *mikvah* to cleanse yourselves. Wash the utensils you use for cooking, too. And do not stay near your husband when you have your monthly."

I bowed my head in embarrassment as did the others. We had already faced the humiliation of sharing the chamber pot and emptying it over the side of the ship. Who wanted to discuss more personal matters?

The Senhora reviewed holidays and the appropriate foods for festivities with us. She repeated recipes over and over until we memorized them.

"The sauce used for partridges is *almodrote*. Use Cafalan cheese, garlic and fresh eggs. And make sure your birds are well taken care of. Do not allow them to get dirty. Stir everything into a broth and let it simmer on the fire."

I dared to ask a question. "If one cannot find a partridge?"

Senhora Solomon's mouth frowned at my interruption, her tongue darting in and out, yet she answered with patience. "*Volanteria,* any flying bird, will do. Doves, capons, ducks, geese. They need to be slaughtered the proper way. Trim the fat away with your thumbnail like this." She demonstrated and continued, "If you have to make a funeral meal, serve eggs in their shell according to our *kashrut* laws. It means that they have not been contaminated. They symbolize our eternal existence, one the Creator made without beginning or end."

I did not know how I would remember it all, but I knew I wanted to keep the lessons close to my heart. She opened small cloth bags tied with string and passed them around for us to smell. They were spices—mint, rosemary, galingall, cumin, lavender and saffron. I took a deep breath with each one and closed my eyes. The fragrances transported me back to the warmth of *mi abuela's* kitchen, the aroma of her cooking.

"You must grow your own herbs and share them with each other. Holidays will be confraternity events. Make *hamin* for Shabbat with chickpeas and spinach. If you lack the spinach, use cabbage," she told us, her hands checking the pins in her coiled hair.

We learned we could still be harmed for our Judaizing ways because our faith was not sanctioned, even in Amsterdam, a tolerant society.

"Our customs have always made us seem like foreigners. Be careful not to sing under your breath. Some think prayers cross our lips. After the servants clean your oil lamps, do not let them see you put in a new wick two hours before twilight. Hide your olive oil. Christians fry in lard." She gazed down at her skirt as she smoothed the fabric over her corpulent knees. "One can never be too careful." Then she looked up at us, her eyes unyielding.

My head spun like a wheel with information. Often I fell asleep, the ancient knowledge tumbling like bolls of cotton in the wind. The days passed with haste when there was so much to learn. And, I was going to be someone's wife! Who would it would be? Would he care for me? What would he look like? I envisioned myself with fine clothes, satin against my skin, the smell of orange blossoms in my bath. Maybe I would be a woman of substance with servants and a fine husband and beautiful children. A part of me wanted to fulfill my duty of being a wife. Another small fragment wandered to a place of solitude and independence, one where Grazia resided, a woman on her own.

Time floated by studying Senhora's lessons and watching the horizon. We spent hours fixing each other's hair and pinching our cheeks to bring the bloom back.

Near the end of our two-month journey, after we left the coast of India and headed toward the Canary Islands, a terrible squall rocked the boat. The incessant rolling and tossing continued day and night, sliding the benches from one side to another in the cabin. Few of us could climb into our rope hammocks that swung back and forth with the ship's motion.

Before long we had retched our meals in the corners of the room. Worse, we were not steady enough to use chamber pots. The floor became slippery with our waste. The Captain sent someone to check on us but he gasped in repulsion when he opened the door. The horrible stench forced me to keep a handkerchief over my nose and mouth. The sisters clung to one another, wailing to Jesus and Mary to save them. Senhora Solomon hushed them.

Perhaps my previous sea crossing inured me as I did not lose my meals like the others. I was queasy, a strong taste of unwelcome bile reaching the back of my throat, but not ill. I sat on a bench, my feet planted, balancing myself, my hands holding tight as we swayed. Even our steadfast chaperone could not weather this storm. The only one with a bed, she moaned with each wrenching of the ship, the crack of the three-mast sails making her grimace.

When I sensed a lull I made my way to the deck, a pitcher under my arm. I brought the others water from a wooden drum that was nailed down. The rain beat on my face but at least I did not smell the foul air. The monkeys began to scream when they saw me, their red mouths and sharp white teeth gaping in fear, black-brown shiny coats flat with rain. The birds huddled together, their vibrant colors now indistinguishable. I looked out into the grayness, sea and sky blended together. I could not see the other two ships at our side.

My compatriots' parched pale lips slurped water from the ceramic cup that I held. When they finished, their heads fell backward, unsupported by thin necks. Would I be the only survivor? I thought for sure they would die without nourishment. By the third day the captain stopped checking on us or sending any meager supplies.

Another day passed. The Senhora motioned to me. Her bed alone had not shifted, perhaps because of her girth. Even her heavy oak trunk had scraped across the floor to the other side of the room. Her once-coiled hair lay in tangled strings, blanched skin stretched across her cheekbones, damp forehead dripping sweat. I could not hear her whisper and bent closer to the pallet. Her breath was foul with the sea sickness and I recoiled.

"Bellina, this barrage is endless. We must be traveling in circles not to be out of it by now. Bring something for the others. Even if it will not stay down, they must try to eat," her voice a hoarse whisper. "I cannot arrive with dead bodies."

"*Si*, Senhora."

"Be careful on deck. The waves can sweep you away." With effort she lifted her hand and pointed a finger at me, "Tell the Captain he cannot abandon us because we are women."

"Si, Senhora." My angry stomach rumbled. I stood up and prepared to go.

"Bellina," she said through parched and cracked lips, her tongue not able to find moisture. "Of all the girls, you are the brightest, the most capable."

"Thank you, Senhora." I nodded and curtsied out of respect. I wished I had verbena tea for her.

"Never mind thanking me. I see your strength. If I do not complete this journey, my brother, Saul, has been chosen for you." She turned on her side and faced the wall.

"Senhora, you will not die. Everyone feels that way."

"Go, go." She waved me away with her hand.

Starving, I ventured up the stairs holding tight to the ropes. Howls of air greeted me, gusting and whipping my hair. A monster wind ripped at me, trying to pry my hands loose. My fingers gripped against the force, my drenched clothes fluttering like escaping birds, then gluing themselves to my body. The ropes holding the monkeys and parrots whipped in the violent wind, the cages shaking with rage.

The Senhora's words beseeched me to get food for the others, just as Grazia had once done for me. Determined to make my way to the quarterdeck, I held the ropes and rolled with the ship.

The canvas sails with their red crosses billowed and flapped as the masts squealed with pressure. Blinding salt spray burned my eyes; a torrent of rain stung my skin. Tornados of wind jerked the boat and it listed to its side.

I fell and grasped a thick coil of rope, my fingers tensing. The animals' cages shook, their tattered ropes shredding. With a roar they broke loose and the trapped animals were tossed into the sea, their piercing screams gobbled by the wind. I began to sob. What difference would it make if I let go now? The incessant rain soaked past my skin, luring me to loosen my grip. Was there harm in giving up? Sleep was no longer my enemy, but a welcome relief to the pain of hanging on to a rope.

My hands, bleeding, were washed clean, stinging with salt water. My eyes fluttered and images of a warm fragrant bath lured me, clean dry linens stacked beside it. I loosened my fingers.

At this angle I could slip away into the darkness and sleep forever. The long, low sides of the carrack were an invitation to give way, a chance to disappear without a trace of being on this earth. Who would know? Or care?

"Bellina! Bellina!" I lifted my head. Who is calling? Someone wants me. *Mi abulela*? Grazia?

"Yes? Who is it?"

"Bellina."

"Yes, I am here." I turned my rain-soaked face toward the source of the voice. Nothing.

"Bellina, hold tight. Do not let go."

The sound disappeared in the howl of the wind.

I could not give up.

I remained there for an hour or more, forcing myself to stay awake, holding firm with all my might, hiding my head in the crook of my arm.

When the vessel righted itself after what seemed an eternity, I saw one of the masts had fallen, cracking the railing near the top cabin. The sail ballooned and puffed, dragging in the turbid water, crippling the ship. I knew we would all die.

Angry at God's cruelty I pulled myself to my knees. No longer sure-footed on the slippery decks, I crawled, clinging to cables, toward the main cabin.

As I struggled with the door I could see through a rain-smeared window the captain, navigator and six of his sailors poring over a map, leather-bound log books, charts and compasses laid out on a table. With supreme effort against the gale winds I pulled open the door and tumbled inside. It was a few minutes before my crumpled, panting mess was addressed.

"Still here, eh?" the captain said, looking me up and down. Old and wrinkled and burned by the sun, his penetrating eyes were absent of compassion. He wore a big leather belt with a sword at his side and fingerless gloves, his white ruffled collar filthy with wear.

I caught my breath and made my voice loud. "We need food." I straightened to my full height, emboldened, demanding.

"So do we," said a boatswain whose mean mouth and hard eyes frightened me. He glared at me, his stocking cap covering most of his hair hanging in greasy strands.

I lifted my chin. "You must have something we can eat. The girls are starving."

A few of the men laughed. The captain moved away from the maps and came toward me, angry, mouth smirking.

"In case you are unaware, our mast is down and much of our cargo has been ripped away. We have lost the salted cod, flour and olive oil. We have no more food." The captain spit on the floor near my skirt. I backed up, my stomach churning with fear.

"I can think of something else to satisfy my hunger," said the first mate, grinning. A stringy beard surrounded his brown, rotted teeth and bleeding gums. Sores on his skin were probably from the sailor's disease that so many had. He lurched across the room and pressed himself onto me, his unwashed odor making me gag.

The others in the room laughed and snarled, vicious dogs at prey. One of them took off his neckerchief and wiped drool from his mouth. For the first time I noticed young boys in the back, Indian slaves kidnapped from Brazil, their dark faces devoid of expression, black bangs covering their eyes.

"No food and Pablo only thinks of his other hungers," said another deckhand with huge, brawny fists. He opened and closed them while a few laughed.

Their amusement infuriated me and I pushed at him with my ripped, trembling hands. My efforts were futile. He grabbed my wrists, nails poking my skin, and pinned them to my side, his knee dividing my skirts. I felt his wet mouth grapple at my lips, his tongue probing like a wretched worm. When I turned my head to the side he lunged at my neck biting me so hard I screamed. The men guffawed, elbowing each other.

"Help me with this one. She's the beauty of the lot. The rest are miserable wenches." He turned my chin with two dirty fingers. "She has the eyes of a pirate's emeralds."

"Yes," chimed in the one with the huge hands. "Let us get the rest of the bitches."

"No!" I screamed this with such force my heart pounded wildly. Involuntary tears streamed down my face, thinking about the poor weak souls in the hull of the ship.

"What? A volunteer to save the others? Hah! Someone trying to get into heaven," said my tormentor.

"*Shema Yisroel*," I said with a murmur, moving my head from side-to-side, trying to shake his odor away from me.

"An excellent idea. We can all have her and leave the others alone." He breathed into my face. "A damned martyr."

Suddenly, he gave a violent pull at my skirts. The top layers ripped away like paper to one thin cotton slip and my underclothes. I trembled, chicken bumps covering my body. I bit my lip and tasted blood.

I thought all was lost, but the God who created the storms also created a saving wave. A surge of colossal proportions rolled the ship with such enormous intensity that the boatswain ripped away from me, slamming into the wall and crashing onto the floor, crying out, writhing in pain. His leg and knee twisted at an awkward angle, a tree branch struck by lightning.

Heaving to catch my breath, rage seethed through me. The captain squinted, glancing at the wicked man on the floor, announcing a diagnosis, "Broken."

He stared at me, a thumb motioning in my tormentor's direction. "Will bother you no more. Go back to your cabin. I will send a bit of food I have stashed, though it may be moldy." Then he turned away to the others watching in horror. "Here, help me get him up on the table. Told you not to mess with them Jew bitches. Known to have powers."

I bent down and grabbed my torn skirts, making my way on the slippery decks covered with sea salt. The storm had eased and a bleak charcoal sky appeared. Again, I saw no sign of the other ships.

Before I reached our room I heard wailing. My heart pounded. I forgot about the aching bite on my neck and ran the rest of the way, bursting through the door. The girls were gathered around the Senhora's bed, some with their hands covering their faces, a few saying Hail Mary's, others banging their heads against the wall muttering the *kaddish*.

When they saw me, they looked up, cries interrupted. "She's dead, she's dead. She began to choke and now she's dead. What will become of us? Oh God in Heaven, why is our fate to be abandoned in a cruel world?" It was hard to think in the confusion. Did she die because I left our quarters? Was it my fault?

"What happened to your skirts?" asked a petite one with agate black eyes.

"It is not your concern."

I knew we had to take care of the body. "We must wash and wrap her in white cloth. Take the bed coverings. Then we will say prayers and bury her at sea. Jewish law says she cannot remain this way."

Food soon arrived in an old basket. I cajoled the sailor to help us move the Senhora to the deck for she was heavy and we could not do it alone. He watched me with suspicion but returned with a few others who kept their eyes cast downward, no doubt afraid of my powers. We rolled her wrapped body onto a piece of canvas sail and lifted her to the top deck.

Afterward, as we watched the white caps envelop the Senhora, I stood with the others remembering her orders to breathe and fill our lungs. We went below in silence. There was not much appetite for our meal of moldy ship biscuits, almonds, a small piece of mutton and wine. No one touched the bit of bacon.

After a brief stop in shallow waters close to an island coast we waited while repairs were done to the broken mast by the enslaved Indians. I could not watch as they climbed high into the bird's nest to steady it. I followed seagulls circling overhead as phosphorous fish swam the waters. Fortunately, some of the sailors caught fish for us that we prepared over a small fire with the Senhora's spices.

In the next few days we approached another shore in the distance. We had divided the Senhora's clothes among us and although it was too big for me, I wore her skirt of black velvet and a silk shawl covering my shoulders.

The others said I should have it because I had saved them. I protested but in the end took it. I liked fine things. I held my family's precious candlesticks and prayer book in a basket over my arm.

As the ship got closer a group of men came into view. I stood proud, my spine straight with determination, remembering my grandmother's words of faith. My sea-sisters had elected me to speak for them. I had to tell the Senhora's brother of her death.

We disembarked, as the group of men stood by, surveying us. The tallest, dressed in a silk coat, gold buttons gleaming in the light, and wearing a white ruffled collar and top hat, came toward me. He had a short beard and kind, welcoming eyes as he reached out his hands.

"Welcome to Amsterdam. I am Saul Solomon and you are to be mine."

Chapter 30

Alegra

Granada, Spain
June 5, 1999

I am marrying the Professor tomorrow, a June bride with a happy ending just like my corny *telenovela*. My future starts with a man who loves me, a deep soul connection that makes me feel whole. With intelligence and kindness he's transported me to where I must have come from, partly by reading his novel. I love Grazia and Bellina. They're my emotional release.

I'm vulnerable in love and inept at explaining my emotions, afraid my fragile heart might break. At first, I hesitated to confess how I felt to him. After a solid evaluation of my options, *Mama always said fall in love with your heart and your head*, I have made a decision.

Harold Guzman and I can make a life together, one where we exchange ideas, explore new places and share companionship. I love him. Even if he does drive me crazy with snoring so loud it threatens to shake loose ceiling plaster. Okay, I exaggerate a bit. You would, too, if you had to survive sisters like mine.

Hal's older and grumpier, with unkempt ways, but he's the most endearing and stimulating man I've ever met. A romantic, too. I've never fascinated any man.

He watches me take a bath in the evening, sitting on the edge of the tub as my breasts float in the water, singing pieces of operas and reading revised parts of his novel to me. He tells me he's smitten with me, a dated term at best as I drift in the water happy, very happy.

The day of the big event I wake up nervous and bloated. What if I'm too chubby to fit into my white lace dress? I touch my top lip and feel fine down. Will it cast a shadow in the photos? Damn! My sisters would kill me. I should have taken care of this at a waxing place and started a diet two months ago. I throw off the covers and step onto the cold tile floor of the bathroom to peer in the mirror. I know who can help me in my dilemma. I head for the kitchen.

Manuelita, our occasional housekeeper, follows my hand motions when I point to my top lip. I speak Spanglish and can't think of a word for depilatory. With an aha she leaves for a few minutes and returns with a teaspoonful of white cream that she places in a piece of tin foil.

I spread it generously on my lip. She holds up ten fingers and points to the clock. I nod. I go back to the bathroom to sit on the toilet seat and wait, glancing at my watch every thirty seconds.

When it begins to sting after five minutes I rush to the sink, wait for the hot water to choke itself through the pipes and wash it off, expecting to see a hairless top lip. Instead, small berry-red pimples have erupted. "No," I wail.

I'm finally getting married at thirty-five and the area above my mouth looks like a baboon's ass. Or is it a mandrill? I melt into a sobbing heap, prostrate on the bathroom floor. "I can't get married today. A bride with pustules?" I let out a God-awful sound and curl into a ball.

Manuelita does her best to comfort me by offering me another cream, but I shake my head no. She disappears. I pull myself up and re-examine my lip in the silver-framed mirror. My fuchsia duck-lip sends me into another spasm of sobs. Hal hustles up the hallway, slippers slapping the floor.

"What's all the commotion? Why is my beautiful bride upset?" I lock the door. He cannot see me like this.

Through the door I hear Manuelita return, bargaining with the Professor to leave me alone. She placates him enough so that he shuffles away mumbling about jittery brides and nonsense. She bangs on the door with her fist.

"I am not coming out," I shout, hanging my head. What am I going to do? Manuelita continues to pound the door with the heel of her hand. I glance in the mirror again, shrieking in horror.

"Señorita, Señorita, I can solve *su problema.*"

"Really?" I say with sarcasm, sliding myself back onto the floor, leaning against the cabinets.

"*Si, abre la puerta.*"

I brush tears away with the back of my hand, pulling myself upright by way of the sink. I stare in the mirror again, hoping this nightmare will have disappeared. I touch the puffy places with my index finger. It's worse. My lip has erupted in little purple pustules. I agonize, renewing my cries with the thought of my sister, Marta, yelling at me about not spending my special day at a spa.

"Señorita." Manuelita knocks harder.

"No Professor?" I ask.

"No, Señorita Alegra. No señor."

I open the door a crack. Her upturned palm holds two flesh-colored band-aids.

We marry in Judge Rinaldo Reyes cluttered office. He's a short man with oily black hair combed back from his forehead, squinty eyes and a pronounced Castilian lisp. He wears a caca brown suit and a fancy silk-striped tie.

After brief introductions, the judge motions us through a doorway to his wife and daughter who are to be our witnesses. They appear in modest dresses and nod to us. My heart begins to jack-hammer. This is it.

It's warm and the overhead fan doesn't give much of a breeze. The judge removes his jacket, and instead of putting it over the back of his desk chair, he swings it around, resting it on his shoulders like a cape.

Hal shifts nervously beside me. He grabs my hand and it's damp. The judge picks up his official book and begins to recite our vows in heavily-accented English. I am being married by a short, squinty man with a lisp who is dressed like Dracula.

In moments the ceremony is over. I am Mrs. Harold Guzman. Mama would be happy for me. Hal pulls me toward him, kissing me with vigor and enthusiasm, wrapping me tightly in his arms. Self-conscious with witnesses staring, I don't linger. When we pull apart Hal is smiling with one of my band-aids dangling from his chin.

After a brief taxi ride we cuddle on a train ride to Marbella, a coastal city filled with the fragrance of jasmine. We check into our suite at the Oro Hotel off the Plaza de Naranjas. I collapse onto the bed with its peach duvet and lots of floral pillows. The room is sexy and quiet and I'm very happy. I touch my swollen lip. Thank Goodness it's receding.

I relish the luxury of a big marble tub every evening, sleeping late toward the noon hour in the morning. We breakfast on the terrace overlooking the square, an array of fresh oranges and pineapples, warm baguettes, jellies and aromatic coffee delighting our senses.

I love people watching. Seniors envelop each other's arms while teen girls rush by them in short skirts, the eyes of swaggering men shifting toward them. Mothers push baby strollers, sunlight shielded from their babies' faces with diminutive hats. I throw my head back and let the sun wash my face.

We sightsee daily during our five day respite. My favorite excursion is to Cuevas de Nerja where huge caves are covered with stalactites and stalagmites. We arrive there by bouncing on an old bus filled with tourists and locals. A solemn, wrinkled woman sits across from me with a dead chicken, its pink-purple feet sticking out of newspaper.

During our long descent into the belly of the mountain, down dark stairs with rock-cold walls, the temperature drops and I shiver, pulling my sweater close to me. Dramatic lighting casts shadows as Star Wars music reaches a crescendo. It's commercial but I love it, especially the end when we reach the Hall of the Cataclysm, with the largest stalactite column in the world. I giggle to myself about the cataclysms we've been creating.

A frazzled mother with three children clinging to her reads from a guidebook. "It took one trillion drops of moisture to make this. Isn't that interesting?" Her kids aren't listening. The two girls hit each other and the boy picks a scab on his knee until it bleeds. He complains, pointing to the dribble of red sliding down his leg.

I turn away. This huge column evokes something in me. Prickly bumps spread across my body. I can't believe it. I'm a hot, turned-on maniac in Birkenstocks. I touch my neck and it's warm. Hal is fascinated with the enormity of the phallic structure, too, straining his neck to take it all in. I can't wait to get him back to the room and into bed. My sisters would be proud of me. I have lost all inhibitions and represent a newer, more mature version of Madonna.

But our bliss is marred on day four. As I learn later, most honeymooners have a fight. After a late breakfast on the terrace, a morning of lovemaking, a stroll to the Cortijo de Miraflores, an old sugar mill renovated into a museum, a nap and a late seafood dinner on the docks, I feel content and satiated.

I'm sitting up in bed, Hal's manuscript on my lap. Sighing with satisfaction I read a few more pages, but then throw down the manuscript. "OhmiGod! Bellina's marrying a stranger? Where's her spunk? Don't you think the romance should have been with Senhora Olivia's son?" Men know nothing about women.

Hal comes out of the bathroom with a towel wrapped around his waist and another draped around his neck. "That's what they did in those days. You know that. Women didn't have choices. And, if I don't build some tension in the novel it'll be boring." He pats his face with the damp towel and drops it on the bed.

Hal's oblivious to my concern about the spread. I kick the towel to the floor with my foot, sputtering, "Her family's gone, Grazia abandoned her. Either have her find true love or go out on her own." I emphasize this by clutching the manuscript to my chest, adjusting my white cotton gown to cover my legs. I am no longer feeling sexy.

"Alegra, you're such a romantic. Some people marry for love and then divorce a few years later. What happened to the passion? Orthodox Jews and Indian families pick spouses for their children. It's a much better system," he says with finality, heading back to the bathroom.

"Do you think my mother would've picked you for me?" I call after him.

He returns with his toothbrush and mumbles a garbled response. "She would've loved me." He puffs himself up a bit, smoothing his chest with his free hand, his belly no longer sucked in.

"She would have been impressed with your intellect," I say under my breath, "but she would have been really annoyed with your grumpiness and chauvinism," I announce with clarity.

He removes the toothbrush from his mouth and white spittle covers his lips. "Me, grumpy? A chauvinist? I've championed women's rights for years. Well, the intelligent ones who were capable of research."

"That's exactly what I'm talking about. You don't think I'm your equal. You're impossible." I slam the papers on the bed and fold my arms across my chest.

There's silence as he stares at me like I'm an alien, then dismisses me with a wave and heads back to the bathroom. I hear water and know he's rinsing his mouth. He returns and points his index finger at me.

"I'm difficult? Have you looked at yourself? You've had one weird mood swing after another."

His words sting me. I jut out my chin to announce, "Any woman with eggplant-sized pimples on her top lip the day of her wedding knows that's a reason for hysteria. Ask anyone." Then I begin to blubber. I never should have married him. I never should've married anyone. I'd be better off alone.

Hal comes over and sits on the bed next to me, stroking my arm. "I married you because I thought you'd be reasonable. Not like all those other silly women." He pulls my hands away from my face and hands me a tissue.

I blow my nose, snorting inadvertently, and then giggle a bit. "Marta hates when I do that."

"I can't wait to meet your wicked sisters when we return to Miami." He dries my tears with a swipe of his thumb. "Come on, Alegra, I love you. I'm not that bad, am I?" He gives me a sly grin.

"You're mean and impossible and—" I've run out of words. I breathe a sigh of relief. "I think you're a lovable teddy bear." But of course, I'm not finished and neither is he.

"Now. Back to the book. What are you going to do with Bellina? Grazia's disappeared into the jungle. Will we hear from her again?" I'm annoyed at this turn of events for two women whose lives are tied to mine.

He sighs, pauses for a moment and reaches into his bathrobe pocket. He is ignoring my concerns. "Close your eyes. I have something for you."

When I open my eyes a sparkling diamond Star of David appears on a white gold chain resting in the palm of his hand. "Oooh, for me?" I'm surprised and awed.

"Who else? A wedding present."

Suddenly, my heart falls. "But I'm not really a Jew. Can I still wear it?"

"Watch," he says. He gives the top of the star a tug and it falls away. In a split second it has become what looks like six connected miniature butterflies. I don't know what to say. I am touched by his sweetness and the significance of the gift. He pushes them together and they become a star again. He repeats it a few times until I can see how he is doing it.

"Where did you find such a magical piece of jewelry?"

"I had it replicated from an articulated design used by the *conversos*. The women wore the star under their clothes near their heart and could turn it into butterflies for safety. They risked themselves everyday to stay true."

I pull myself forward and kiss him on the lips. "I love it and you. It's beautiful. Thank you."

"Stand up," he says, taking the star from me. He turns me around by my shoulders, closing the clasp around my neck. The butterflies nestle on my chest.

I turn to face him. He draws me close and strokes my hair. We embrace and I feel something hard against my leg. He whispers, "In the meantime, don't forget to Google 16th century Amsterdam."

Chapter Thirty-one

Bellina

1 Elul 5284, (10 August 1524)
Amsterdam, Netherlands

My fate changed as I set foot on the dock. No longer a servant I was the bride-to-be of a successful man. The rush of being readied by others in the congregation for marriage remains hazy. I remember the buzz of brides, murmurs of excitement, trembling hands, the scent of flower blossoms and perfumes.

Still, there must have been something I missed, a time where I thought for a moment, will I be happy? Will he love me? Will I always feel so alone? It may have scattered across my mind, fluffs of dandelion in a breeze, but I did not dwell on it for very long. I wished Grazia to be by my side.

Not only was I to be a married woman with all the privileges it endowed but a piece of my soul would find a home. Saul, a large man, broad-shouldered like his sister, may she rest in peace, was chosen for me. Kind and pleasant-faced with fawn eyes, he looked at me with love and tolerance of my endurances. Holding my face in his hands, he whispered, "Tell me, Bellina, tell me."

At first I shook my head, unwilling to give up secrets embedded in the dark reaches of my mind. Later, I told him vignettes of my life, scraps of memory, nightmares that coerced me to call out in my sleep.

I described the force of the Church and how it destroyed us, the cruel priests and the *auto-de-fe's*, our countrymen who turned against us and even Jews who sealed our fate with betrayal. My tales tumbled forth until I sobbed and could not speak. My tears could fill a sea.

Maybe that is what God had in mind. Can He see what has happened to His people who are flung to so many shores? My circumstances whirled by me, my powerlessness, my inability to control my fate. Slices of my odyssey spilled out–the blood and stew on Antiga's floor, the abandonment of Grazia, ships filled with sickness, and most of all, the deaths of my grandparents who haunted me.

I had shoved the memory of that day in the Lisbon courtyard to the far reaches of my mind. If it struggled to be heard, I pushed it farther away. But I could not keep it submerged forever. The heat and hunger, people with their packages and belongings, waiting, hoping they could leave. Their sounds pierced the air--cries, prayers, the haranguing of the heretics, a lonely violin solo. And my grandmother, that moment in time where she reached toward *mi abuelo* in response to his shouts, the clashing of swords, the aggression of metal against metal, and the moans of those nearby. Above it all, *mi abuela's* shrieks, her committed bravery to slit her own throat, blood painting her chest crimson.

Selfish, yes, to leave us alone, yet acceptable to release her from more torment. My grandparents loved each other and stayed connected through God until the end. The deaths of my grandparents flung me into an uncertain world. The warmth of their kitchen, the cooking aromas, the Sabbath candles stay with me, bring me comfort. I vow to create cherished memories for my own.

After the wrenching of these stories, Saul would hold me, stroking my hair and take me to him.

My children were born from this weeping. The first to arrive was a little boy I named Hermando after my grandfather. My joy was incomprehensible. Motherhood made evil memories fade, a ship disappearing in the horizon. Our second, a girl I named Hanna, after the mother I never knew, had green eyes like mine. I loved them beyond all expression. This became the family I lost.

Our community of *conversos* became cousins to me. We shared recipes, books, thoughts and prayers. In that comfort I conceived again and again, only losing one to the influenza. I could not mourn for long. We are now a family of eight, four girls and two boys, the second girl named Estrella after her grandmother.

Saul has been good to me with his powerful way of expressing himself, words flowing together like poems. Only he can lift me from my melancholia. He brings tulips to cheer me, their throats blushed with pink. He knows my appreciation of beauty. And, although he travels often to expand commerce with other converso merchants in places as far flung as Italy and India, he always returns to see me and ours with joy.

My life among the Hollanders has been a beginning, all previous events another journey where I felt diminished, lost, subject to the whims of others. Now, as a wife and mother, a person of importance married to a prosperous diamond merchant, I have a sense of dignity.

It is not just the silks and taffeta I wear, which I know to be far superior then the Senhora's; it is much more than that. I feel the calmness of a glassy sea, predictable, relieving sameness of religious ritual that takes me back to our ancient culture in Spain. I feel free to learn, encouraged by my husband. I keep a journal and write my thoughts daily.

Sometimes I write letters to Grazia that will never be sent, angry tomes about her abandonment. However, by the end of each entry I am grateful. After all, if she had not left would I have returned to the continent? I might have remained a servant on a sugar plantation in Brazil, willing to forego a future rather than leave my only relative.

I feel God's good guidance in my choices as though He has empowered me with delicious rewards. I know this when my Saul whispers words of adoration, as I brush my lips across my children's cheeks and I see their innocent faces illuminated in the Sabbath candles.

My feelings about Amsterdam are profound. I am safe, finally. Although accepted by the liberal people of the Netherlands, we do not flaunt our faith. Our distrust of others who have betrayed us does not allow us to be careless. Our Judaism is private and fulfilling. I belong.

Secretly, I finger the necklace Saul presented to me on our wedding day. It is a Star of David on a platinum chain set with faceted, colorless diamonds that remains hidden under my clothes, cool against my collarbone. And, as a reminder of our trials, it can be changed in an instant with a press of my finger to fall away and become miniature butterflies that float across my chest. It is an exquisite piece that reminds me where I have come from, what I have endured.

It is in this state of glory that I receive an unexpected letter that rocks me from my foundation.

Chapter Thirty-two

Bellina

21 Elul 5284 (30 August 1524)
Amsterdam

An envelope arrived, one made from rough paper stock, and I recognized the familiar hand of my aunt. I settled into my husband's comfortable velvet chair with carved legs and arms. The fire cast lingering shadows on the cool gray walls. My hands trembled as I broke the blue seal with my thumbnail. The letter slid out and I smoothed the folds of paper on my lap.

Pesach, 5282 (Passover, 1522)
Recife, Brazil

My dearest Bellina, daughter of my beloved sister, Hanna,
I think of you at this time because of the seders in our
home, hidden from the world, reciting God's blessings, a
celebration of freedom. When it was Purim few weeks ago,
a time of joy, I remembered how God's mercy saved us from
wicked Haman, the prime minister who planned to destroy
all the Jews on the thirteenth of Adar. The precious memories
of our family at the time of the festivals give me comfort.
From my lovely finca by the sea I write this, one of many
letters I have composed, some only in my head. I have felt
guilt at the way I departed from you almost twelve years ago
and ask your forgiveness. I hope this letter finds you with
ease and before more seasons have passed. It has traveled
through many hands to reach your community. If it does
it is only because of reliable missionaries who have offered
assistance. Some missives I fear, though sent, may languish
at the bottom of the sea. Others I did not have the courage to

send.

    I am well. In the beginning Rupert and I had many chal-
lenges as we made our way to freedom. I became schooled in
the ways of survival. Without machetes to clear our path it
would have been an impossible journey. The jungle can be an
inhospitable place. Spiders the size of plates and miniscule
bugs gnawed my skin raw as I stomped through mangrove
swamps. My arms and face were scratched by branches and
hanging vines, their thorns a special torture. We lost some
in our party of ten. Our numbers shrank and grew as we
received help from the native peoples who joined us along
the way. Without their knowledge of our path we would have
perished.

    Between the thick foliage and savannas there are vil-
lages, unseen by anyone. Although they risked their well-
being because of hatred for the Europeans, I was shocked by
women who wore no covering, striding with nursing young
at their breasts, bared for all to see. The leaders showed us
exotic fruits and nuts we could eat and the places to sleep.
The safest spot was in a tree trunk after it had been checked
for snakes. Cats and monkeys dwelled in the upper branches
of the trees shading the jungle floor. Also, I saw a creature
covered in hair that hung upside down clinging to branches
with its claws.

Snakes? The squirming hideous creatures were sometimes caught and
their skins displayed on the plantation, but the thought of Grazia near them
shocked me. I reached for a glass of port next to me. The sweet liquid bathed
my mouth, giving me courage to continue.

    I was struck by colors and sounds in a world that I had
only peered into from the edges. The verdant forest was a
wonderment with its myriad of greens, leaves as big as my
body, flowers that defy description. Sounds echoed around

*me. Did you know monkeys have a language? That birds con-
verse with one another? That they compete for attention? Yet
sometimes it was so silent I could hear my heart beating.*

*The dangers were many. Escobar, a cousin of Rupert's, was
mauled by a large cat, sleek and shiny black as he. We left his
scarred, bloody body and ran for our lives. A tribesman with
muddied hair who helped us drink water from giant leaves
was squeezed to death by a snake the size of a tree trunk. I
felt terrified much of the time, but with all that our family
has endured, my will to live was strong. Rupert had me in
his grip.*

*When we first made our way out of the jungle to the shore,
relief flowed over me. I know I must have been unrecognizable as a woman with Rupert's flour sack pants and my hair
shorn from matting. The Hollanders were kind to us. No one
asked for identification papers or a certificate of marriage.
I must tell you immediately, may Papa's soul rest in peace,
I saw to a marriage contract. Later, a transient rabbi who
came to help the many conversos who had settled nearby,
blessed us. There is a strong spirit of community here as we
work hard to carve a life from the resources around us.*

*At first it was awkward, a white woman and an African,
but today as I watch our three beautiful children playing in
the wild pampas, shrieks of laughter sailing in the wind, I
know that mi madre would be proud.*

Proud? My grandmother would be horrified and my grandfather would
have disowned her. Ah, but did it make a difference? It was a new world
where we must search for the truth and protect those we love. I am resigned
as I read on.

*One, my eldest, Estrella, named after Mama, has the green
eyes of clear waters and skin the color of cocoa. She reminds
me of your comely face, the way you looked at me, quizzical,*

yet trusting. My middle child, Leah, is a robust girl, dark as ebony with the long legs of a runner. My last, a son, Hermando, thrills us with pleasure every day as he lurches forward and backward on the new legs of a baby. His cinnamon face is so like his Papa's. It was late to start a family so I am grateful to God in the Highest that he has blessed me with such good fortune. You will be pleased to know I will school them in our faith as our mothers have done before us.

But I get ahead of myself. It took me many years to follow your trail and only with the help of Rupert's mother, Antiga, who remained in the employ of the Palumbo family due to her exceptional culinary skills, was I able to find you. She has passed in recent time, but not before she assisted us in tracing your steps.

Are you well? The Senhora, may she burn in hell with her elegant ways, said you were lost at sea on a boat to Amsterdam. It took time to learn the truth.

It was quite by accident I met a family of Hollanders who traveled to our shores. They spoke of a Senhora Bellina, one of the most beautiful women in the Netherlands, who started a school of Hebraic studies. To my delight I learned you are a respectable married woman with children of your own. I wish you well, my sweet Bellina. I pray you have found solace from our tumultuous lives.

I, too, am at peace, although we still live in fear of the long arm of Torquemada and his Inquisition. They search in Mexico and Peru, but here a flash of the machete keeps most at bay.

I do not flaunt my beliefs. In secret we light the candles for the Sabbath bride and say the shema. I close my eyes and beckon the evening, the vision of our life in Spain but a sad memory. Tomorrow we will celebrate our passage from Egypt for Pesach. Matzo is baking in a community oven as I write this missive. This festival, in particular, has great meaning for me. Freedom from oppression drove me to this place.

As for Rupert, he started on the docks, his strong shoulders

*lifting and baling. With his stalwart will and roped back he
soon became a leader. He traded his sweat for a small piece of
property on the northeast coast. Land thick with brazilwood
trees is the source of red dye so popular with the Europeans.*

*Remember how Papa taught me everything about textiles?
At first my sewing skills were in demand but soon I became a
merchant, dying bolts of cloth pigeon blood, crimson and pale
rose. I mixed colors with insects and leaves, traded reds for
blues, made purples that drove people wild with envy until
they lined up waiting to buy my goods.*

*Rupert is a hard worker and with his cadre of African
friends he manufactured more, traded for goods we needed,
bought additional land and built us a home. He is not the
slave you once knew. His raw intelligence thinks ahead of
what will be desired next. Today others work for us farm-
ing, making dyes, cutting cloth, everything a new frontier
expects. They toil for hours, anxious to trade earnings for
knives, tools, any metal object of value.*

*Papa would be impressed to see his Grazia dealing with
tradesmen and Mama would be proud of my finery. I even
replicated her beautiful velvet cape and trimmed it with
the plumage of exotic birds. Some of my travails may have
coarsened me, but in this world I am viewed as a lady.*

*My head is filled with so many thoughts. If you were next
to me—-ah, how I treasure the moments we clung together
whispering words of encouragement--there would be much to
talk about, but in a letter I must reveal myself.*

*I have harbored a secret for many years, believing it was
for the best, taught that way by my parents. Also, my loyalty
to those who brought me into this world deserved respect. But
in this New World old rules are expendable.*

*A woman's shame mars a whole family. Your mother, my
sister Hanna, did not die in childbirth. I do not know if she
is alive, but when I last saw her she resided in the Convento*

*de San Francisco in Granada where Papa banished her
for having you without the benefit of marriage. The sisters
required a dowry for her as the bride of Christ and father
cursed as he paid it.*

    *I believe Mama would have come back for my sister and
your mother if it had not been for the expulsion. But alas,
she could only save you. And what a tale that was. I watched
Papa almost drop your tiny wriggling red body into the sea
with waves crashing as loud as Mama's sobs.*

    *My complicity in all this has washed me with guilt. At
first, I could not say anything. Later, what difference did it
serve? But, now, with a family of your own, there lies the
chance to touch your mother.*

    *Please do not despair over your illegitimacy. It is not im-
portant. You are alive for a reason, a light of our faith. Find
your mother, dear one. Hurry. Meet her soon. If she is alive,
many years have passed for her. Let her know that her blood
lives on, albeit in children who do not know her. Search, Bellina. Know my sister, a sweet beauty whose raging passion
took her from us.*

    *I fear I will not see you again in this life. We are separated
by continents and oceans but perhaps we might communi-
cate with one another. I bless you, love you and wish you
well. I am happy as I sit in my atrium filled with tropical
flowers in a myriad of colors and tiny white birds whose
wings hum in constant motion. We are all children of God.*

    With My Sincerest Kindness,
    Your Loving Aunt Grazia

I could not speak. One hand covered my pounding heart and the other
lifted the port to my lips.

Chapter
Thirty-three

Alegra

November 3, 2000

The past year seems like a dream. I have returned as a married woman to Florida. With Hal's year of sabbatical behind us, an almost-finished novel in his briefcase and a wedding band on both of our fingers, I feel a sense of accomplishment. I'm thrilled with my happy ending. I never expected to find love at that job interview. Was it just over a year ago? I thought my dreary life with a mama's boy was destined to take me into old age. Now my future expands every day.

Yes, I realize I've walked away from my freedom, one that's sometimes interrupted by a crusty professor, but it's worth it. He makes me laugh. Hal has given me more than I left with—a history, a tradition, a sense of place and time, a spiritual grounding. And he loves me. I feel like my thirsty roots have been saturated with water.

After selling Mama's house and Hal's condo, which was easier than trying to fix it up, we've settled into a home in Coral Gables built in the 1950s close to the university.

Winding streets and lush foliage seem sleepy compared to the hustle of Eighth Street and Miami or Coconut Grove and its hoards of tourists. Our pink cottage on Majorca sits back from the street surrounded by golden-flowering hibiscus hedges and shaded by giant banyans whose toes break through green Saint Augustine grass. Inside, it's light and less cluttered than either of us have ever lived. We've replaced carpeting with white tile and hung framed watercolors from the market in Granada.

When Hal's busy I work in the garden, read, listen to music. I need time to think about who came before me, my parent's life in Cuba, their parents and those before them--where they all came from, what their exile was like from Spain and Portugal. No matter what, their blood courses through me, even if I don't know their names.

Were they resolute in their beliefs? Or did they convert and give up like many others? Sarah Aroeste and her *Ladino* poems sing to me as I work in my garden out back. I grow tomatoes, scallions, squash and lettuce to harvest for our Friday night dinners.

I think about Grazia, Bellina and their families. Would Grazia have been content to stay at home following the traditional life? Recently we started to invite other professors, some graduate students and a few neighbors to join us for shabbat.

As a professor's wife I have class privileges, an esteemed member of the university community. I'm auditing European history and English Lit so I can catch up to my smart husband. I hustle across campus, textbooks in hand, a bit nervous at being an older student, but thrilled to sit among the others and proud to be learning.

Even Irma, my glamour-puss sister and Marta, my hypochondriac one, are impressed with my new status. Irma, a recent redhead, is dating a seventy-year-old retired doctor. They play tennis every day and he's even letting her decorate his Miami Beach condo in an African motif. She's great at spending other people's money, but I wonder what he thinks about the zebra drapes and leopard rugs. Butter, my former cat, has abandoned me for a tiger-striped chair.

Of course Marta has another incurable illness, a lethal strain of Lyme disease. "Alegra, I have so many symptoms I can't even get out of bed in the morning." She pants, "I can hardly breathe."

"Do your joints ache?" I ask. This is the first time she's had a disease that didn't start with an A.

"Ay, I have that, too. I'm so weak I cannot put on make-up. But the good news is Sammy is going to start a business." She fans herself with a plastic surgery brochure.

"Really? What?"

"Dog obedience classes."

I laugh out loud. Heaven help us. I bless their vicious dog that started me on this journey.

Mostly my sisters leave me alone. It's friendly when we get together because Hal is a novelty. They stare at him when he expounds on ancient armor as though they've never been with someone brilliant.

I've been reading the Old Testament. The first commandment states, "Thou shall have no other gods before me." It resonates, an endless echo. That statement separated and caused cruelty to a group of people, allowing others to be dictators of our faith. I suppose I'll never have all my questions answered but the exploration intrigues and encourages me.

With tears in my eyes this Friday night, I acknowledge all the women who whispered a prayer, lit a candle, spoke a Hebrew name through thousands of years. What strength did it take for them not to accept the Father, the Son and the Holy Ghost? I feel connected to those who suffered, were betrayed by others, burned alive, tortured because they would not give in. These prayers are for them.

Hal and I light candles and say the blessings over the bread and the wine, looking into each other's eyes. I sip red wine and tear off a piece of *challah* for us to share.

When I put my glass down, Hal kisses me on the cheek and picks up my hands, beaming, "*Shabbat shalom.* I am so proud of you and your efforts to reclaim your rich heritage."

I beam at him, lowering my eyes, self-conscious with his compliment. When I look up, I say, "Thank you. I'm grateful for you. And the adventures to come. I am only sorry we didn't meet sooner in our lives and shared more, maybe had a family."

He's silent for a few minutes. Clearing his throat he asks, "Have you ever thought about children?"

I can't respond and look away as I swallow. It's something I had ruminated about as the years passed and Saul never asked me to marry him. Eventually, I learned to accept reality. I wasn't going to do it on my own without the benefit of a committed partner.

Suddenly, I get an uneasy feeling. How odd that we haven't discussed this in our four months of marriage. I dismiss it with a slight shrug. After all, he's been a somewhat crotchety bachelor of fifty. Diapers and crying? I'm too old for such adventures. We both look away.

With oven mitts I bring a brisket smothered in onions and mushrooms to the oval table in the dining room. The aroma of its juices makes my mouth water. There's a steaming bowl of fresh vegetables from our garden on the table. We sit down to start our meal. For a few minutes it's only the sounds of utensils against the plates.

"Well?" he asks me, expectant, his last question still hanging in the air.

I don't know what to say. Finally, I respond before I pick up my fork, looking him square in the eyes. "I let the idea go when I turned thirty." Hal gazes at me, his hazel eyes watery.

"Would you like to think about it now?"

My eyebrows shoot up. "What? You'd consider children? Really? Noisy kids?" He looks at me quizzically and I soften even more. My voice sounds mushy. "Messy, wonderful babies?"

Hal takes a sip of wine and smiles. He adjusts his glasses on to his nose and clears his throat. "Now let's not get carried away. Maybe one and then we can negotiate."

I am so excited I can hardly speak. With shaking hands I push back my chair. It scrapes against the ceramic tile as I leap up to throw my arms around Hal almost knocking off his glasses. My face is an inch from his. "You're serious? You'll make a baby with me?" I rub his neck and kiss his head leaving a trace of lipstick.

Hal grumbles a bit. "We have plenty of time for monkey business. Sit down and finish your meal. This is a perfectly good brisket." Then he gives me a dreamy look. "We're going to be very busy working on our new project together."

Chapter Thirty-four

Bellina

21 Elul 5284 (30 August 1524)

Shards of sealing wax dropped from Grazia's letter as it fell from my hands. My mother alive? How could that be? I was thirty-five years of age so she would be fifty, an old woman. Had she survived?

My initial shock turned to dismay. My grandparents and Grazia were complicit in a lie, weaving sad yet delightful stories about a lovely young woman and her grief-stricken husband. And none of it was true. Anger simmered and boiled inside of me for days until it became a tempest, the untruths echoing in snatches of conversations. I could not sleep and instead paced for hours. In daylight my fury twisted my emotions. Finally, tears came.

The guilt I felt for so long–that I was the cause of my mother's death—washed away. Over and over I repeated, she did not die because of me, she did not die. My vision of her passing with loving souls wishing her to the angels became a private nightmare. She had done the unthinkable and the family conspired not to tell me, including Grazia who had been my most intimate confidant.

I stayed in bed for days and finally, after a week, sat staring into the fireplace ravaged by my thoughts. She had done a common thing, pregnant without the blessing of marriage. A whore!

What did that make me? A woman without proper parentage. Would it matter to my husband that I was not of fine stock? They covertly erased a life by plotting and plying me with inveracities. She was punished for indiscretions that, although not acceptable, caused her to be left behind. Did she worship the divisive trinity with grace or despise the shackles of it? Did she know what hell the Church wrought on her own kind?

As I waited for Saul in our sitting room, I reached for a glass of port next to me, a tremor in my hand causing me to spill a bit. He had been most tolerant of this news.

After my initial shock and anger dissipated, I thought of my mother in a more sympathetic light. After all, she had been abandoned. She must have been frightened as a young woman left in the care of others, especially the cruel church. Had she died of loneliness? Or did she remain passionate for her lost love? Did the baby taken away from her steal across her thoughts? I hurled my port toward the fire, the shattered glass splintering my heart.

In moments I thought of a new reality. What if she were alive? Alive! Could it be? Had she survived the sanctimonious life? I stood, knees shaking, using the chair for support. Then I must go to her. I must find her and tell her she has a daughter and grandchildren. Perhaps the reward for banishment was survival.

At first I was insistent with my husband that I travel to Spain and find my mother. Saul would not hear of such a thing. "Are you without your mind? What if you are caught? They will burn you at the stake. What about us and your children?"

I cajoled him for hours, begging and pleading to help me in some fashion. I promised him the world to allow me to go. "Please, I must know. I have to see her," I repeated endlessly, sometimes shrieking and banging my fists on his chest.

"You do not know if she is alive. Hysteric," he muttered more than once with disgust.

I spoke to his back. "I could speak to those who knew her, find out what happened when the convent doors shut."

Our disagreements lasted for days, me with a thread of hope and, Saul, usually patient, forbidding me to mention my mother. He was adamant while I cried for hours. Finally, after drying my tears on a particularly anguishing day, he agreed to help me. However, I had to give up the idea of traveling to Spain. He could not permit such a reckless venture.

After remaining quiet about the subject for more than a month he brought me good news. Maybe he changed his mind because of my persistence or maybe it was the idea that our children had one grandparent still alive. Or perhaps it was simple curiosity and a desire to make me happy. He did not say. I know he cared for me deeply and that my grief overwhelmed him.

Through my husband's tangled web of *conversos* he had access to those who swore allegiance to the Church. Some of our most devout had disappeared into the netherworld of Catholic hierarchy. Others traded surreptitiously with us.

In Amsterdam the Church had fallen into disfavor for their lack of tolerance. In a few places the power was in the hands of the nobility and burghers. Saul promised to contact those he knew who could make such transfers to bring my mother to me.

Arrangements could be made for gifts, bribes in actuality–a signet ring with a small diamond or perhaps a strand of pearls from the East. Or even an exquisite tapestry from the Loire region in France to grace a private chapel.

Some priests, who enjoyed the fruits of trade, welcomed French wines and cheese. Ah, I thought to myself, no wonder the people starve and the priests are fat. Our motley group of believers scattered across lands and fastened together by one God, brought me hope.

Our celebrations were small and private, Rosh Hashanah, Yom Kippur and Sukkoth in the fall and the Celebration of Lights in the winter.

The converso community, who traded goods with each other, began to restrict travel. Their reputations meant people came to them. The dangers were many as my grandfather had said–pirates, robbers, lack of food. However, for this unique cargo Saul went in person, crisscrossing Europe beyond the Pyrenees, along sea routes, and finally, returning with the news that the maps were being written to bring my mother to me.

She was alive! My joy flowed in the form of tears. The woman who shepherded me into this world was alive. I fell to my knees and thanked God in gratitude.

Chapter Thirty-five

Bellina

7 Nissan 5285 (10 April 1525)

Word came that the transfer was complete. On a crisp spring day a week before Passover I traveled to the Sisters of Christ abbey outside of Amsterdam with my oldest son, Hermando and daughter, Estrella.

The fields bloomed with tulips and poppies. The carriage my husband had arranged sped by the banks of the canals to a small village. Our transportation waited outside the high walls. It had been many years since I was forced to enter a Catholic structure and my heart fluttered wildly. Would they trap me? Was this a trick of some sort?

The chanting of nuns with pure and sweet voices slipped across the breezeway behind us. In a courtyard of fragrant roses and tinkling fountains, psalms were sung, the words low and humming, bees in the garden of my mind. We passed refectories and chapels and were left to wait in a stark anteroom.

Suddenly, I am in the present. There is no past. Only now. I know she is here. I feel it. Hair stands up on the back of my neck and tiny beads of sweat dot my forehead. A draft rustles my skirt. My throat is so dry I cannot swallow.

How did she feel when the nuns took me from her arms? Did she scream and cry? I am a mother now. I understand that unbreakable bond. I would die if someone forced my children from me.

I have dressed with care, my gown of the newest brocade. My son wears a chambray wine-colored wool coat. My daughter and I display large crosses to show faith. Even in this tolerant climate we are cautious. The diamond necklace of butterflies rests against my skin. I finger a rosary, the glass beads still familiar in my hand after so many years. I can repeat the decades but choose not to, instead moving my lips in prayer reciting the *shema.* The necessities of a duplicitous life have never left me.

The door opens slowly and I am confronted with the Mother Superior, an imposing figure in dark robes, her hair covered. I cross myself before her and kneel. Her pallor is one of skin that has not been outside these walls or seen the gift of sunshine. Refusing to reward me with a smile, her eyes, dark and hard, make me feel tiny. She motions me to stand. It is rumored that her brother, a cardinal, who appointed her to this position, wields great power in the Netherlands. I bow with respect.

"This is highly irregular," she says in a hoarse whisper. The children move close behind me, their sweet breath at my back. She pauses and I wait without exhaling. Saul has instructed me to say little, warning me that she will make a show of objection. Payments have been made and I am not to interfere. Louder, she says, "This arrangement is not possible."

"What?" My eyes open wide in surprise. And then I remember his words. Be patient. Be obsequious. I lower my eyes. "Please, Mother." Church bells sound and I know time is passing at an excruciating pace.

"Perhaps your husband could show more respect for our work here."

"Yes, Mother."

"The Feast of the Annunciation will be soon." She reminds me. "The day after Palm Sunday."

"Yes, Mother." Did Saul forget something?

"A case of wine," she whispers and motions us to follow. A wave of disgust makes me feel ill, so that I don't want to continue. Will it really be my mother?

The Mother Superior leads us down a long passageway into the bowels of the convent, far from the entry. A panicky wave rises in me. How will I escape? I cough, nervous with the closeness.

After we climb down steps to a basement area she stops at a large wooden door. We enter a small vestry, empty except for a large tapestry on the wall of silk and gold thread portraying the Virgin and her son, halos around their heads. I stare at the intricate stitches, probably from child nuns in Brussels.

I have learned these things from my husband. He has brought me exquisite gifts from his travels including a *millefleurs*, a tapestry of a thousand flowers that hangs in our bedroom for warmth.

The air, chilly and damp, feels heavy with tension. Will my Spanish flow freely from my lips after all this time? Portuguese and Flemish roll from my mouth daily. Two unlit candelabras stand in the corners reminding me of our own Sabbath candles. My anxiety wanes and I become calm in the dimness. Small rays of light from beveled windows near the ceiling gleam down, checkering across the floor. I wait, my heart thumping a steady loud rhythm. There are no chairs, only a hard wood table. Gray flagstones cover the floor.

A diminutive woman with a slight stoop enters and stands in the shaft of light, her face gracefully unlined of creases. She looks perplexed, as though someone has awakened her. She turns to the Mother Superior, "Why am I here?" Her child-like voice is fearful as are her frightened eyes. Green eyes. Eyes like mine.

I cannot utter the word *mother*. A large silver cross with their savior glints in the spot of sunlight. I am struck by how she is a reflection of me—the shape of her face, the aquiline nose, pale eyes darting the room.

What is she thinking? Her hair is covered, face solemn. She appears older than I imagined. The convent offers protection but not an easy life. She cocks her head to hear.

"Is there trouble?" she asks the Mother Superior in a soft voice.

The Mother Superior gives me a harsh look, her eyes menacing as if to say, "This insignificant nun can do you no good. Whatever it is, get on with it."

"May we have a few moments alone?" I ask with boldness. I know Saul has already paid handsomely for this privilege.

The Mother Superior shakes her head no.

"Please, a private family matter." I do my best to keep my tone less urgent. Does she know me? Maybe I am erased from her mind.

My mother looks terrified. I can see she has no idea why she is here. She does not recognize me. Would she remember my birth so long ago? That I am her daughter? Has she forgotten the threads of her life?

I lift my head. "Your request will be granted by my husband this week."

The Mother Superior, her face stern, backs out of the room. "Be brief. She is weary from her travels and the many avenues that have brought her here. Heaven can only know what urgency you have created."

I can barely hear my mother when she asks, "What do you want of me?" Her hands flutter to her head as though there is a fly buzzing nearby.

I press my fingers into the children's backs to move them closer. I could not decide whether to bring them. At first I thought it a bad idea because it would unnerve all of us. Later I decided it might be the only chance for them to cast eyes on their grandmother. They are silent because they know who she is. She might embrace them or flee and scream for salvation.

I approach and reach for her hands. Her eyes are fixed on mine without recognition. "Mother?" The word chokes in my throat.

She shakes her head no and pulls her hands away. I glance toward the door. Have they brought the wrong nun?

"You have traveled a long way through irregular channels. I am your daughter and these are your grandchildren." I wait, my heart palpitating.

No. She shakes her head. Tears well in her eyes.

"Do you know your parent's names?"

She seems so distant, her eyes blinking. Will she faint? She closes them. Without looking at me she says, "Hermando and Estrella."

"The same as my children. And your sister's name is Grazia."

"Grazia," she says in a whisper, her cheeks pale with shock.

She opens her eyes, clear and cool as a hidden lake.

"Grazia raised me. You are my mother."

"But. . .but I thought you were all dead. They said my baby died of the influenza." She blinks in disbelief. "What of my parents?"

I shake my head no as I stare into her eyes, ones I longed to see for my entire life. "No, Mother, it is only me. I am here."

She cannot accept or absorb what I am telling her. Suddenly agitated she begins to move about the room, an animal trapped in a cage. "How can this be?" she repeats. She goes to a corner and then whirls around to look at me. "You are Jews?"

"Yes, Mother." My body reacts to the confession and I become damp under my arms, on my face, around my waist. "A secret." My finger touches my lips.

She walks the perimeter of the room covering it in a few strides, returning to me, her face inches from mine. A torrent of tears wets my shoulder as she collapses in my arms. I can hardly hold her as I begin to cry, unable to stop a lifetime of tears. The children come closer and hold me as well.

"Your survival?" she asks between sobs.

"It is a long story." I wipe my face with the back of my hand. "Will you come home with us? All you have to do is tell the Mother Superior you are comfortable with that decision. It has been arranged. We live in a fine house near the *Oude Kerk*, the Old Church. Come. Listen to our tale, the family history. You can return in a few days if it does not please you."

She steps back, tears streaming down her cheeks. "No, I know of no other life outside the convent." She glances at the children who wait in awe, their expressions shocked at our raw emotions. Estrella looks at this stranger with hope.

"Please. Learn who we are. Hermando is our oldest. There are four more at home waiting to meet you. I cannot express how I feel about finding you, finding my own *sangre*."

She stares at me. She may reject the idea of leaving the cloistered world she knows. My husband warned me of her possible resistance. "She may not survive away from the enclosed walls of rituals not unlike the fish who flop and thrash at the docks," he told me.

My apprehension makes me daring. I cannot resist this opportunity. "Come," I whisper, clasping her hand as I would a child, holding her elbow. Estrella takes her other one and we lead her toward the door, up the stairs, past the maze of rooms and nuns singing in the courtyard, toward the light.

And so I return that afternoon with the woman who bore me, a nun in a habit with extraordinary green eyes and a will of iron. After introductions to our family and a hearty meal, I read her Grazia's letter.

My mother blinks, a non-believer of such fantasy. Next I share the story of her parents and the two expulsions. She is not angry, only saddened. She listens, hands folded, quiet with contemplation.

I watch her in prayer on bended knees in our garden. Each day as my tale unfolds she understands how much of what happened to us was sanctioned and conspired by the church. Soon her habit is discarded and replaced with a simple robe.

"Will I burn in Hell?" my mother asks me when I see her in it the first time. I take her in my arms.

"No, Mother. You are still a Jew. We do not believe in hell."

Epilogue

Alegra

I rock my beautiful green-eyed Estrella on a cushioned teak lounge chair in our Florida room. I sing a *Ladino* lullaby I have learned. She looks up at me with such mommy-love, her ebony hair in cochungos around her face. I press her to my breast and she sucks hungrily, a finger touching her velvet skin. I rest my head back in gratitude.

It's taken almost two years for the University of Miami Press to publish Hal's novel. In the local media and a few scholarly journals *The Blind Eye* has been hailed as "a literary achievement," "an extraordinary insight into Sephardic life in the 16th century," and "a well-researched historical narrative of superior importance." Several universities have asked him to be a visiting professor including the University of New Mexico where descendants of *conversos* are acknowledging their past, even exploring DNA testing to discover their roots.

Hal's proud of his accomplishments. I don't know where his inquisitive mind will lead him next, but I see lots of books piled next to his side of the bed. He's informed me the earliest Jews to colonize America were Sephardim escaping the Dutch colony in Brazil. Poor souls had their goods stolen by pirates and arrived penniless.

I'm on for the ride. I've got my baby. I run my finger over her lips and she smiles back at me. What could be better? I'm surprised I've taken to motherhood with such enthusiasm. Irma, who has bought Estrella two dozen baby Guess and Versace outfits, and Marta, who has dire warnings about every childhood disease, dote on our little star. I am smitten. My world is lit.

Hal's a good papa although changing diapers is not his forte. You would only have to see him fussing over her to know that Estrella is a daddy's girl. We spend hours playing with her and agree that after finding each other, she's the best thing that's ever happened to either of us.

At night when she is asleep all I want is for him to hold me tight so I know all this is true.

Author's Notes for
The Blind Eye—A Sephardic Journey

Through a previous novel based on family history I explored Jewish people from Eastern Europe known as Ashkenazi. What I wanted to familiarize myself with were Sephardim who claim their heritage from Spain, Portugal, Africa and the Middle East.

Although my own background is not Sephardic I became fascinated with families who were denied the right to practice their faith for centuries. Indeed, the persecution they suffered in fifteenth and sixteenth century Spain and Portugal foreshadowed what was to come in Europe hundreds of years later.

I had so many questions: Why were these educated people threatening? Was it their belief in one God? Their ability to read? Or was it economics? How did they keep their faith and traditions when everything was done to either blend them into the hierarchy or torture them into abandoning their faith? What role did the Catholic Church play? How does one hold on to a belief system that risks lives? What strength does one have to exhibit to defy ultimate power?

My research began with reading history, attending lectures and conferences and joining the Society for Crypto-Judaic Studies. I also visited Spain and Portugal, particularly the Alfama district in Lisbon where three major events took place. I searched for historical accuracy, including documentation by Bishop Coutinho, an observer of significant events during the time period. I also utilized historical figures such as the apostate, Levi ben Shem-tob and Rabbi Simon Maimi. One of the highlights of my trip was spending the day at the Maritime Museum in Lisbon, the Museu de Marinha, located at the mouth of the Tagus River and Belem, the exit port for those fleeing the Inquisition. I could almost see the ships leaving and the chaos on the shore.

As an author of historical fiction I was interested in every aspect of daily life—what people ate, how they made pan de la aflicción in secret, the spices they used, what they wore, how textiles were made, how they got names like Pereira, Oliveira or Abulafia, the ships they used such as caravels or taforeias and the names of the streets they walked. Typically, novelists use ten percent of research they accumulate.

I wanted details that would make the reader identify with my characters. Their journey follows many who fled Europe and were able to reach South America and later, the United States in the 1500s. Indeed, the first Jews who reached the shores of New York were Sephardim fleeing persecution. I must acknowledge books by David M. Gitlitz such as A Drizzle of Honey and Secrecy and Deceit as well as Israel Abrahams', Jewish Life in the Middle Ages.

The story took shape when I thought about people today who trace their heritage back to the expulsion in 1492 by Queen Isabella. A contemporary Cuban-American woman who searches for her identity formed a parallel narrative that utilized some of my satirical skills.

Crypto-Jews knew their identity and history as it was passed on in families. Today the revival of Ladino, the language that blends Hebrew and Spanish, is kept alive by jazz artist and songwriter, Sarah Aroeste, a treasure of times past.

Reader's Guide
The Blind Eye A Sephardic Journey

1. The author blends humor into historical fiction. What are the parallels between the two narratives of Grazia in the 15th century and Allegra in the 20th?

2. Why were the Jews cast out of Spain in 1492 and then five years later in Portugal?

3. The Blind Eye is written from the points of view of Grazia, Bellina and Alegra. What binds these generations of women together?

4. What are the similarities and differences between the roles of the women who are centuries apart?

5. How do Grazia and her mother keep their religious traditions alive?

6. What role did the Church play in The Inquisition?

7. The attitude of the Dutch people was one of tolerance. How does this play out in the novel?

8. Grazia and Bellina learn many lessons as life catapults them forward. What does Alegra learn without the perspective of historical events? Does her Cuban history influence her?

9. Three events—the massacre at Rossio Square, the kidnapping of the children and the mass conversion—are documented. Could this happen again?

10. How did the ending of the novel tie Grazia, Bellina and Alegra together? Was it satisfying?

Acknowledgements

A special thank you to all my readers in the Scottsdale Writer's Group, Deborah Ledford, Virginia Nosky, and Judy Starbuck who read my story in its roughest form. The First Prize for an Unpublished Manuscript from the Arizona Author's Association gave me great encouragement. I also appreciated the editor's eye of CiCi McNair.

Marcia Fine is the author of five novels, two historical fiction and three satires. She has shifted careers numerous times; however, she has kept the same husband. She resides in Arizona.

Other Novels by Marcia Fine

Gossip.com
Boomerang - When Life Comes Back to Bite You

The Blind Eye
First Prize Arizona Authors Association

Stressed in Scottsdale
First Prize Satire/Humor, Arizona Publishing Association
Silver, Living Now Awards
Honorable Mention, Arizona Author's Association

Paper Children
Finalist:
USA Book News Book of the Year,
Foreward, Book of the Year,
Eric Hoffer Award

CPSIA information can be obtained at www.ICGtesting.com
Printed in the USA
BVOW08s1058250315

393232BV00002B/391/P